The American College Teacher

National Norms for the
1989-90 HERI Faculty Survey

by

Alexander W. Astin
William S. Korn
Eric L. Dey

Higher Education Research Institute
Graduate School of Education
University of California, Los Angeles

March, 1991

COOPERATIVE INSTITUTIONAL RESEARCH PROGRAM

The Cooperative Institutional Research Program (CIRP) is a national longitudinal study of the American higher education system. Established in 1966 at the American Council on Education, the CIRP is now the nation's largest and longest empirical study of higher education, involving data on some 1,300 institutions, over 8 million students, and more than 100,000 faculty. To maximize the use of these data in research and training, the CIRP was transferred to the Graduate School of Education at UCLA in 1973. The annual CIRP freshman and follow-up surveys are now administered by the Higher Education Research Institute at the University of California, Los Angeles, under the continuing sponsorship of the American Council on Education.

AMERICAN COUNCIL ON EDUCATION

The American Council on Education (ACE), founded in 1918, is a council of educational organizations and institutions. ACE seeks to advance education and educational methods through comprehensive voluntary and cooperative action on the part of American educational associations, organizations, and institutions.

HIGHER EDUCATION RESEARCH INSTITUTE
University of California, Los Angeles

The Higher Education Research Institute (HERI) is based in the Graduate School of Education at the University of California, Los Angeles. The Institute serves as an interdisciplinary center for research, evaluation, information, policy studies, and research training in postsecondary education. HERI's research program covers five broad areas: the outcomes of postsecondary education; academic administration and institutional management; faculty performance; federal and state policy assessment; and educational equity.

CIRP PROJECT STAFF

Alexander W. Astin, Professor and Director
Eric L. Dey, Associate Director
William S. Korn, Assoc. Director for Operations
Ellyne R. Berz, HERI Office Manager   Robin Bailey, Assistant to the Director

CIRP ADVISORY COMMITTEE

Estela M. Bensimon
Center for the Study of Higher Education
The Pennsylvania State University

Peter Ewell
National Center for Higher Education
Management Systems

Hugh Fordyce, Director of Research
United Negro College Fund

Weldon Jackson, Vice President
Morehouse College

Charles McClain, Commissioner
Missouri Coordinating Board for Higher Education

George Neely, Jr., Executive Vice President
Fisk University

Amaury Nora
College of Education
University of Illinois at Chicago

Earl Richardson, President
Morgan State University

Deborah Teeter
Director, Institutional Research
University of Kansas

Robert H. Atwell (ex-officio)
President
American Council on Education

Elaine El-Khawas (ex-officio)
Vice President
American Council on Education

Additional copies of this report may be purchased from the Higher Education Research Institute, Graduate School of Education, 320 Moore Hall, University of California, Los Angeles, CA 90024-1521. Please remit $12.00 with your order.

ISBN 1-878477-04-8

The American College Teacher

National Norms for the
1989-90 HERI Faculty Survey

Table of Contents

List of Tables

Acknowledgements

We are especially indebted to our colleague, Ron Opp, who managed the complex and often frustrating task of collecting the data. Special thanks are also due to Jeff Milem, who played a key role in questionnaire design. We also want to acknowledge the considerable assistance we received from the small army of students and staff who participated in the data collection: Ellyne Berz, Sylvia Hurtado, David Hsieh, Theresa Mahoney.

Finally, we want to express our appreciation to the thousands of faculty who took time out of their busy lives to complete the questionnaire. This is just the first, single tabulation of their responses, and we are currently working on a number of more sophisticated analyses which we hope will enhance our understanding of American college teachers, their institutions, and their students.

The American College Teacher

National Norms for the
1989-90 HERI Faculty Survey

The American College Teacher*

This report summarizes the highlights of a national survey of college and university faculty that was carried out by the Higher Education Research Institute (HERI) in the fall and winter of 1989–90. The results reported here are based on the responses of 35,478 full–time college and university faculty members at 392 two–year colleges, four–year colleges, and universities across the country. For this report, a 'faculty member' is defined as any full–time employee of an accredited college or university who spends at least part of his or her time teaching undergraduates. Although the survey also covered academic administrators in these same institutions, only those administrators who spend at least some time teaching undergraduates are included in the results.

The Survey Instrument

The survey questionnaire was designed in conjunction with a national study of the outcomes of general education programs funded by the Exxon Education Foundation. Earlier pilot studies done at the Higher Education Research Institute had suggested that a major determinant of the outcomes of general education programs is the types of faculty members employed at the institution and their particular style of interacting with students. Accordingly, the questionnaire content focused heavily on issues such as how faculty members spend their time, how they interact with students, their preferred methods of teaching and examining students, their perceptions of the institutional climate, and their primary sources of stress and satisfaction. The final survey instrument included a number of questions addressing each of these issues in addition to demographic and biographical information. The instrument also included a section allowing individual institutions to ask their faculty members a set of up to ten locally–developed additional questions (see Appendix B for a copy of the survey instrument).

* The collection of data for this report was supported in part by a grant from the Exxon Education Foundation.

Institutional Sampling

Although the original Exxon grant was designed to study a selected sample of 53 institutions comprising a diverse set of approaches to general education, the omnibus nature of the survey instrument prompted a decision to invite other institutions across the country to participate in the survey for a nominal fee. Letters of invitation to participate in the survey were subsequently sent to the chief academic officers at some 2,500 other institutions. The response to the invitation was far greater than expected: an additional 379 institutions agreed to administer the survey, bringing the total institutional sample up to 432. Of those 432 institutions, 40 were dropped from the national data base because of low response rates, leaving 392. A careful examination of the characteristics of the participating institutions revealed that every major type of institution was well–represented. Accordingly, the decision was made to prepare national 'norms' for faculty at different types of institutions. This report thus covers twelve different norm groups: all institutions, all four–year institutions, all two–year institutions, public universities, private universities, public four-year colleges, private four-year colleges (combined and broken down by three subgroupings of private four-year colleges: nonsectarian, Roman Catholic, and Protestant), and public and private two–year colleges.

Weighting Procedures

In order to approximate as closely as possible the results that would have been obtained if all college and university teaching faculty in all institutions had responded to the survey, a multistage weighting procedure was employed. The first set of weights was designed to adjust for response bias *within* participating institutions. Thus, the entire faculty at each institution was sorted into twelve categories representing all combinations of gender (male or female) and rank (professor, associate professor, assistant professor, instructor, lecturer, other). The ratio between the number of faculty in the institution and the total number of respondents in each category was used as the first corrective weight. Thus, if there were 20 female full professors and 10 of those responded, each of these respondent's weights would be 2.0 (20 divided by 10). This within-

2

institution weight, which is designed to correct for any response bias related to the gender or rank of the faculty member, adjusts the total number of respondents up to the total number of faculty at the institution.

To develop the second level of weights, institutions were sorted into 23 stratification cells based upon type (two-year, four-year, university), control (public, private-nonsectarian, Roman Catholic, Protestant), and, for four-year institutions, selectivity (defined as the average admissions test score of the entering freshman class). This last stratification variable—institutional selectivity—is designed to control for the 'quality' or prestige of the institution. Within each of these stratification cells, faculty in all institutions in the population were sorted into the same 12 gender by rank categories described above. Data from all participating institutions within each institutional stratification cell were then combined, and the weighted number of respondents (using the first weight described above) was then determined separately for each of the gender by rank combinations. Thus, for each gender by rank combination within a stratification cell, we had two values: the total number of faculty in the higher education population, and the weighted number of respondents to our survey. The ratio between these two totals became the second weight, which was designed to correct for between-stratification cell differences in institutional participation. The final weight used for each respondent consisted of the product of the two weights (that is, the within-institution weight and the between-institution weight).

Table 1 shows the total number of institutions and total number of institutional participants by stratification cell, together with the total number of faculty members, faculty surveyed, and faculty respondents for each cell.

Table 1

Institutional and Faculty Participation, by Stratification Cell

	Institutions			Faculty			
	Total	Partici-pating	Used in Norms	Total	Sampled[1]	Respon-dents[1]	Used in Norms
Public universities							
Low selectivity	56	15	13	39,298	15,615	8,127	4,609
Medium selectivity	38	4	4	38,779	3,631	2,041	1,363
High selectivity	23	9	6	23,083	9,688	3,951	1,779
Private universities							
Low selectivity	25	5	5	10,355	2,764	1,507	1,146
Medium selectivity	19	3	2	10,637	1,423	675	338
High selectivity	25	5	4	15,790	3,314	1,540	745
Public four–year colleges							
Low selectivity[2]	209	39	36	46,871	8,250	4,771	3,700
Medium selectivity	96	21	18	34,276	7,703	4,151	2,920
High selectivity	42	8	8	14,533	3,036	1,667	1,343
Nonsectarian four–year colleges							
Low selectivity[2]	183	23	19	9,369	2,572	1,506	935
Medium selectivity	61	13	10	6,737	1,840	946	523
High selectivity	83	31	28	8,254	4,629	2,646	1,969
Very high selectivity	48	16	16	6,892	2,674	1,586	1,382
Catholic four–year colleges							
Low selectivity[2]	81	19	18	4,420	1,659	1,152	853
Medium selectivity	59	16	16	4,713	1,873	1,231	933
High selectivity	33	7	7	3,857	1,096	639	526
Protestant four–year colleges							
Low selectivity[2]	218	36	35	11,566	2,729	1,945	1,557
Medium selectivity	70	21	20	5,620	1,854	1,335	1,068
High selectivity	46	21	21	4,778	2,604	1,702	1,474
Two–year colleges							
Public	866	92	85	84,674	11,448	7,128	5,351
Private	132	5	4	3,578	237	175	116
Black colleges							
Public	59	5	5	9,634	955	463	357
Private	56	18	12	3,717	1,885	690	491
All institutions	2,528	432	392	401,431	93,479	51,574	35,478

[1] Includes respondents who were not classified as full-time undergraduate faculty.
[2] Includes institutions with unknown selectivity.

4

Survey Response

Responses to the survey exceeded our most optimistic expectations. Of the 93,479 questionnaires mailed out, useable returns were eventually received from 51,574, constituting a 55.2 percent response. We believe that there are several factors that may have contributed to the high response rate. First of all, we believe that the questionnaire addresses a wide range of issues of concern to faculty members (faculty respondents were told that their institution would receive a profile of faculty responses to each item). And even though the questionnaire contained nearly 200 questions, it did not appear to be of excessive length (it was limited to only four pages; see Appendix B) and required a minimal amount of reading coupled with a maximum amount of responding. Finally, the response rate was substantially increased by the fact that a second wave of questionnaires was sent to nonrespondents approximately four weeks after the first wave was sent.

Initially we assumed that the high response rate could be attributed to several other factors: a covering letter written by the institution's chief executive officer (or other high-ranking administrator) and the fact that each institution provided a current, up-to-date list of their faculty. However, the Higher Education Research Institute has recently supplemented this sample of faculty respondents with surveys of an additional 75 institutions (supported by a National Science Foundation grant) in which the covering letter came from UCLA and commercial name and address files were used rather than names and addresses provided by the institution. Considering that up to ten percent of the names and addresses from the commercial lists were probably invalid, the 46 percent overall rate of response from these 75 institutions was impressive.

Since it was necessary to identify each questionnaire recipient in order to be able to follow up on nonrespondents with a second wave of questionnaires, we decided to imprint the faculty member's name and address directly on the questionnaire. Although it may have been preferable to use a code number rather than the name and address, we wanted there to be no ambiguity in the respondent's mind as to the fact that he or she was being identified. We hoped that any concerns about confidentiality raised by printing the name and address directly on the questionnaire would be mollified to some extent by the fact that the completed questionnaires were returned to a commercial processing center (and then to us at the Higher Education Research Institute) rather than to the institution. This procedure ensured that there would be no way for the responses of any individual faculty member to be known to the institution.

In spite of these hopes and precautions, we received a good deal of critical mail from some of those surveyed. While many of the critical comments focused on particular survey questions, by far the most common complaint concerned the imprinting of the name and address on the questionnaire. While there is no way to know for sure how the normative figures have been affected by these concerns about privacy, it should be emphasized that the number of critical letters received (approximately 500) is really quite small, given that 93,479 surveys were mailed out, and given that we were surveying college and university faculty who pride themselves on their critical skills. Only a minority of those faculty who took the trouble to write critical letters refused to complete their questionnaires.

Definitions

As already noted, only those full-time employees who were engaged in teaching undergraduates were included in the normative data reported here. Thus, full-time administrators, full-time researchers, or faculty members who teach *only* at the postgraduate level have been excluded. More specifically, a respondent was included in the normative data if one of the following conditions were met: the respondent was a full-time employee at his or her institution (question #2)

AND   noted teaching as his or her principal activity (question #1) AND either taught at least one undergraduate-level course (question #17) OR taught no classes at all in the most recent term (this last condition is included for teachers on sabbatical leave or those currently engaged in research)

OR   taught at least two courses in the last term (question #17), at least one of which was at the undergraduate level

OR   did not indicate that he or she taught any specific types of courses, but did indicate spending at least 9 hours per week in scheduled teaching (question #16).

Results

Complete results of the faculty survey, reported separately for men, women, and all faculty, are provided in Section II (also see Appendix A, which shows that this survey agrees well with a recent National Center for Education Statistics faculty survey in terms of age, race, academic rank, and highest degree held). In this section we have abstracted highlights of the current HERI survey of faculty for discussion and interpretation. Results will be presented separately under six headings: background characteristics, professional goals, teaching, research, job satisfaction and stress, and perceptions of the institution.

Background Characteristics

Demographic and background characteristics of the faculty are shown in Table 2. The much-discussed aging of American college and university faculty is clearly demonstrated by the results: one-fourth of all faculty are 55 or older, and well over half are 45 or older. Only about one faculty member in ten (10.2 percent) is younger than 35. Public and private universities have more younger faculty than other types of institutions, but they also have slightly more older faculty. Clearly, the faculty at universities appear to be more *variable* with respect to age than the faculty at two- and four-year colleges. Well over half of college faculty have been at their current institutions for ten years or longer, and over 16 percent have been at their current institution for twenty-two years or longer. Private institutions appear to have more recently-hired faculty than public institutions. This latter finding is further reflected in the fact that more professors in public than private institutions are tenured.

The largest differences in Table 2 are reflected in the highest degree held by faculty members. While three-fourths of four-year institutions' faculty hold a doctorate degree, fewer than one faculty member in five at two-year institutions holds the doctorate. As would be expected, the highest proportion of faculty holding doctorate degrees (more than 80 percent) is found in the universities, whereas the highest percent with Master's degrees (60-plus percent) is found among faculty at two-year institutions.

Table 2
Background Characteristics, by Type of Institution (Percentages)

Background characteristics	All	Universities		Four-year colleges		Two-year colleges	
		Public	Private	Public	Private	Public	Private
Age							
Less than 35	10	11	16	9	13	7	13
35-44	31	30	32	29	34	30	39
45-54	35	33	27	38	31	40	38
55 or more	24	27	26	25	22	24	20
Highest Degree Held[1]							
Bachelor's	3	1	1	1	2	10	4
Master's	28	13	8	22	29	60	70
Doctorate	61	81	87	69	62	16	18
Year Hired by Current Institution							
Before 1967	16	19	21	16	17	11	15
1967-1981	46	45	40	46	38	58	44
Since 1981	37	36	40	37	45	31	41
Tenured	67	70	66	68	57	71	55
Race							
White	90	92	93	87	92	91	97
Black	4	1	2	7	4	4	3
Asian-American	3	4	3	4	2	2	0
Hispanic	1	1	0	1	1	2	0

[1] Figures may not add to 100% because 'other' (e.g., professional) degrees are not included.

These last findings are consistent with the salary data (Table 3). More than twenty percent of the faculty in public and private universities are paid $70,000 or more, compared to less than ten percent in four-year colleges and less than five percent in two-year colleges. Conversely, universities have the fewest faculty members (less than 15 percent) making less than $40,000.

Two interesting inconsistencies emerge from the salary data reported in Table 3. First, although only 8.9 percent of the faculty in public four-year colleges make $70,000 or more, less than twenty percent (19.5 percent) of their faculty make below $40,000. Private nonsectarian four-year colleges, by contrast, find 37.9 percent of their faculty making below $40,000. Thus, despite the dearth of highly paid faculty in the public four-year colleges, the salary 'floor' in most of these institutions appears to be substantially above that in many of the private four-year colleges. Among other things, these results show that the *variability* in salaries paid at the private four-year colleges is considerable.

Table 3
Faculty Salaries, by Type of Institution

Type of Institution	Percentage making	
	$70,000 or more	Less than $40,000
Private universities	29.2	11.4
Public universities	23.6	14.5
Private nonsectarian four-year colleges	9.0	37.9
Public four-year colleges	8.9	19.5
Public two-year colleges	3.4	30.9
Protestant four-year colleges	1.4	52.7
Catholic four-year colleges	1.2	49.5
Private two-year colleges	0.0	75.3

Note: To convert salaries to a 12 month basis, 9 and 10 month salaries have been inflated by a factor of 2/9.

Professional Goals

Table 4 shows the percentages of faculty members who rate various professional goals as either 'essential' or 'very important.' Practically every faculty member (98 percent) rates 'be a good teacher' as a very important goal. Next in line is 'be a good colleague' (80 percent), followed by 'engage in research' (59 percent). As would be expected, professors in universities are much more likely to give a high priority to research (79-85 percent) compared to professors in two-year colleges (24-25 percent). Professors in universities give lower priority than professors in other

9

types of institutions to good colleagueship, providing services to the community, participating in committee or administrative work, and—perhaps surprisingly—engaging in outside activities. It would thus appear that the high priority given research by professors in universities causes them to give lower priority to practically all other major professional goals, with the possible exception of teaching.

Table 4
Professional Goals of Higher Education Faculty, by Type of Institution (Percentages)

Goals rates either 'essential' or 'very important'	All	Universities		Four-year colleges		Two-year colleges	
		Public	Private	Public	Private	Public	Private
Be a good teacher	98	98	96	98	99	99	99
Be a good colleague	79	76	75	80	83	85	83
Engage in research	59	79	85	61	54	25	24
Engage in outside activities	52	49	48	54	54	55	57
Provide services to the community	43	36	34	46	45	52	48
Participation in committee or administrative work	29	23	19	31	32	36	35

Given the continuing controversy over the relative priorities assigned to research and teaching, it is important to determine just how faculty members approach the potential conflict between these two very important functions. Table 5 shows results from several questions relating to this issue. In the first set of questions, faculty members were asked to indicate their 'principal activity.' Given how we defined 'teaching faculty' (see above), it is not surprising that a large majority (90 percent) of college faculty say that teaching is their principal activity; research and administration are identified as principal activities by only six and three percent, respectively, of college faculty. As would be expected, the percentages giving research as their principal activity are substantially higher (14 and 18 percent) in the public and private universities. Virtually no faculty members in the two-year colleges identified research as their principal activity.

Table 5
Faculty Interest and Involvement in Research and Teaching, by Type of Institution (Percentages)

		Universities		Four-year colleges		Two-year colleges	
	All	Public	Private	Public	Private	Public	Private
Principal activity							
Teaching	90	82	78	93	95	95	94
Research	6	14	18	2	1	0	0
Administration	3	3	3	4	3	3	5
Other	1	1	0	1	1	2	1
Do interests lie primarily in teaching or research?							
Very heavily in teaching	37	17	11	34	42	70	75
Leaning toward teaching	35	35	32	42	42	25	17
Leaning toward research	24	42	45	21	15	5	8
Very heavily in research	4	7	12	3	1	0	1
Hours per week spent teaching classes							
Less than 9	34	61	72	24	20	8	9
More than 12	34	12	6	30	33	78	70
Hours per week spent doing research							
None	20	5	4	14	24	52	54
1-4	28	18	14	33	38	32	32
More than 12	23	42	49	20	11	3	2
Agree 'strongly' or 'somewhat' that							
Institutional demands for doing research interfere with my as a effectiveness as a teacher	27	44	35	32	16	6	4

A somewhat different picture emerges, however, when we inquire about faculty *interests*. Faculty members were asked to indicate their relative degree of interest in research versus teaching along a four point scale ranging from 'very heavily in teaching' to 'very heavily in research.' More than one-quarter of all faculty members indicate that their interest either 'leans' more toward research than teaching or is 'very heavily' in research. In the public universities this figure is nearly half (49 percent), whereas in the private universities more than half of the faculty (57 percent) prefer research over teaching. Thus, the number of faculty who prefer research over teaching is more than four times larger than the number who see research as their principal activity.

Here we have impressive documentation for the 'research versus teaching' conflict: even though nine faculty in ten identify their principal job activity as teaching, many of these admit to having a greater interest in research. Faculty who report such discrepancies between job responsibilities and personal preferences are most numerous in the universities, but they exist in substantial numbers in all types of institutions.

When asked whether they believe that institutional demands for doing research interfered with their teaching effectiveness, more than one-quarter of the faculty agreed that they did. Consistent with the data on interests, faculty who work in universities are most likely to see research demands as interfering with their teaching. It is also pertinent to note that about one-third (32 percent) of faculty who teach in the public four-year colleges feel that institutional demands for doing research interfere with their teaching effectiveness. Considering that these institutions produce fully one-third of all the baccalaureate degrees in the country and that they represent our principal teacher training institutions, this finding should be a cause for concern.

What is especially interesting about these results is that a faculty member's belief that pressures to do research interfere with teaching bears little relation to their interest in research versus teaching: 28 percent of those whose interests lean more toward teaching report that research demands interfere with their teaching, in contrast to 29 percent of those whose interests lean more toward research. Within the public universities, however, a relationship *does* exist: 52 percent of those faculty members whose interests lean more toward teaching, contrasted to only 36 percent of those whose interests lean toward research, say that research demands interfere with their teaching. Interestingly enough, this relationship does *not* appear to result from differences in teaching loads at the public universities, since those with the lowest teaching loads (less than nine hours) are only slightly less likely (43 versus 46 percent) than those with the highest teaching loads (more than eight hours) to report that research demands interfere with their teaching.

In short, the conflict between research and teaching appears to be greatest among professors who teach in our public universities, with the majority of those whose primary interests lie in teaching reporting that their teaching effectiveness is compromised by demands to do research.

Differing patterns of faculty interests by institutional type are further reflected in the time spent teaching classes. Faculty members in universities spend the least time teaching classes, whereas faculty in the two-year colleges spend by far the most time. Indeed, more than three-fourths of the community college faculty (78 percent) teach more than twelve hours of classes per week, contrasted with only about one-third of the four-year college faculty and about ten percent of the university faculty.

The reverse pattern can be observed for time spent doing research. More than half of the two-year college faculty spend *no* time in research, in contrast to less than one-fourth of the four-year college faculty and only about five percent of the university faculty. (It is probably the case that this latter group includes many administrators and lecturers.) By contrast, nearly half of the university faculty spend more than twelve hours per week doing research, compared to less than one-fourth of the four-year college faculty and less than five percent of the two-year college faculty.

In summary, even though most college faculty recognize that teaching is their principal activity, a substantial number (including half of the university faculty) prefer research over teaching. At the same time, more than one–quarter of all college and university faculty feel that institutional demands for doing research interfere with their teaching. Even though the faculty in the universities have by far the lowest teaching loads, they are the most likely to feel that institutional demands for doing research interfere with their teaching. In the next two sections we shall examine the faculty's involvement in research and teaching in greater detail.

Teaching

Faculty preferences for different instructional methods are shown in Table 6. The most frequently used method is the class discussion (used in 'all' or 'most' courses by 70 percent of the faculty), followed by 'extensive lecturing' (used by 56 percent of the faculty in all or most courses). All other methods are used regularly by only small minorities of faculty members.

Table 6
Instructional Methods Used by Higher Education Faculty, by Type of Institution (Percentages)

Methods used in 'all' or 'most' courses	All	Universities		Four-year colleges		Two-year colleges	
		Public	Private	Public	Private	Public	Private
Class discussions	70	66	67	71	73	71	63
Extensive lecturing	56	61	64	54	48	53	62
Independent projects	34	35	32	36	35	32	24
Cooperative learning	26	24	19	27	28	29	23
Experiential learning/field studies	19	18	14	20	19	20	14
Group projects	16	16	12	17	16	15	14
Student-developed activities	15	12	11	17	15	18	17
Multiple drafts of written work	12	11	12	12	15	12	13
Graduate teaching assistants	8	18	26	4	1	1	1
Student-selected topics	8	8	8	9	9	9	8

Somewhat surprisingly, there are few differences by type of institution in faculty preference for particular instructional methods. Professors in universities and in private two-year colleges show the greatest propensity toward extensive lecturing, while faculty in private four-year colleges do the least lecturing. And, as would be expected, faculty in the universities are by far the most likely to use graduate teaching assistants in their courses. Otherwise, the faculty in different types of institutions use very similar pedagogical approaches.

What kinds of goals do faculty have for their undergraduate students? Table 7 shows the percentages of faculty who rate various student developmental goals as either 'essential' or 'very important.' Developing the 'ability to think clearly' is a near-universal goal for college faculty in all types of institutions (99 percent). Faculty are also quite strong and consistent in their desire to increase the 'desire and ability to undertake self-directed learning' (93 percent). Enhancing students' self-understanding (67 percent) is the next most important goal endorsed by faculty, followed closely by 'helping students develop personal values' (63 percent), 'preparing students for employment after college' (62 percent) and 'developing moral character' (56 percent). Providing for students' emotional development is endorsed by only 40 percent, while the least popular developmental goal is to prepare students for family living (19 percent). Generally speaking, faculty who teach in universities give lower priority than faculty in all the other types of institutions to goals other than developing the ability to think clearly. Faculty in all three types of public institutions—universities, four-year colleges, and community colleges—give somewhat higher priority to preparing students for employment after college than do their counterparts in the private institutions. Faculty in private two- and four-year colleges give relatively high priority to 'affective' outcomes such as personal values, moral character, and family living.

Research

Table 8 shows the amount of time spent on research and scholarly writing by faculty in different types of institutions (Table 8 presents a finer breakdown of the data reported in Table 5). Nearly one-fourth of the professors in private universities (23 percent) spend more than twenty hours a week in research and scholarly writing, followed by 18 percent in the public universities. This would suggest that a significant minority of the faculty in public and private universities devote more than half of their time to research and writing. Table 8 also shows an interesting result with the breakdown of private four-year colleges into subgroups: substantially more of the

Table 7
Faculty Goals for Undergraduates, by Type of Institution (Percentages)

"Very Important" or "Essential" Goals	All	Universities		Four-year colleges		Two-year colleges	
		Public	Private	Public	Private	Public	Private
Develop ability to think clearly	99	99	99	100	100	99	99
Increase desire and ability to undertake self-directed learning	93	92	91	93	94	92	88
Enhance students' self-understanding	67	60	58	69	74	72	79
Help students develop personal values	63	55	54	64	74	68	81
Prepare students for employment after college	62	55	42	65	58	78	64
Develop moral character	56	47	49	54	68	63	77
Prepare students for graduate or advanced education	53	49	52	55	58	42	47
Provide for students' emotional development	40	30	30	38	49	49	62
Enhance the out-of-class experience of students	40	35	29	44	48	47	54
Teach students the classic works of Western civilization	37	33	38	37	44	28	39
Prepare students for family living	19	11	9	18	24	27	37

faculty in the private-nonsectarian colleges spend a significant amount of time in research, when compared to the faculty in the denominational colleges.

Table 8

Time Spent on Research and Scholarly Writing, by Type of Institution (Percentages)

Type of institution	Hours per week		
	More than 20	More than 12	None
Private universities	23	49	4
Public universities	18	42	5
Public four-year colleges	6	20	14
Private nonsectarian colleges	4	14	21
Catholic colleges	2	8	23
Protestant colleges	1	8	28
Two-year public colleges	1	3	52
Two-year private colleges	0	2	54

What does all this time spent in research activities produce? Table 9 shows the publication rates of faculty by type of institution. As would be expected, the typical faculty member in a public or private university publishes far more than faculty members in other types of institutions. Almost half of the faculty in public universities (46 percent) and more than half in the private universities (52 percent) have published more than 10 articles in academic or professional journals, as compared to less than 25 percent of the faculty in four-year colleges and less than 5 percent of the faculty in two-year colleges. The large majority of faculty in two-year colleges have *never* published an article in an academic or professional journal.

Table 9
Publications by Higher Education Faculty, by Type of Institution (Percentages)

Type of publications	All	Universities		Four-year colleges		Two-year colleges	
		Public	Private	Public	Private	Public	Private
Articles in academic or professional journals							
None	28	11	8	23	32	62	71
More than 10	25	46	52	21	13	3	1
More than 50	5	10	13	2	1	0	0
Chapters in edited volumes							
None	66	47	37	68	74	91	93
Five or more	8	15	20	6	4	2	0
Books, manuals or monographs authored or edited							
One or more	48	58	62	48	40	36	15
Five or more	8	12	15	7	5	4	2
Professional writings accepted or published in last two years							
None	45	22	16	43	52	82	85
Five or more	13	26	30	10	6	1	2

Similar differences by institutional type can be observed with chapters published in edited volumes. Over half of the faculty in public and private universities have published chapters in edited volumes, compared to only about 30 percent in four-year colleges and fewer than 10 percent in the two-year colleges. Somewhat surprisingly, differences by institutional type are much smaller when it comes to the publication of books: more than one-third (36 percent) of faculty in two-year colleges have published one or more books, compared to 48 percent of the faculty in public four-year colleges and 58 percent in the public universities. However, when it comes to professional writings accepted or published during the past two years, great institutional differences remain: more than three-fourths of the faculty in public and private universities have published writings in the last two years, in contrast to about half of the faculty in four-year colleges and fewer than 20 percent in two-year colleges. Similarly, more than one-fourth of the faculty in public and private universities have had *five* or more writings accepted or published during just the past two years.

In summary, these findings dramatize the great differences by institutional type in the involvement of faculty in research and writing. University faculty are not only much more involved in research activities, but they also produce much more in the form of published output than do faculty in other types of institutions. As expected, the majority of faculty in the two-year colleges spend no time in research and a large majority have never published an article in a professional journal. Faculty in the public and private four-year colleges fall in between those in the two-year colleges and the universities in terms of their research involvement and productivity. Involvement is greatest in the public and nonsectarian four-year colleges and least in the religiously affiliated colleges.

Job Satisfaction and Stress

How satisfied are college and university faculty with their jobs? Table 10 shows the percentages of faculty who are very satisfied or satisfied with eleven different aspects of their jobs. Somewhat surprisingly, faculty show their greatest level of satisfaction (83 percent) with 'autonomy and independence.' Upon reflection this finding certainly conforms to the notion that tenure and academic freedom provide faculty with a great deal of autonomy. This result is not consistent, however, with the impression that faculty members frequently complain about external threats to their autonomy, although it might well be that faculty have come to value their autonomy so highly that they protest vigorously any real or imagined threats to it.

Table 10
Job Satisfaction of Faculty, by Type of Institution (Percentages)

Percent who were 'Very Satisfied' or 'Satisfied' with	All	Universities		Four-year colleges		Two-year colleges	
		Public	Private	Public	Private	Public	Private
Autonomy and independence	83	85	89	80	84	81	85
Undergraduate course assignments	78	77	80	75	80	78	78
Job security	75	74	74	75	70	79	71
Relationships with other faculty	75	69	74	74	80	80	82
Graduate course assignments	72	75	78	71	68	41	72
Overall job satisfaction	69	66	75	65	71	74	74
Competency of colleagues	68	65	75	63	74	71	69
Working conditions	65	66	75	58	66	64	63
Relationships with administrators	52	48	53	49	58	53	57
Teaching load	50	58	64	42	45	49	43
Opportunity for scholarly pursuits	45	53	62	38	39	44	33
Salary and fringe benefits	44	44	51	39	40	52	42
Visibility for outside jobs	43	46	59	38	40	42	39
Quality of students	38	38	59	32	43	30	25

Given that nearly two-thirds of the faculty respondents hold tenure, it is not surprising that 'job security' produces a relatively high degree of satisfaction (75 percent). Relationships with other faculty (75 percent) and course assignments, both undergraduate (78 percent) and graduate (72 percents) are generally seen as satisfying, although course *load* is not (51 percent). Next in order are overall job satisfaction (69 percent), competency of colleagues (68 percent), and working conditions (65 percent). Faculty are least satisfied with visibility for outside jobs, salaries and fringe benefits, and with the quality of their students.

Not surprisingly, those faculty members who are tenured are much more likely to report satisfaction with job security (89 percent) than those who are not tenured (44 percent). Interestingly enough, whether or not the faculty member holds tenure does not affect his or her satisfaction with autonomy and independence (84 and 93 percent, respectively, for tenured and nontenured respondents).

Although the satisfaction patterns are quite similar from one kind of institution to another, there are some differences that should be noted. Not surprisingly, faculty at public and private universities are more satisfied with their teaching loads and opportunities for scholarly pursuits than faculty at other types of institutions. Faculty at private universities are most satisfied with the quality of their students, whereas faculty at private two-year colleges and at all types of public institutions are the least satisfied with the quality of their students. When asked if they would still want to be a college professor if they had it to do over again, 80 percent of the faculty said 'probably' or 'definitely' yes, and 12 percent said 'not sure.' Only 7 percent said 'probably no' and 2 percent 'definitely no.' Differences by type of institution were minor.

What sources of stress do faculty members report? By far the most common sources of stress are time pressures and lack of a personal life (see Table 11), both of which are seen as significant sources of stress by more than four out of five faculty members. Next in line are teaching load (65 percent), household responsibilities (64 percent) and committee work (58 percent). Interestingly enough, students are seen as a source of stress much less often than committee work, colleagues, and faculty meetings.

Although sources of stress show very similar patterns across different types of institutions, there are a few interesting differences. Not surprisingly, 'research and publishing demands' and 'fundraising expectations' are seen as sources of stress more frequently by university professors than by professors in other types of institutions, whereas 'teaching load' is most likely to be seen as a source of stress in the two-year and four-year colleges. Consistent with findings reported in earlier tables, faculty in the public four-year colleges are more likely than those in the four-year private colleges to report 'research or publishing demands' and 'fundraising expectations' as significant sources of stress.

Table 11
Sources of Stress for College Faculty, by Type of Institution (Percentages)

'Extensive' or 'Somewhat' source of stress in past year	All	Universities		Four-year colleges		Two-year colleges	
		Public	Private	Public	Private	Public	Private
Time pressures	84	85	85	83	87	79	82
Lack of a personal life	80	80	81	79	83	77	81
Teaching load	65	59	58	69	71	66	70
Household responsibilities	64	62	62	62	68	65	69
Committee work	58	59	50	61	57	54	75
Colleagues	54	58	51	57	53	50	45
Research or publishing demands	50	73	71	57	45	12	12
Faculty meetings	50	51	43	52	48	47	65
Students	50	48	45	49	54	54	63
Review/promotion process	46	52	44	50	45	35	45
My physical health	38	36	36	38	38	41	36
Children's problems	32	31	29	31	31	35	35
Child care	29	28	30	27	31	29	41
Subtle discrimination	29	29	25	33	28	28	26
Care of elderly parent	26	25	22	27	27	28	31
Marital friction	24	24	25	24	23	24	22
Fund-raising expectations	21	31	25	21	15	13	17
Long-distance commuting	17	13	16	19	16	20	18

Perceptions of the Institution

How do faculty members perceive their institutional climates? Table 12 shows thirteen institutional priorities as perceived by the faculty that show interesting patterns across different types of institutions (Section II shows the complete set of 22 institutional priorities that faculty were asked to rate). To 'promote students' intellectual development' and to 'create a positive undergraduate experience' each are widely perceived as having high priority: 76 percent and 68 percent, respectively, of the faculty say it is a 'high' or 'highest' institutional priority. However, four of the top six priorities have to do with the money and status of the institution, including increasing on maintaining institutional prestige (75 percent), enhancing the institution's national image (62 percent), raising money for the institution (58 percent), and economizing or cutting costs (54 percent).

All of the remaining items shown in Table 12 are checked as a high or highest priority by less than 45 percent of the faculty respondents. The three lowest priorities are to 'help solve major social and environmental problems' (26 percent), to 'facilitate involvement in community service activities' (23 percent; see Section II), and to 'help students learn how to bring about change in American society' (21 percent).

A number of differences in institutional priorities can be seen across different types of institutions. Perhaps the most interesting differences occurred between public and private institutions. With almost no exceptions, private two-year colleges, four-year colleges, and universities are seen as giving greater priority than their public counterparts to student developmental goals (promoting intellectual development, creating a positive undergraduate experience, developing leadership ability among students, and enhancing students' out-of-class experience), developing a sense of community among students and faculty, and enhancing the institution's resources and reputation (enhancing institution's national image, increasing or maintaining institutional prestige, and raising money). Universities, compared to four-year colleges and two-year colleges, give much higher priority to hiring faculty stars, conducting basic and applied research, raising money, and enhancing the institution's national image and prestige. Two- and four-year colleges (especially the private ones) give greater priority than the universities to developing a sense of community among students and faculty and to student developmental goals (creating a positive undergraduate experience, developing leadership ability among students, and enhancing students' out-of-class experience). Few differences by type of institution occurred with respect to priorities given to economizing and cost-cutting, helping solve major social and environmental problems, and helping students learn how to bring about social change.

Table 12
Institutional Priorities as Perceived by Faculty at Different Types of Institutions (Percentages)

'Highest' or 'High' institutional priority	All	Universities		Four-year colleges		Two-year colleges	
		Public	Private	Public	Private	Public	Private
Increase or maintain institutional prestige	75	80	87	71	78	68	73
Promote students' intellectual development	76	71	84	72	86	76	80
Enhance institution's national image	62	78	85	57	64	37	46
Create a positive undergraduate experience	69	52	72	69	86	74	82
Raise money for the institution	58	64	78	53	72	39	62
Economize and cut costs	54	59	57	54	50	52	58
Conduct basic and applied research	44	81	74	42	24	11	6
Develop a sense of community among students and faculty	41	26	35	38	61	48	61
Develop leadership ability	38	26	32	38	54	40	60
Hire faculty 'stars'	27	50	47	20	13	11	11
Enhance students' out-of-class experience	29	17	27	29	44	30	43
Help solve major social and environmental problems	26	26	26	25	31	24	18
Help students learn how to bring about change in American society	21	15	16	22	31	22	20

Table 13 shows how faculty at different types of institutions perceive their institutional climates as reflected in twenty different statements. The greatest degree of consensus (between 69 and 76 percent agreement) occurs with respect to five statements about the faculty: that they are committed to the welfare of the institution, strongly interested in undergraduates' academic and personal problems, positive about the general education program, and sensitive to the issues of minorities. A majority of faculty (between 50 and 60 percent) also agree that administrators consider student and faculty concerns when making policy, that student affairs staff have the support and respect of faculty, and that students of different racial/ethnic origins communicate well with one another.

Relatively small percentages of faculty believe that 'there is a lot of racial conflict here' (12 percent), that the campus administration cares little about what happens to students (24 percent), that there is little trust between minority student groups and campus administrators (37 percent), or that the curriculum suffers from faculty overspecialization (28 percent). One of the most negative features of the perceived institutional climate is that only a small minority of faculty (27 percent) feel that 'most students are well-prepared academically' or that there are many opportunities for faculty and students to socialize with each other (38 percent).

Consistent with the results reported earlier, faculty in the private institutions are more likely than their public institution counterparts to agree that their colleagues are interested in the academic and personal problems of undergraduates, that administrators consider student and faculty concerns when making policy, and that there are many opportunities for faculty and students to socialize with each other. Faculty in the public institutions, on the other hand, are more likely than their private counterparts to believe that the curriculum suffers from faculty overspecialization and that the campus administration cares little about what happens to students. Faculty in the universities (especially the public universities) are the most likely to report problems with ethnic/racial minorities, as revealed in their greater propensity to see 'a lot of campus racial conflict' and 'little trust between minority student groups and campus administrators' and their lower endorsement of the item, 'students of different racial/ethnic origins communicate well with

Table 13
Faculty Perceptions of the Institutional Climate, by Type of Institution (Percentages)

Agree 'strongly' or 'somewhat' that	All	Universities		Four-year colleges		Two-year colleges	
		Public	Private	Public	Private	Public	Private
Faculty are committed to welfare of the institution	76	68	76	72	87	81	88
Faculty are strongly interested in academic problems of undergraduates	74	62	68	77	90	84	94
Faculty are interested in students' personal problems	74	58	61	71	89	85	97
Faculty here are positive about the general education program	72	63	76	66	79	84	85
Most faculty here are sensitive to the issues of minorities	69	65	67	68	73	73	74
Administrators consider student and faculty concerns when making policy	60	52	56	58	71	63	75
Students of different racial/ethnic origins communicate well with one another	59	50	51	58	62	70	76
Student affairs staff have the support and respect of faculty	58	55	54	56	67	61	78
Administrators consider faculty concerns when making policy	50	46	53	46	62	50	50
Students here resent taking courses outside their major	43	41	29	47	40	47	48
There are many opportunities for faculty and students to socialize with each other	38	28	40	35	59	37	64
Many courses include minority group perspectives	36	33	30	37	37	40	21
Many courses include feminist perspectives	29	28	30	25	32	31	15
The curriculum here has suffered from faculty overspecialization	28	42	37	27	21	16	9
There is little trust between minority student groups and campus administrators	28	41	35	27	19	18	12
Faculty feel that most students are well-prepared academically	27	24	51	22	38	20	18
Institutional demands for doing research interfere with my effectiveness as a teacher	27	44	35	32	16	6	4
Many students feel like they do not "fit it" on this campus	25	29	32	26	24	18	21
Campus administrators care little about what happens to students	24	31	21	27	13	23	17
There is a lot of campus racial conflict here	12	21	11	10	9	5	7

26

one another.' This greater degree of racial conflict may result in part from the large size and impersonality of the research university, but it may also have to do with the larger enrollments of ethnic minority groups at these institutions (especially the public universities). Researchers at the Higher Education Research Institute are currently investigating these and other possible explanations for this finding (Hurtado, 1990).

A potentially troublesome finding is that only 27 percent of the faculty feel that most students are well-prepared academically. Given that 'quality of students' turned out to be the least satisfying area for faculty (only 38 percent were satisfied with student quality), it would appear that a majority of college and university faculty in the United States do not respect their students' academic preparation and academic skills. That most faculty would have so little regard for their students' abilities could represent a major source of difficulty in trying to establish more trust and better relationships between students and faculty.

The final table (Table 14) shows faculty views on a variety of controversial issues. Although it is not surprising that a solid majority of college faculty (76 percent) believe that college grading is too easy, it is somewhat surprising to see a comparable degree of support (74 percent) for the idea that 'colleges should be actively involved in solving social problems.' This high figure is somewhat more surprising, given that only 26 percent of these same faculty members believe that helping to 'solve major social and environmental problems' is a high institutional priority (Table 12). This discrepancy suggests that institutional and individual faculty priorities may be considerably out of line when it comes to the issue of the university's involvement in solving social problems. It may well be that administrators who wish to focus more of their institutional energies on addressing critical social problems might find a large untapped reservoir of faculty support for such initiatives. Fewer than ten percent of college faculty feel that racial discrimination is no longer a problem in America, and only minorities of faculty agree that unionization has benefitted the teaching-learning process, that the chief benefit of college is to increase one's earning power, or that college officials have the right to ban persons with extreme views from speaking on campus.

Table 14
Faculty Views on Controversial Issues, by Type of Institution (Percentages)

Agree 'strongly' or 'somewhat'	All	Universities		Four-year colleges		Two-year colleges	
		Public	Private	Public	Private	Public	Private
Grading in colleges has become too easy	76	78	79	78	76	70	72
Colleges should be actively involved in solving social problems	74	75	71	75	76	70	75
Tenure is an outmoded concept	37	36	34	35	39	40	43
Faculty unionization has enhanced the teaching-learning process	32	28	21	33	28	45	32
The chief benefit of a college education is that it increases one's earning power	25	20	14	26	18	38	27
College officials have the right to ban persons with extreme views from speaking on campus	20	13	16	17	26	27	36
Racial discrimination is no longer a problem in America	7	7	7	7	5	8	7

Although fewer than one-third of the faculty (32 percent) agree that 'tenure is an outmoded concept,' it is interesting to note that this many faculty question the value of tenure given that they personally stand to benefit substantially from the tenure process. As would be expected, those without tenure are much more likely than tenured faculty (52 versus 29 percent) to believe that tenure is an outmoded concept. Still, it is remarkable that more than one-fourth of all tenured faculty feel that tenure is outmoded.

There are only a few differences in faculty views by type of institution that merit comment. Professors in public institutions (especially in community colleges) are more likely than their private institution counterparts to believe that faculty unionization has benefitted teaching and that the chief benefit of a college education is to increase earning power.

Summary

This report is based on survey data collected in 1989-90 from a national sample of 35,478 faculty members at 392 colleges, universities, and community colleges. Data have been weighted to approximate the results that would have been obtained if all college faculty in all accredited institutions across the country had responded. Following are some of the survey highlights:

- Although the large majority of faculty (90 percent) see teaching as their principal activity and virtually all faculty (98 percent) give 'good teaching' a high priority, more than one-quarter (28 percent) prefer research over teaching and more than one-quarter (27 percent) feel that institutional pressures to do research and publish interfere with their teaching.

- Although 80 percent of college faculty spend at least some of their time in research and scholarly activities, fully one-fourth of the four-year college faculty and 62 percent of the community college faculty have never published an article in a scholarly journal. At the other extreme, one of every ten faculty employed by universities have published fifty or more articles.

- Time spent in research activities varies markedly by type of institution. Half of the faculty in private universities spend more than twelve hours per week doing research and writing, compared to less than 20 percent of faculty in four-year colleges and only 3 percent in the community colleges.

- Faculty are most satisfied with their autonomy and independence and job security. Two-thirds of the faculty report high levels of overall job satisfaction, and 80 percent would 'probably' or 'definitely' become a college professor if they had it to do over again. Faculty are least satisfied with their salary and fringe benefits and with the quality of their students.

- Considering that almost three-quarters of the faculty do not feel that students are well-prepared academically, it would appear that most new college students will first have to prove themselves academically to their faculty mentors before they will be able to gain faculty trust and respect.

- Although universities (especially private universities) have the lowest teaching loads and the greatest degree of faculty involvement in research, faculty at these institutions also experience the greatest degree of conflict between their teaching responsibilities and the demands of research. This conflict is most severe in the public universities. Similarly, among professors in four-year colleges, those in the public institutions experience the greatest conflict between research and teaching.

- Compared to their private counterparts, professors in public institutions give higher priority to preparing students for employment and conducting research.

- Faculty in all types of private institutions give greater priority than their public counterparts to the students' affective development, to fundraising, and to enhancing the institution's image and reputation.

- Faculty in the universities, compared to faculty in other types of institutions, see their institutions giving more priority to enhancing the institution's national image, increasing or maintaining institutional prestige, raising money, and hiring faculty 'stars.'

- Although two-thirds of all faculty are tenured, more than one-third (including 29 percent of those with tenure) feel that 'tenure is an outmoded concept.'

References

Hurtado, S. *Campus Racial Climates and Educational Outcomes*. University of California, Los Angeles, Unpublished Doctoral Dissertation, 1990.

National Center for Educational Statistics. *Faculty in Higher Education Institutions, 1988*. Contractor Report. Data Series DR-NS OPF-87/88-I.27. Washington, D.C.: NCES, March, 1990.

National Normative Data for

the 1989-90 HERI Faculty Survey

ALL FACULTY

	ALL			Universities		Four-year Colleges					Two-year Colleges	
	Insts	4-yr	2-yr	Pub	Priv	Pub	All Priv	Nons	Cath	Prot	Pub	Priv
Age as of December 31, 1989												
less than 30	2.2	2.3	1.7	1.9	3.5	1.6	3.1	2.9	2.2	4.0	1.6	4.3
30 - 34	8.0	8.8	5.3	8.7	12.0	7.2	9.8	10.0	8.9	10.0	5.1	8.7
35 - 39	13.4	13.8	12.0	13.2	14.9	12.9	15.6	15.9	15.7	15.1	11.6	20.0
40 - 44	17.3	16.9	18.9	16.7	17.2	16.2	18.0	18.3	18.7	17.3	18.8	19.1
45 - 49	18.9	18.1	21.7	17.6	15.4	20.1	17.2	16.6	17.1	18.0	21.9	16.5
50 - 54	15.7	15.0	18.2	14.9	11.1	17.4	13.9	14.4	13.0	13.5	18.4	11.3
55 - 59	12.8	12.9	12.4	13.7	10.7	13.8	11.7	11.7	11.7	11.6	12.7	7.1
60 - 64	8.3	8.6	7.2	9.3	10.0	8.2	7.7	7.4	7.8	8.0	7.1	7.8
65 - 69	2.9	3.0	2.2	3.4	5.0	2.3	2.5	2.4	3.8	2.1	2.2	2.7
70 or more	0.5	0.5	0.5	0.5	0.4	0.4	0.6	0.5	1.1	0.4	0.4	2.6
Academic Rank												
professor	33.7	36.2	25.1	40.5	40.8	34.5	30.0	31.3	21.6	32.8	25.3	18.9
associate professor	25.7	28.5	15.9	27.7	26.0	30.0	28.8	28.5	33.5	26.4	16.0	13.7
assistant professor	23.3	26.4	12.4	23.4	26.2	27.1	30.0	27.9	35.3	30.2	12.1	19.7
lecturer	1.8	2.1	0.5	3.2	3.7	1.3	1.0	1.1	1.0	0.7	0.5	0.9
instructor	13.1	5.3	40.8	3.6	1.5	5.7	9.0	9.6	7.3	9.1	41.1	32.9
other	2.3	1.5	5.3	1.7	1.7	1.4	1.3	1.6	1.3	0.8	4.9	14.0
Administrative Title												
not applicable	77.5	77.8	76.6	82.7	81.5	78.0	68.3	70.6	67.3	65.6	77.4	57.6
director or coordinator	9.2	9.2	9.2	8.6	8.0	9.6	10.2	10.5	10.9	9.4	8.9	17.7
department chair	8.6	8.2	9.9	3.6	6.1	7.6	17.0	15.1	17.0	19.7	9.4	21.2
dean	0.2	0.2	0.2	0.1	0.2	0.2	0.4	0.2	0.2	0.6	0.1	0.0
associate or assistant dean	0.4	0.4	0.2	0.5	0.4	0.3	0.5	0.2	0.4	0.8	0.2	0.9
vice-pres, provost, vice-chanc	0.1	0.1	0.1	0.1	0.1	0.0	0.1	0.0	0.1	0.2	0.0	0.0
president, chancellor	0.0	0.0	0.0	0.0	0.0	0.0	0.0	0.0	0.0	0.0	0.0	0.0
other	4.0	4.0	3.9	4.5	3.7	4.2	3.4	3.1	4.0	3.6	4.0	2.6
Principal Activity												
administration	3.3	3.4	3.0	3.2	3.3	3.6	3.4	3.3	3.4	3.4	2.9	5.2
teaching	89.9	88.3	95.3	82.1	77.9	93.3	95.3	95.2	95.4	95.4	95.4	93.9
research	5.7	7.4	0.1	13.7	18.4	2.0	0.5	0.8	0.3	0.3	0.1	0.0
services to clients and patients	0.6	0.5	1.0	0.7	0.2	0.5	0.3	0.2	0.5	0.3	1.0	0.0
other	0.5	0.5	0.7	0.4	0.2	0.6	0.5	0.5	0.4	0.6	0.7	0.9
Racial Background (1)												
White/Caucasian	90.4	90.2	91.1	91.6	93.3	86.8	91.7	88.8	96.2	93.4	90.9	97.4
Black/Negro/Afro-American	4.0	3.9	4.0	1.4	2.0	7.0	4.0	5.2	0.8	4.2	4.1	2.6
American Indian	0.9	0.8	1.2	0.9	0.4	1.0	0.6	0.7	0.5	0.6	1.3	0.0
Asian-American	3.2	3.4	2.2	4.2	2.8	3.8	2.1	2.6	1.7	1.5	2.3	0.0
Mexican-American/Chicano	0.8	0.5	1.7	0.8	0.2	0.6	0.3	0.3	0.5	0.3	1.7	0.0
Puerto Rican-American	0.4	0.5	0.2	0.4	0.1	0.2	1.1	2.1	0.2	0.1	0.2	0.0
Other	2.1	2.2	1.7	2.6	2.3	2.2	1.8	2.1	1.8	1.3	1.8	0.0

ALL FACULTY

	ALL			Universities		Four-year Colleges					Two-year Colleges	
	Insts	4-yr	2-yr	Pub	Priv	Pub	All Priv	Nons	Cath	Prot	Pub	Priv
Highest Degree Earned												
bachelor's (B.A., B.S., etc.)	3.2	1.3	9.9	1.0	0.6	1.2	2.1	2.7	1.5	1.6	10.1	4.3
master's (M.A., M.S., etc.)	28.1	18.9	60.8	12.6	8.2	22.3	28.5	24.7	32.2	31.8	60.4	69.6
LL.B., J.D.	0.7	0.6	0.8	0.5	0.5	0.8	0.6	0.7	0.8	0.4	0.9	0.0
M.D., D.D.S. (or equivalent)	0.4	0.4	0.4	0.6	0.2	0.6	0.2	0.2	0.1	0.2	0.4	0.0
other first professional	0.6	0.7	0.4	0.7	0.3	0.7	0.8	0.8	0.7	0.7	0.4	0.0
Ed.D.	4.7	5.0	3.6	3.7	1.0	8.3	4.2	4.1	2.6	5.4	3.6	2.6
Ph.D.	56.3	68.5	12.8	76.9	86.2	61.1	57.9	61.2	56.6	54.0	12.7	15.7
other degree	4.0	3.5	6.0	3.1	2.3	3.8	4.2	4.0	3.9	4.6	6.0	5.2
none	2.0	1.1	5.4	0.8	0.7	1.2	1.5	1.5	1.6	1.3	5.5	1.7
Field of Highest Degree (2)												
agriculture or forestry	1.4	1.5	1.1	3.1	1.0	1.0	0.2	0.4	0.0	0.2	1.2	0.9
biological sciences	6.1	6.4	5.2	7.1	6.3	5.9	6.0	5.6	6.3	6.3	5.2	6.4
business	6.4	6.2	7.4	5.3	5.7	7.2	6.1	5.6	8.8	5.5	7.4	5.4
education	15.0	12.9	22.5	10.6	2.9	18.2	13.8	12.9	11.9	16.2	22.4	26.2
engineering	5.1	5.7	3.2	8.9	8.1	4.2	1.9	2.9	1.4	0.8	3.3	0.0
English	6.8	6.3	8.5	5.7	5.7	5.9	8.0	8.3	7.3	7.9	8.3	12.8
health related	4.8	3.8	8.4	4.0	1.7	4.6	3.5	2.5	5.0	3.9	8.5	5.4
history or political science	6.5	7.1	4.1	6.6	10.9	6.3	7.1	7.7	6.7	6.3	4.1	4.6
humanities	8.2	9.4	3.7	8.5	15.8	5.7	12.9	11.9	14.4	13.4	3.5	8.4
fine arts	8.3	8.6	7.1	9.1	4.9	8.7	9.9	9.5	7.4	11.8	6.8	13.7
mathematics or statistics	5.6	5.3	6.3	4.6	6.3	5.5	6.0	5.9	6.1	4.5	6.4	4.5
physical sciences	6.8	7.3	5.0	7.3	9.5	6.6	7.4	8.1	6.4	6.9	5.1	3.7
social sciences	12.5	13.8	8.1	13.6	17.8	13.1	12.9	13.7	12.9	11.6	8.2	6.3
other technical	1.5	1.1	2.7	1.0	0.9	1.3	1.2	1.4	1.5	0.7	2.8	0.0
other non-technical	5.0	4.5	6.7	4.8	2.4	5.8	3.2	3.6	3.8	2.2	6.9	1.8
Year Highest Degree Earned												
1951 or earlier	2.6	2.3	3.6	2.3	3.5	2.1	2.1	2.3	2.2	1.9	3.6	2.6
1952 – 1956	3.2	3.5	2.1	4.2	6.5	2.5	2.3	2.7	2.1	1.9	2.2	0.9
1957 – 1961	5.7	6.0	4.6	7.6	7.3	4.7	5.1	5.4	5.7	4.2	4.7	0.9
1962 – 1966	11.3	11.4	11.1	13.3	11.6	10.8	9.6	10.6	8.1	8.9	11.1	10.4
1967 – 1971	17.8	17.5	19.0	18.5	14.2	19.6	14.7	14.8	12.6	15.6	19.0	18.2
1972 – 1976	18.0	17.4	20.1	16.1	15.1	18.8	18.5	17.4	20.4	19.2	20.4	14.7
1977 – 1981	15.6	15.3	16.9	13.8	14.6	15.8	17.4	16.8	19.6	17.0	16.8	20.0
1982 – 1986	16.5	16.9	15.0	15.2	17.3	16.3	19.4	19.3	19.2	19.5	14.7	22.7
1987 – 1989	9.2	9.7	7.6	9.0	10.0	9.3	11.0	10.8	10.2	11.8	7.5	9.5
Degree Currently Working Toward												
bachelor's (B.A., B.S., etc.)	1.7	0.5	6.2	0.1	0.9	0.5	0.6	1.3	0.2	0.1	6.5	0.0
master's (M.A., M.S., etc.)	4.7	1.9	14.4	1.0	0.7	2.2	3.2	3.4	2.5	3.3	14.6	9.3
LL.B., J.D.	0.3	0.3	0.3	0.4	0.0	0.2	0.3	0.5	0.0	0.2	0.2	1.6
M.D., D.D.S. (or equivalent)	0.1	0.1	0.3	0.0	0.0	0.2	0.2	0.2	0.2	0.2	0.2	1.6
other first professional	0.2	0.2	0.3	0.1	0.1	0.1	0.4	0.3	0.7	0.4	0.2	1.6
Ed.D.	3.4	2.5	6.4	1.0	0.3	3.8	3.9	3.7	3.4	4.4	6.3	7.8
Ph.D.	12.3	11.7	14.4	6.8	5.6	14.5	17.3	16.1	19.2	17.8	14.6	12.6
other degree	2.2	1.7	4.2	1.1	0.7	2.1	2.3	2.3	2.0	2.6	4.1	6.2
none	75.1	81.2	53.7	89.6	91.6	76.5	71.7	72.1	71.9	71.1	53.3	61.0

ALL FACULTY

	ALL			Universities		Four-year Colleges					Two-year Colleges	
	Insts	4-yr	2-yr	Pub	Priv	Pub	All Priv	Nons	Cath	Prot	Pub	Priv
Department of Current Faculty Appointment (2)												
agriculture or forestry	1.6	1.8	0.9	3.5	1.6	1.3	0.1	0.3	0.0	0.0	0.9	0.9
biological sciences	5.6	5.8	4.8	5.9	5.8	5.6	5.8	5.3	6.3	6.3	4.8	5.7
business	8.6	8.2	10.2	7.0	6.9	9.6	8.6	8.2	12.3	7.0	10.2	10.3
education	8.5	8.9	7.2	7.9	2.2	12.1	9.1	7.9	7.3	11.9	7.0	13.1
engineering	4.9	5.6	2.5	8.9	8.9	3.8	1.7	2.7	1.1	0.6	2.6	0.0
English	7.4	6.7	10.1	6.0	5.6	6.3	8.7	9.0	7.6	9.0	9.9	14.2
health related	5.9	4.5	11.0	4.8	2.5	5.5	3.8	2.4	6.5	4.3	11.3	3.7
history or political science	5.7	6.5	2.7	6.4	9.5	5.6	6.6	7.0	5.9	6.3	2.7	2.8
humanities	8.0	9.2	3.6	7.8	16.6	5.4	13.0	12.2	14.2	13.5	3.4	8.6
fine arts	8.6	9.2	6.5	9.8	5.0	9.5	10.1	9.6	7.1	12.4	6.2	13.3
mathematics or statistics	6.1	5.7	7.6	5.2	5.4	5.9	6.3	6.1	6.3	6.6	7.6	8.4
physical sciences	6.7	7.1	5.4	6.6	8.2	6.9	7.4	8.0	6.5	7.1	5.5	3.8
social sciences	12.1	12.9	9.2	12.5	16.0	12.6	12.4	13.4	11.4	11.3	9.2	10.4
other technical	3.7	2.3	8.5	1.8	2.2	2.7	2.7	3.4	2.9	1.5	8.8	1.9
other non-technical	6.5	5.6	9.7	6.0	3.9	7.2	3.7	4.4	4.6	2.2	10.0	2.8
Year Appointed to Current Position												
1951 or earlier	1.9	2.0	1.7	1.9	2.1	1.8	2.3	2.3	3.0	1.8	1.7	0.9
1952 – 1956	1.2	1.4	0.3	1.6	2.6	0.8	1.6	1.6	1.6	1.5	0.3	0.9
1957 – 1961	3.3	3.8	1.3	4.2	5.3	2.8	4.0	3.8	4.5	4.1	1.3	0.9
1962 – 1966	9.8	10.4	7.6	11.2	10.6	10.8	8.8	9.8	6.8	8.3	7.4	12.6
1967 – 1971	18.8	17.6	23.1	19.1	13.9	20.6	12.7	13.6	11.1	12.4	23.5	14.3
1972 – 1976	13.7	12.2	18.7	13.0	12.0	12.9	10.3	9.9	10.4	10.7	19.0	12.5
1977 – 1981	14.0	13.5	15.9	12.9	13.6	12.9	15.0	14.1	17.6	15.0	15.9	17.0
1982 – 1986	18.7	19.3	16.7	18.2	19.4	18.9	21.4	21.3	20.8	22.0	16.5	22.2
1987 – 1989	18.6	19.8	14.7	18.0	20.5	18.4	23.9	23.6	24.2	24.1	14.5	18.8
Tenured?												
yes	66.8	65.7	70.7	70.1	65.5	67.8	56.5	57.7	53.9	56.2	71.3	55.4
no	33.2	34.3	29.3	29.9	34.5	32.2	43.5	42.3	46.1	43.8	28.7	44.6
Year Received Tenure												
1951 or earlier	0.4	0.3	0.7	0.4	0.1	0.3	0.5	0.4	1.0	0.3	0.7	0.0
1952 – 1956	0.4	0.4	0.1	0.6	0.7	0.2	0.5	0.5	0.6	0.4	0.1	0.0
1957 – 1961	1.8	2.2	0.4	2.5	4.1	1.3	2.1	2.3	2.0	1.7	0.4	0.0
1962 – 1966	5.8	6.6	2.8	7.3	9.2	5.2	6.4	6.6	5.3	6.6	2.8	3.7
1967 – 1971	17.7	17.8	17.6	18.7	17.3	18.3	15.4	16.4	12.6	15.3	17.7	14.3
1972 – 1976	24.8	23.9	27.8	23.8	20.0	26.7	21.4	22.8	19.9	20.2	28.0	23.2
1977 – 1981	18.6	18.3	19.8	19.1	18.7	18.4	16.4	15.3	17.0	17.6	20.0	12.6
1982 – 1986	18.7	18.5	19.2	17.3	18.5	18.1	21.8	20.9	22.6	22.6	19.2	17.8
1987 – 1989	11.8	11.9	11.6	10.3	11.4	11.7	15.7	14.8	19.0	15.2	11.0	28.5
Primary Interest												
very heavily in teaching	36.7	27.2	69.9	16.5	10.8	33.6	41.8	36.0	45.0	48.4	69.7	74.8
leaning toward teaching	35.4	38.6	24.2	34.7	32.1	42.4	42.0	42.9	42.7	40.3	24.6	16.5
leaning toward research	24.0	29.3	5.5	41.9	45.1	21.2	14.9	19.2	11.6	10.7	5.4	7.8
very heavily in research	3.9	4.9	0.4	6.9	11.9	2.8	1.2	1.9	0.7	0.6	0.3	0.9

ALL FACULTY

	ALL			Universities		Four-year Colleges					Two-year Colleges	
	Insts	4-yr	2-yr	Pub	Priv	Pub	All Priv	Nons	Cath	Prot	Pub	Priv
Marital Status												
married (currently)	75.9	75.8	76.2	78.1	76.1	74.3	74.4	74.7	64.6	79.3	76.1	79.5
separated	1.3	1.4	1.1	1.4	0.9	1.6	1.4	1.5	1.9	0.9	1.2	0.0
single (never married)	10.9	11.5	8.8	9.6	11.7	11.4	14.5	11.8	25.0	12.5	8.6	12.8
single (with partner)	2.4	2.5	2.1	2.3	4.9	2.1	2.0	2.9	1.3	1.0	2.1	0.9
single (divorced)	8.3	7.8	10.2	7.5	5.7	9.4	6.8	8.0	6.5	5.3	10.4	5.2
single (widowed)	1.2	1.1	1.7	1.1	0.8	1.3	1.0	1.1	0.6	1.0	1.7	1.7
Spouse's or Partner's Education												
8th grade or less	0.2	0.1	0.3	0.1	0.2	0.2	0.1	0.1	0.0	0.1	0.3	0.0
some high school	0.5	0.3	0.9	0.3	0.2	0.5	0.3	0.2	0.5	0.3	0.9	0.9
completed high school	4.3	3.5	7.2	3.5	2.6	4.0	3.5	3.9	3.9	2.7	7.4	1.9
some college	12.4	10.7	18.6	11.2	7.5	11.3	10.8	10.4	9.4	12.0	18.8	15.0
graduated from college	19.3	18.5	22.3	18.4	17.3	18.2	19.8	19.7	16.5	21.7	22.2	26.0
attended grad/prof school	10.5	10.8	9.4	11.2	11.5	10.4	10.8	11.1	9.3	11.0	9.3	13.2
attained advanced degree	39.1	42.1	28.8	43.4	48.2	40.4	39.3	41.0	36.1	38.5	28.7	31.9
does not apply	13.6	13.9	12.5	11.9	12.6	15.3	15.6	13.7	24.3	13.6	12.5	11.1
Father's Education												
8th grade or less	19.9	18.9	23.7	18.2	14.5	21.8	17.9	16.8	20.9	17.7	23.7	23.4
some high school	11.0	10.1	14.0	9.6	9.6	10.7	10.3	9.8	11.0	10.6	14.2	9.0
completed high school	22.6	21.8	25.6	22.0	19.0	22.3	22.1	21.8	24.0	21.6	25.5	28.0
some college	13.7	13.7	13.6	13.2	13.6	14.2	13.7	13.1	13.3	14.8	13.6	13.5
graduated from college	12.9	13.7	10.2	14.2	15.4	12.3	14.0	14.7	13.9	13.1	10.1	13.5
attended grad/prof school	4.9	5.4	3.4	5.7	6.3	4.9	5.1	5.2	4.4	5.5	3.4	3.6
attained advanced degree	15.0	16.5	9.6	17.1	21.6	13.8	16.8	18.5	12.5	16.8	9.6	9.0
Mother's Education												
8th grade or less	14.4	13.9	16.1	13.5	10.4	15.8	13.3	13.2	15.5	12.2	16.2	14.5
some high school	11.0	10.4	13.1	9.0	10.0	11.8	10.5	10.2	10.9	10.6	13.2	11.6
completed high school	33.3	32.6	36.1	33.8	30.0	32.0	33.0	32.5	34.2	33.1	36.2	33.3
some college	16.4	16.4	16.1	16.2	16.9	16.2	16.8	15.6	17.5	18.2	16.0	19.8
graduated from college	14.7	15.6	11.6	16.2	18.3	14.4	15.0	15.9	12.9	14.9	11.5	13.5
attended grad/prof school	4.0	4.2	3.2	3.9	5.8	3.6	4.5	4.8	4.1	4.4	3.1	5.4
attained advanced degree	6.3	7.0	3.6	7.3	8.6	6.2	6.9	7.9	4.9	6.6	3.7	1.9
Base Institutional Salary in Thousands (3)												
less than 20	0.5	0.4	1.1	0.1	0.1	0.2	1.4	1.4	1.3	1.5	1.0	3.6
20 – 29	7.3	6.5	10.0	3.2	2.9	4.4	16.2	13.7	14.6	20.7	9.5	24.4
30 – 39	17.0	15.7	21.5	11.2	8.4	14.9	27.5	22.8	33.6	30.9	20.4	47.3
40 – 49	27.7	26.7	31.2	23.3	20.2	32.2	26.9	23.9	30.2	29.3	31.5	23.8
50 – 59	19.6	19.9	18.1	19.7	18.2	23.8	14.8	17.2	13.5	12.0	19.5	0.9
60 – 69	15.2	15.6	14.1	19.0	20.2	15.9	8.2	12.0	5.6	4.2	14.7	0.0
70 – 79	6.0	7.0	2.4	9.5	9.0	6.9	2.6	4.4	1.1	0.9	2.5	0.0
80 – 89	3.7	4.6	0.7	8.0	9.5	1.5	1.8	3.4	0.0	0.4	0.7	0.0
90 – 98	1.2	1.5	0.1	2.5	4.5	0.2	0.4	0.8	0.0	0.1	0.1	0.0
99 or more	1.6	2.1	0.1	3.6	6.2	0.3	0.2	0.4	0.0	0.0	0.1	0.0

ALL FACULTY

	ALL			Universities		Four-year Colleges					Two-year Colleges	
	Insts	4-yr	2-yr	Pub	Priv	Pub	All Priv	Nons	Cath	Prot	Pub	Priv
General Activities												
held academic admin position....	38.9	41.2	30.7	38.7	42.1	40.9	44.8	44.5	48.4	43.3	30.5	36.3
award for outstanding teaching..	30.8	30.4	32.2	30.6	25.1	32.4	30.0	29.2	29.2	31.7	32.2	32.6
spouse or partner an academic..	33.1	32.9	33.9	31.3	29.6	34.7	34.4	33.8	29.3	37.8	33.7	38.7
commute a long distance to work.	18.3	17.1	22.8	14.3	16.5	20.0	17.0	18.9	18.6	13.3	23.2	14.1
research/writing on women/gender	18.7	20.7	11.6	20.6	22.4	19.3	22.2	22.7	24.1	20.5	11.7	9.7
research/writing on race/ethncty	18.3	20.0	12.2	20.2	18.4	20.7	19.5	21.1	18.3	17.9	12.4	7.2
have dependent children.........	53.8	53.2	55.9	54.2	51.2	52.7	53.3	53.3	49.2	55.7	55.7	62.0
am a U.S. citizen...............	94.7	93.8	97.9	93.1	89.3	94.9	95.6	94.4	96.7	96.6	97.8	99.1
interrupted career for hlth/fam.	9.9	8.8	13.8	7.9	6.5	9.6	10.0	9.2	12.0	10.0	13.8	13.9
considered career in acad admin.	40.2	40.4	39.4	40.7	33.7	42.6	40.1	40.3	39.9	39.8	39.4	41.3
plan working beyond age 70......	35.2	37.6	27.0	38.4	43.3	34.5	38.1	39.2	41.2	34.8	26.7	33.4
General Activities in the Last Two Years												
had one or more firm job offers.	34.5	33.8	36.9	31.6	34.5	33.6	37.0	36.7	36.8	37.5	37.1	32.5
part in fac development program.	53.6	47.2	75.9	32.5	30.6	54.9	65.5	60.2	70.6	70.1	75.8	78.1
developed a new course.........	69.1	70.6	63.6	67.3	74.4	69.0	75.7	75.9	77.6	74.5	63.8	60.2
considered early retirement.....	30.2	28.3	37.0	29.7	20.8	32.6	23.8	24.4	22.3	23.8	37.3	29.8
considered leaving academe......	37.5	37.3	38.2	37.9	31.2	38.4	37.8	38.4	39.3	36.1	37.9	43.8
Teaching Activities in the Last Two Years												
taught honors course...........	18.0	19.8	11.4	20.5	30.5	15.6	19.1	20.8	18.2	17.0	11.2	16.1
taught interdisciplinary course.	34.3	37.0	24.5	34.2	41.9	33.8	43.0	46.3	35.9	42.1	24.4	26.8
taught general education course.	45.2	45.4	44.2	35.2	32.6	53.4	54.6	51.6	48.8	61.9	44.0	48.9
taught develop/remedial course..	14.6	10.4	29.4	7.0	4.9	13.0	14.4	15.1	14.4	13.4	29.5	27.6
taught ethnic studies course...	6.2	7.0	3.5	5.7	6.8	7.3	8.6	9.1	7.4	8.6	3.5	2.1
taught women's studies course...	5.1	5.6	3.3	4.9	6.3	4.8	7.4	8.2	7.4	6.4	3.4	2.1
team-taught a course...........	35.6	37.0	30.4	38.7	38.4	33.7	38.9	39.5	32.5	41.6	30.5	27.3
worked w/students on resrch proj	62.7	70.2	34.3	77.2	78.1	66.6	60.6	64.5	57.7	56.5	34.1	37.5
attd racial/cultural workshop...	27.1	24.4	36.5	18.8	17.3	28.6	29.9	30.1	36.7	25.7	37.4	16.6
attd women's/minorities workshop	17.2	16.1	21.3	12.5	13.4	16.7	21.9	23.8	27.3	16.0	21.7	10.2
held faculty senate/council ofc.	25.6	24.7	28.9	21.9	22.8	26.5	27.0	26.6	29.8	26.0	28.9	28.0
used funds for research.........	42.7	50.9	11.4	62.0	66.3	42.3	38.8	43.5	34.9	34.0	11.3	14.6
served as a paid consultant.....	46.3	49.3	35.7	52.8	55.9	49.1	40.5	42.2	41.6	37.4	36.3	20.5
Research Working Environment												
work essentially alone..........	67.6	68.0	66.1	63.1	64.9	69.3	75.0	74.2	72.9	77.4	65.7	76.3
work with one or two colleagues.	25.0	26.2	20.4	30.5	29.5	25.3	19.6	20.4	21.9	17.0	20.6	15.4
member of larger group..........	7.4	5.7	13.5	6.4	5.6	5.4	5.4	5.4	5.3	5.6	13.7	8.2

ALL FACULTY

HOURS PER WEEK SPENT ON:	ALL			Universities		Four-year Colleges					Two-year Colleges	
	Insts	4-yr	2-yr	Pub	Priv	Pub	All Priv	Nons	Cath	Prot	Pub	Priv
Scheduled Teaching												
none	0.3	0.4	0.2	0.6	0.6	0.2	0.1	0.1	0.2	0.1	0.2	0.0
1 – 4	7.2	8.6	2.2	12.2	18.5	5.0	3.4	3.6	3.5	3.1	2.2	3.8
5 – 8	26.2	32.1	5.0	47.7	53.1	19.6	16.9	21.2	14.6	11.9	5.1	4.8
9 – 12	32.0	36.9	14.9	27.1	21.9	45.0	46.9	45.1	53.4	45.8	14.8	19.1
13 – 16	17.6	13.5	32.1	6.6	3.6	18.6	21.1	18.3	19.5	26.0	31.6	46.6
17 – 20	10.1	5.7	25.6	4.0	1.2	7.6	7.6	7.2	6.5	8.8	25.9	20.0
21 – 34	5.9	2.5	18.0	1.6	0.9	3.3	3.5	3.9	2.0	3.7	18.5	4.8
35 – 44	0.5	0.3	1.4	0.1	0.0	0.5	0.4	0.5	0.3	0.3	1.5	0.0
45 or more	0.1	0.1	0.4	0.0	0.0	0.1	0.1	0.1	0.2	0.2	0.3	0.9
Preparing for Teaching												
none	0.3	0.3	0.2	0.5	0.5	0.2	0.1	0.2	0.2	0.0	0.3	0.0
1 – 4	8.4	8.4	8.4	10.4	10.7	7.5	5.7	6.2	5.0	5.4	8.4	10.5
5 – 8	22.9	23.0	22.7	26.0	26.4	22.1	17.9	19.3	17.1	16.5	22.6	25.5
9 – 12	25.2	25.0	25.9	25.9	26.3	24.9	23.0	23.2	22.9	22.8	26.0	22.7
13 – 16	17.3	17.3	17.3	16.7	16.9	17.1	18.8	18.7	18.2	19.4	17.3	17.0
17 – 20	13.8	13.8	13.7	11.5	10.8	15.2	16.4	15.9	17.2	16.7	13.9	9.4
21 – 34	9.4	9.6	9.0	7.3	6.6	10.0	13.8	12.5	15.3	14.9	8.9	10.3
35 – 44	2.0	1.9	2.0	1.1	1.2	2.2	3.2	3.0	3.3	3.3	1.9	3.7
45 or more	0.7	0.7	0.7	0.6	0.5	0.7	0.9	0.9	0.9	0.9	0.7	0.9
Advising/Counseling of Students												
none	2.6	2.5	2.9	3.2	1.6	2.7	1.7	1.7	1.8	1.7	2.9	1.9
1 – 4	56.6	55.9	59.0	59.3	62.2	52.4	52.8	51.6	51.9	55.0	58.9	61.1
5 – 8	29.5	29.9	27.9	27.8	26.4	31.4	32.5	33.9	33.4	30.1	28.1	22.7
9 – 12	8.0	8.3	6.9	6.8	7.4	9.5	9.3	9.0	9.7	9.4	6.7	12.4
13 – 16	2.0	2.1	1.5	1.5	1.5	2.6	2.3	2.4	1.7	2.4	1.6	1.0
17 – 20	0.9	0.9	0.7	0.9	0.7	0.8	1.1	1.2	0.9	0.3	0.9	0.9
21 – 34	0.4	0.3	0.7	0.4	0.2	0.3	0.3	0.0	0.2	0.3	0.7	0.0
35 – 44	0.1	0.1	0.2	0.0	0.0	0.1	0.1	0.0	0.2	0.1	0.2	0.0
45 or more	0.0	0.0	0.0	0.0	0.0	0.0	0.0	0.0	0.1	0.0	0.0	0.0
Committee Work and Meetings												
none	4.6	4.2	6.3	4.6	5.6	3.1	4.5	4.7	4.0	4.5	6.5	3.7
1 – 4	68.8	67.0	75.5	63.8	70.8	66.0	71.1	69.9	71.0	72.8	75.3	80.2
5 – 8	20.6	22.5	14.1	24.1	18.5	23.9	20.0	20.4	20.8	18.9	14.3	10.5
9 – 12	4.3	4.7	2.8	5.4	3.8	5.3	3.2	3.5	2.8	2.9	2.7	4.7
13 – 16	1.1	1.2	0.8	1.5	1.1	1.2	0.9	1.1	1.0	0.5	0.8	0.9
17 – 20	0.3	0.3	0.4	0.5	0.1	0.4	0.2	0.2	0.3	0.2	0.4	0.0
21 – 34	0.1	0.1	0.1	0.1	0.1	0.2	0.1	0.0	0.0	0.2	0.1	0.0
35 – 44	0.0	0.0	0.0	0.0	0.0	0.0	0.0	0.0	0.0	0.0	0.0	0.0
45 or more	0.0	0.0	0.0	0.0	0.0	0.0	0.0	0.0	0.0	0.0	0.0	0.0

ALL FACULTY

HOURS PER WEEK SPENT ON:	ALL			Universities		Four-year Colleges					Two-year Colleges	
	Insts	4-yr	2-yr	Pub	Priv	Pub	All Priv	Nons	Cath	Prot	Pub	Priv
Other Administration												
none	36.5	35.2	41.0	36.1	31.6	37.0	33.2	33.5	34.3	32.0	41.2	35.0
1 – 4	38.6	38.9	37.3	40.4	43.5	37.0	37.3	37.6	37.0	37.2	37.3	38.1
5 – 8	11.5	11.7	10.8	11.2	11.9	11.0	13.3	12.7	12.9	14.4	10.7	13.5
9 – 12	5.8	6.1	4.8	5.4	6.8	5.9	7.1	7.2	7.4	6.7	4.8	5.2
13 – 16	3.0	3.2	2.5	2.6	3.3	3.5	3.4	3.4	3.0	3.7	2.5	2.1
17 – 20	2.3	2.5	1.7	2.2	1.7	2.8	3.0	3.0	2.9	3.1	1.6	3.1
21 – 34	1.7	1.8	1.5	1.5	1.1	2.2	2.1	2.1	2.1	2.2	1.5	2.1
35 – 44	0.4	0.4	0.4	0.5	0.2	0.3	0.3	0.4	0.3	0.3	0.3	1.0
45 or more	0.2	0.2	0.2	0.1	0.0	0.3	0.2	0.1	0.3	0.3	0.2	0.0
Research and Scholarly Writing												
none	20.2	11.9	51.7	5.4	3.8	13.5	23.6	20.5	23.0	28.4	51.6	53.8
1 – 4	27.9	26.9	31.7	17.7	14.2	33.3	38.1	34.3	41.6	41.7	31.6	33.2
5 – 8	16.4	18.2	9.4	17.0	16.6	19.8	18.4	19.4	19.2	16.4	9.5	7.0
9 – 12	12.4	14.6	4.2	18.3	16.4	13.7	9.4	11.6	8.0	7.0	4.2	4.0
13 – 16	7.3	8.9	1.3	11.6	12.7	7.8	4.7	6.2	3.7	3.1	1.2	2.0
17 – 20	6.7	8.3	1.0	12.2	13.4	5.9	3.1	4.1	3.0	2.0	1.1	0.0
21 – 34	6.3	7.8	0.5	12.4	14.5	5.6	2.1	3.0	2.6	1.0	0.5	0.0
35 – 44	1.8	2.2	0.1	3.5	5.4	0.9	0.5	0.7	0.3	0.3	0.1	0.0
45 or more	1.0	1.2	0.1	2.0	2.8	0.5	0.2	0.3	0.1	0.1	0.2	0.0
Consultation with Clients or Patients												
none	68.8	68.5	69.9	66.4	70.2	66.9	73.0	72.7	71.2	74.4	69.7	74.9
1 – 4	20.7	21.0	19.7	22.5	20.1	21.9	18.2	18.2	18.8	17.8	19.8	17.4
5 – 8	6.3	6.4	6.1	6.6	5.9	7.0	5.3	5.5	5.6	4.8	6.1	6.6
9 – 12	2.2	2.1	2.1	2.3	2.6	2.1	1.8	2.1	1.5	1.5	2.3	0.0
13 – 16	0.8	0.8	0.8	0.9	0.6	0.8	0.7	0.7	1.0	0.5	0.8	0.0
17 – 20	0.6	0.6	0.6	0.8	0.3	0.6	0.7	0.7	0.7	0.5	0.6	0.0
21 – 34	0.4	0.4	0.4	0.5	0.1	0.4	0.3	0.0	0.7	0.4	0.5	1.1
35 – 44	0.1	0.1	0.1	0.1	0.3	0.1	0.1	0.0	0.3	0.1	0.1	0.0
45 or more	0.1	0.1	0.2	0.0	0.0	0.2	0.0	0.3	0.0	0.0	0.2	0.0
Number of Days Spent Off-Campus for Professional Activities												
none	12.4	10.9	17.6	10.1	8.2	11.3	12.9	13.6	14.3	11.0	17.5	20.3
1-2	14.3	11.9	22.8	9.0	8.5	13.0	16.0	14.1	18.9	17.2	22.7	24.7
3-4	23.7	22.1	29.2	17.7	17.6	23.8	28.4	26.5	28.1	31.2	29.2	29.2
5-10	29.8	31.9	22.4	33.8	29.2	32.8	29.1	29.9	26.2	29.6	22.6	18.7
11-20	13.3	15.4	5.9	19.0	22.7	13.3	9.5	10.9	8.5	7.9	6.0	5.3
21-50	5.0	6.0	1.5	7.9	11.7	4.2	3.0	3.6	3.0	2.2	1.4	1.8
50+	1.6	1.8	0.6	2.6	2.2	1.5	1.1	1.4	0.9	0.8	0.7	0.0

ALL FACULTY

	ALL			Universities		Four-year Colleges					Two-year Colleges	
NUMBER OF:	Insts	4-yr	2-yr	Pub	Priv	Pub	All Priv	Nons	Cath	Prot	Pub	Priv
Articles in Academic or Professional Journals												
none	28.7	19.2	61.9	10.7	8.1	22.8	32.0	28.5	33.6	36.2	61.5	71.0
1-2	18.8	17.8	22.4	12.3	9.9	21.4	24.3	21.5	26.6	27.1	22.5	20.2
3-4	13.1	14.4	8.3	11.4	12.4	17.2	15.8	16.3	16.8	14.5	8.4	5.3
5-10	14.8	17.6	4.9	19.2	17.9	17.9	14.7	16.8	13.4	12.5	5.0	2.7
11-20	10.7	13.3	1.4	18.2	18.9	10.3	7.7	9.6	6.4	5.8	1.5	0.0
21-50	9.4	11.8	0.8	18.2	19.7	8.1	4.0	5.3	2.5	3.2	0.8	0.9
50+	4.6	5.9	0.2	10.0	13.2	2.3	1.4	2.1	0.7	0.9	0.2	0.0
Chapters in Edited Volumes												
none	66.0	58.8	91.0	46.5	37.4	67.9	74.2	68.5	78.5	80.0	90.9	92.8
1-2	17.6	20.9	6.0	24.1	24.3	19.5	16.7	18.9	15.7	14.1	6.0	6.3
3-4	8.2	10.2	1.1	14.1	17.9	6.9	5.4	7.4	3.8	3.5	1.2	0.9
5-10	5.6	6.9	0.8	10.4	13.3	4.1	2.7	3.8	1.7	1.8	0.9	0.0
11-20	1.8	2.2	0.6	3.5	5.1	1.0	0.6	0.8	0.2	0.4	0.6	0.0
21-50	0.7	0.7	0.3	1.2	1.7	0.3	0.3	0.5	0.1	0.0	0.4	0.0
50+	0.2	0.2	0.1	0.2	0.3	0.2	0.1	0.1	0.0	0.1	0.1	0.0
Books, Manuals, Monographs												
none	52.4	49.0	64.6	41.8	38.0	52.3	60.1	56.9	62.4	63.3	63.8	84.8
1-2	29.9	31.4	24.7	33.1	34.9	30.9	28.0	28.7	27.5	27.2	25.2	10.8
3-4	9.9	10.7	7.0	13.4	12.5	9.8	7.4	8.8	6.8	5.8	7.2	2.6
5-10	5.5	6.4	2.5	8.4	10.3	5.2	3.3	4.0	2.4	2.9	2.5	1.8
11-20	1.6	1.8	0.8	2.4	3.3	1.2	0.9	1.2	0.6	0.6	0.9	0.0
21-50	0.4	0.5	0.2	0.6	0.9	0.4	0.3	0.3	0.2	0.3	0.2	0.0
50+	0.2	0.2	0.2	0.3	0.2	0.2	0.1	0.2	0.1	0.0	0.2	0.0
Professional Writings Accepted or Published in Last Two Years												
none	45.3	34.8	82.1	21.6	15.8	42.8	51.9	46.4	54.4	58.5	81.9	84.8
1-2	25.7	29.1	13.9	27.6	26.1	31.2	29.5	30.0	30.4	28.2	13.9	11.7
3-4	15.8	19.5	2.8	25.1	28.4	15.8	12.1	15.0	10.8	8.9	2.8	1.8
5-10	10.8	13.6	0.9	21.0	23.9	8.5	5.4	7.2	3.7	3.6	0.9	0.9
11-20	1.9	2.4	0.2	3.8	4.4	1.4	0.7	0.9	0.6	0.5	0.2	0.0
21-50	0.4	0.6	0.1	0.9	1.3	0.2	0.2	0.4	0.1	0.1	0.1	0.0
50+	0.1	0.1	0.1	0.1	0.1	0.1	0.1	0.1	0.1	0.1	0.1	0.0
Professional Goals Noted as Very Important or Essential												
engage in research	58.5	68.0	25.1	78.6	85.2	61.0	54.2	60.1	49.6	48.4	25.1	23.9
engage in outside activities	52.5	51.8	55.0	48.7	48.3	54.4	53.9	54.4	54.6	53.0	54.9	57.2
provide services to the cmty.	43.4	40.9	52.3	35.8	33.6	45.7	44.8	43.4	47.7	45.4	52.4	48.2
participate in comm/admin work	29.2	27.2	36.2	23.0	19.3	30.7	32.1	29.8	37.0	32.7	36.3	35.0
be a good colleague	80.0	78.7	84.4	75.9	74.8	79.7	83.4	82.1	83.0	85.5	84.5	83.3
be a good teacher	98.2	97.9	99.2	97.6	95.5	98.3	99.0	99.0	98.9	99.2	99.2	99.1

ALL FACULTY

	ALL			Universities		Four-year Colleges					Two-year Colleges	
	Insts	4-yr	2-yr	Pub	Priv	Pub	All Priv	Nons	Cath	Prot	Pub	Priv
Evaluation Methods Used in Most or All Undergaduate Courses												
multiple-choice mid-terms/finals	33.7	29.0	49.8	27.3	16.2	35.8	28.0	23.7	31.6	32.2	50.1	42.6
essay mid-terms/finals	40.6	43.9	28.8	42.6	50.3	40.8	47.3	47.6	47.5	46.7	28.5	37.3
short-answer mid-terms/finals	34.0	34.8	31.3	35.3	37.0	32.9	35.8	34.9	36.0	37.0	31.2	35.2
multiple-choice quizzes	16.7	12.4	31.8	10.0	5.9	15.8	14.0	12.1	15.1	16.3	31.9	29.2
short-answer quizzes	24.3	22.1	31.6	19.0	16.9	23.9	26.8	25.3	26.3	29.3	31.3	40.0
weekly essay assignments	14.2	13.2	17.9	12.0	12.1	13.7	14.8	15.7	14.1	13.8	18.2	10.4
student presentations	25.5	27.0	20.4	24.8	22.5	28.0	31.0	32.4	31.1	29.1	20.3	21.9
term/research papers	31.9	35.5	19.3	35.6	39.2	33.1	37.0	38.8	34.8	35.5	19.1	23.6
stdnt evals of each others' work	10.0	10.1	9.9	10.1	6.3	10.7	11.1	11.6	11.7	10.0	9.9	10.4
grading on a curve	22.9	25.3	14.6	29.2	29.8	23.4	19.9	22.1	17.7	18.0	14.3	20.0
competency-based grading	52.4	51.0	57.1	53.0	51.5	49.6	50.1	52.8	48.5	47.2	58.0	36.0
student evaluations of teaching	83.3	86.3	72.7	91.2	88.8	83.2	82.7	84.0	87.1	78.5	72.5	79.1
Instructional Methods Used in Most or All Undergrad Courses												
class discussions	69.6	69.4	70.5	65.9	67.4	71.1	72.9	74.9	71.1	70.9	70.8	63.4
computer/machine-aided instruct.	13.2	11.5	18.8	11.4	9.4	12.5	11.4	12.6	10.7	9.9	18.7	21.2
cooperative learning	26.0	25.2	28.9	23.5	18.7	27.0	28.1	28.3	30.0	26.8	29.2	22.9
experiential learning/field stud	18.8	18.6	19.6	18.4	13.7	20.2	19.1	19.0	19.4	18.9	19.9	14.1
graduate teaching assistants	8.3	10.5	0.5	17.8	26.3	4.4	1.0	1.8	0.5	0.2	0.5	0.9
undergrad teaching assistants	2.9	3.2	2.0	2.6	3.8	2.3	4.9	6.4	2.8	4.1	1.9	2.7
group projects	15.7	15.8	15.3	15.6	11.8	17.0	16.1	16.7	17.9	14.3	15.3	14.1
independent projects	34.1	35.0	31.3	34.5	32.4	36.0	35.4	37.4	34.8	32.9	31.6	23.7
extensive lecturing	55.7	56.4	53.4	61.3	63.5	54.5	48.4	46.0	51.2	50.3	53.1	62.1
multiple drafts of written work	12.4	12.5	11.9	11.3	11.7	12.4	14.8	16.7	14.6	12.1	11.9	12.5
readings on racial/ethnic issues	11.1	11.9	8.3	10.9	11.2	11.9	13.6	14.3	13.3	12.8	8.3	8.1
readings on women/gender issues	10.6	11.4	7.9	10.3	12.5	10.7	13.4	14.6	13.5	11.5	7.9	9.0
student-developed activities	15.3	14.4	18.3	12.3	10.7	17.3	15.0	16.0	16.5	12.7	18.3	16.9
student-selected topics	8.5	8.5	8.5	8.1	7.8	9.0	8.5	9.2	9.1	7.1	8.5	7.9
Goals for Undergraduates Noted as Very Important or Essential												
develop ability to think clearly	99.4	99.5	99.2	99.3	99.4	99.6	99.6	99.5	99.8	99.6	99.2	98.3
increase self-directed learning	92.5	92.9	91.3	92.4	90.8	93.4	93.9	94.3	94.0	93.3	91.5	87.6
prepare for employment	62.0	57.6	77.1	55.4	42.1	65.0	58.0	54.6	61.0	61.3	77.7	63.8
prepare for graduate education	50.7	53.2	42.0	48.8	51.5	54.7	58.1	55.1	56.7	63.1	41.8	46.3
develop moral character	56.3	54.4	63.1	47.0	48.6	54.3	68.0	63.0	69.1	74.7	62.6	77.3
provide for emotional developmnt	39.6	36.8	49.3	29.7	29.8	38.3	48.6	45.3	48.7	53.2	48.8	61.9
prepare for family living	18.7	16.1	27.7	11.1	9.4	18.3	23.6	20.5	22.7	28.7	27.4	37.2
teach stdnts classics west civ	35.4	37.4	28.2	33.0	37.8	37.3	43.7	40.7	45.9	46.7	27.7	38.8
help develop personal values	63.3	61.9	68.1	54.9	53.8	63.5	73.8	69.6	75.1	79.0	67.6	80.5
enhance out-of-class experience	41.6	40.0	47.5	35.3	28.9	43.5	47.4	47.5	45.8	48.0	47.2	53.5
enhance self-understanding	67.3	65.8	72.7	60.2	58.3	68.6	73.7	71.9	74.5	75.9	72.4	78.7

ALL FACULTY

	ALL			Universities		Four-year Colleges					Two-year Colleges	
	Insts	4-yr	2-yr	Pub	Priv	Pub	All Priv	Nons	Cath	Prot	Pub	Priv
NUMBER OF COURSES TAUGHT IN:												
General Education												
none	57.8	59.6	51.4	70.9	68.6	53.0	49.8	52.1	55.3	43.8	51.6	47.3
one	20.2	22.5	12.5	20.0	22.5	22.6	25.6	25.6	18.7	29.2	12.2	18.3
two	10.5	10.7	9.5	6.2	6.5	13.9	14.1	13.0	13.5	15.8	9.6	7.6
three	5.8	4.8	9.1	2.1	1.9	6.9	6.8	6.1	8.1	2.8	9.2	7.6
four	3.0	1.7	7.4	0.5	0.4	2.5	2.6	2.1	3.6		7.6	4.3
five or more	2.8	0.7	10.1	0.3	0.1	1.1	1.0	1.0	0.8	1.2	9.8	15.1
Other BA or BS Undergraduate Credit Courses												
none	11.2	6.9	28.8	7.1	6.6	7.1	6.3	7.3	5.1	5.6	29.1	20.0
one	28.9	33.2	11.6	43.4	52.1	26.2	18.7	19.8	16.8	18.3	11.7	8.9
two	27.3	30.2	15.9	31.4	30.1	29.2	29.8	32.2	27.7	27.6	15.8	18.9
three	17.6	18.2	15.2	13.3	8.6	21.8	25.1	23.5	27.0	26.3	15.0	20.0
four	9.3	8.2	13.7	3.1	1.8	11.5	14.0	11.4	18.1	15.5	13.5	18.8
five or more	5.6	3.3	14.9	1.6	0.7	4.1	6.1	5.8	5.4	6.8	14.9	13.3
Non-BA Credit Courses (developmental or remedial)												
none	87.1	93.8	66.6	95.8	96.0	92.2	92.1	90.8	93.6	93.2	66.3	73.5
one	5.4	3.8	10.4	2.6	3.2	4.6	4.4	4.7	3.9	4.2	10.5	9.3
two	2.9	1.2	7.9	0.8	0.6	1.5	1.7	2.4	1.5	1.0	8.0	5.3
three	1.8	0.6	5.6	0.4	0.1	1.0	0.7	1.1	0.5	0.3	5.6	6.7
four	1.4	0.3	4.8	0.2	0.1	0.3	0.5	0.5	0.2	0.6	4.8	3.9
five or more	1.4	0.3	4.8	0.2	0.1	0.4	0.5	0.5	0.3	0.7	4.9	1.3
Graduate Courses												
none	64.1	56.4	98.6	42.5	36.9	62.3	84.2	81.4	79.8	90.6	98.6	100.0
one	29.6	36.0	0.8	48.2	55.7	29.6	12.7	14.4	15.1	7.3	0.8	0.0
two	5.0	6.0	0.2	7.5	6.8	6.1	2.7	3.2	3.6	1.5	0.3	0.0
three	1.0	1.2	0.1	1.4	0.4	1.6	0.6	0.6	1.1	0.4	0.1	0.0
four	0.2	0.2	0.0	0.3	0.2	0.3	0.2	0.1	0.2	0.0	0.0	0.0
five or more	0.2	0.1	0.2	0.2	0.0	0.2	0.1	0.5	0.2	0.0	0.2	0.0
Political Orientation												
far left	4.9	5.7	2.2	6.5	8.2	4.3	5.3	6.7	4.6	3.6	2.3	1.8
liberal	36.8	39.5	27.1	42.1	48.0	35.7	37.0	40.4	37.8	31.8	27.1	26.9
moderate	40.2	38.8	45.1	37.9	30.8	42.1	39.2	36.6	42.7	40.9	45.0	47.2
conservative	17.8	15.7	25.1	13.1	12.5	17.5	18.3	16.1	14.6	23.4	25.2	23.2
far right	0.4	0.4	0.5	0.3	0.5	0.4	0.2	0.2	0.3	0.3	0.4	0.9
Agrees Strongly or Somewhat												
abolish death penalty	44.0	47.5	31.7	48.6	57.6	42.4	48.3	50.7	52.8	42.3	31.4	38.6
national health care plan needed	80.1	81.4	75.8	81.7	85.2	80.3	80.6	83.5	82.5	75.5	76.0	70.2
abortion should be legalized	76.7	78.5	70.7	83.5	83.5	78.5	68.4	77.1	57.2	61.9	71.1	61.4
grading in college too easy	75.8	77.5	69.6	78.1	79.0	77.6	75.8	74.6	80.0	75.2	69.5	71.9
wealthy should pay more taxes	83.0	83.9	79.8	84.2	83.8	83.4	84.4	85.2	84.7	83.0	79.7	83.1
college can ban extreme speakers	19.6	17.5	26.9	12.6	16.0	17.1	25.9	20.9	26.5	32.7	26.5	36.1
college increases earning power	24.6	20.9	37.6	20.2	13.9	26.0	18.2	19.9	17.4	16.1	38.1	27.0
racial discrim no longer problem	6.8	6.5	8.1	6.8	6.6	6.9	5.3	5.8	5.2	4.6	8.1	7.1

ALL FACULTY

	ALL			Universities		Four-year Colleges					Two-year Colleges	
	Insts	4-yr	2-yr	Pub	Priv	Pub	All Priv	Nons	Cath	Prot	Pub	Priv
Agrees Strongly or Somewhat												
fac interested in students' prob	73.8	70.4	85.4	58.4	60.8	72.7	89.3	84.5	92.4	94.5	84.9	97.3
fac sensitive to minority issues	69.1	68.0	73.0	64.8	67.0	67.6	73.4	72.6	74.9	73.8	73.0	73.6
curriculum overspecialized......	28.3	31.8	15.9	42.3	37.4	27.2	21.0	23.1	20.1	18.5	16.1	8.9
many students don't "fit in"....	25.1	27.1	18.2	28.8	32.2	25.9	24.1	27.7	17.8	22.4	18.1	21.2
fac committed to welfare of coll	76.1	74.4	81.7	67.5	76.3	71.9	87.1	83.6	88.3	91.4	81.5	87.7
courses incl minority perspect.	36.0	35.1	39.2	33.2	29.7	37.3	37.3	41.2	35.4	32.9	40.0	20.8
admin consider student concerns.	59.7	58.8	63.2	51.7	55.9	58.2	71.2	69.4	72.3	73.4	62.6	75.3
fac interest in stdnts acad prob	76.4	74.1	84.6	61.6	67.6	77.2	90.4	88.2	91.1	93.2	84.2	93.8
a lot of racial conflict here...	11.8	13.6	5.5	20.8	11.1	10.4	9.4	11.4	6.8	7.9	5.4	7.2
students resent required courses	42.6	41.4	46.8	41.3	29.0	46.8	40.2	38.6	43.9	40.4	46.8	47.6
ethnic groups communicate well..	59.0	55.8	70.0	50.2	51.4	58.4	62.2	59.7	63.1	65.1	69.7	76.2
admin care little about students	23.8	24.3	22.2	30.8	21.2	26.5	13.2	15.7	11.6	10.6	22.5	16.8
low trust btwn minorities/admin.	27.5	30.4	17.3	41.0	34.7	26.6	19.3	22.4	16.3	16.5	17.5	12.3
fac positive about gen ed pgm...	72.5	69.1	84.1	63.0	75.6	66.0	79.1	74.8	81.8	83.7	84.1	84.9
courses incl feminist perspect..	28.4	28.4	30.4	28.4	30.1	25.0	32.4	36.6	38.3	23.1	31.1	15.1
oppty for fac/stdnt socializing.	38.4	38.5	37.9	28.0	39.6	34.7	58.6	54.2	55.9	66.4	36.8	63.8
admin consider faculty concerns.	50.0	50.1	49.5	45.9	52.7	45.7	61.5	57.9	59.5	67.7	49.5	49.5
stdnts well prep academically...	27.4	29.5	20.2	23.7	50.5	22.1	37.7	36.1	33.3	42.4	20.3	17.6
Stdnt Aff staff supported by fac	58.5	57.7	61.3	54.5	54.3	55.6	66.6	64.8	64.6	70.4	60.6	77.9
research interferes w/teaching..	26.7	32.6	6.0	44.4	34.7	31.9	15.7	18.6	18.9	9.8	6.1	3.5
unionization enhances teaching..	32.4	28.9	44.0	28.0	20.9	33.3	27.8	33.0	25.8	21.6	44.5	31.9
tenure is an outmoded concept...	37.0	36.2	40.0	35.9	34.1	35.0	39.3	38.2	44.2	38.2	39.9	42.7
Issues Noted as Being of High or Highest Priority												
promote intellectual development	76.1	76.1	76.0	70.6	83.7	72.4	85.5	83.4	86.2	88.0	75.8	79.8
help students understand values.	47.4	46.6	50.0	32.3	47.2	43.0	71.9	63.6	80.5	79.2	48.8	77.2
increase minorities in fac/admin	46.9	47.9	43.6	52.3	40.5	52.2	39.0	45.2	37.1	31.0	44.4	24.5
devel community among stdnts/fac	41.0	38.8	48.5	25.5	34.8	38.4	60.6	56.4	64.1	64.3	47.9	61.3
devel leadership abil in stdnts.	37.6	36.8	40.5	25.8	32.0	37.6	53.9	51.2	55.1	57.1	39.7	59.7
conduct basic & applied research	44.5	54.2	10.7	80.5	74.0	41.9	24.4	31.3	19.4	17.3	10.9	6.2
raise money for the institution.	58.3	63.5	40.0	63.7	77.7	53.1	71.5	73.3	67.6	71.1	39.1	62.0
devel leadership abil in faculty	24.0	22.5	29.0	20.2	20.6	23.1	25.9	25.0	26.5	26.8	29.0	28.9
increase women in fac/admin.....	39.2	40.9	33.0	45.2	36.7	42.1	35.2	41.9	35.2	25.6	33.6	20.1
facilitate comm svcs involvement	23.3	23.5	22.7	13.3	25.1	21.6	40.0	36.1	35.2	25.6	22.6	25.3
teach students how to change soc	21.1	20.8	22.2	14.7	15.7	21.5	31.0	30.3	46.7	41.8	22.2	20.1
help solve soc/environ problems.	26.3	27.0	23.9	26.4	25.8	25.1	31.1	30.8	34.0	30.5	24.2	17.6
allow airing of diff opinions...	52.0	52.4	50.7	53.0	54.9	48.1	56.5	58.1	33.6	30.1	51.1	41.3
increase/maintain inst prestige.	75.3	77.5	67.8	80.4	87.0	71.0	77.9	80.0	57.3	53.8	67.6	73.4
devel apprec of multi-cultul soc	46.5	47.2	44.1	45.6	40.0	46.6	54.3	56.3	74.7	76.7	44.2	42.7
hire faculty "stars"............	26.8	31.3	10.8	49.8	47.4	20.5	12.7	15.4	53.6	51.8	10.8	10.6
economize and cut costs.........	54.5	55.1	52.6	58.9	57.4	53.9	50.1	51.4	8.5	11.3	52.4	57.8
recruit more minority students..	46.9	48.8	40.3	50.7	44.0	52.1	43.7	48.7	50.4	48.0	40.5	33.4
enhance inst's national image...	61.7	68.6	37.6	78.0	84.9	56.7	64.3	70.5	43.6	36.5	37.2	46.3
create positive undergrad exp...	69.2	67.7	74.2	52.3	71.8	69.1	85.7	82.6	52.5	62.0	73.9	82.3
create multi-cultural environ...	40.0	40.6	37.7	38.9	35.0	42.4	43.4	47.9	88.1	88.7	37.9	32.2
enhance stdnt's out-of-class exp	28.8	28.2	30.9	17.2	27.2	28.5	43.8	44.0	42.5	37.5	30.4	42.9

ALL FACULTY

	ALL			Universities		Four-year Colleges					Two-year Colleges	
	Insts	4-yr	2-yr	Pub	Priv	Pub	All Priv	Nons	Cath	Prot	Pub	Priv
Attributes Noted as Being Very Descriptive of Institution												
easy to see fac outside ofc hour	33.6	32.1	38.6	20.6	27.6	30.5	53.6	50.1	54.9	57.7	38.2	49.4
great conformity among students	24.6	27.0	16.3	26.2	24.9	22.7	35.7	32.5	37.9	39.1	15.8	27.8
most students very bright	8.9	10.8	2.2	7.0	35.5	4.0	13.6	18.3	4.9	11.8	2.3	0.0
admin open about policies	11.9	10.9	15.6	7.9	8.8	10.1	17.3	16.8	13.6	20.2	15.8	11.2
keen competition for grades	20.1	23.2	9.2	25.4	48.9	13.9	20.6	21.5	20.4	20.2	9.4	2.6
courses more theoret than pract	8.6	10.2	3.0	9.5	20.9	6.2	11.4	14.5	6.7	9.6	3.0	1.8
fac rewarded for advising skills	2.0	2.1	1.4	1.3	2.0	1.6	4.1	4.5	3.4	3.9	1.4	0.9
little std contact out-of-class	11.6	9.4	18.9	11.2	4.3	13.9	2.9	3.4	4.1	1.6	19.6	0.9
faculty at odds with admin	18.6	18.5	19.0	19.8	14.9	21.0	14.7	19.0	13.0	9.5	19.1	17.3
intercoll sports overemphasized	16.1	18.9	6.2	33.0	6.8	15.6	10.0	10.3	6.8	11.3	5.5	22.5
classes usually informal	19.8	18.5	24.6	14.6	16.6	19.2	23.8	27.0	19.9	21.3	24.8	19.9
faculty respect each other	31.7	29.7	38.8	23.3	35.0	24.4	44.1	39.9	44.0	50.2	38.2	52.4
most stdnts treated like numbers	5.9	6.8	2.8	12.1	4.5	6.2	1.5	2.2	1.0	0.6	2.8	0.9
social activities overemphasized	6.6	8.0	1.8	7.7	6.2	6.6	11.5	13.0	6.6	11.9	1.4	13.0
little student/faculty contact	5.1	5.5	3.8	7.5	5.9	5.9	2.0	3.1	1.6	0.7	3.9	1.7
student body apathetic	17.0	14.2	26.6	12.9	7.6	21.4	8.6	9.6	7.8	7.5	27.3	11.2
stdnts don't socialize regularly	6.0	4.7	10.2	4.6	1.5	8.2	1.5	2.0	1.5	0.7	10.7	0.0
fac rewarded for good teaching	9.8	10.3	8.0	6.2	10.8	8.1	19.2	19.8	16.0	20.1	8.0	7.8
student services well supported	18.8	18.3	20.7	15.9	18.1	15.4	25.9	29.0	23.5	22.9	20.5	24.2
Personal Goals Noted as Very Important or Essential												
become authority in own field	66.3	68.0	60.4	73.9	79.0	64.4	59.1	62.2	55.3	56.7	60.6	56.5
influence political structure	20.2	20.2	20.2	19.7	20.3	21.2	19.6	20.7	21.4	17.2	19.9	25.0
influence social values	46.8	46.1	49.2	42.1	42.3	46.3	53.6	51.3	57.0	55.0	48.6	63.0
raise a family	72.4	72.0	73.8	73.2	72.8	70.7	71.9	72.1	64.9	75.5	73.6	77.6
have admin responsibility	12.9	12.5	14.4	11.5	9.9	13.2	14.2	14.8	12.9	13.9	14.5	13.9
be very well-off financially	35.8	34.1	41.8	36.1	30.3	36.8	29.0	32.9	26.8	24.5	42.3	30.2
help others in difficulty	67.3	66.0	71.8	62.4	59.5	66.9	73.3	71.3	75.6	74.8	71.6	75.8
be involved in environ clean-up	43.7	42.6	47.6	40.9	34.3	46.0	44.1	45.2	44.4	42.5	47.5	50.9
develop philosophy of life	80.5	79.8	82.8	77.8	72.1	80.8	85.2	83.0	88.0	86.8	82.8	84.3
promote racial understanding	60.2	60.6	59.1	58.1	57.3	61.1	65.1	65.1	66.9	64.1	58.8	66.4
obtain recog from colleagues	53.3	57.5	38.7	65.0	70.4	52.8	47.1	51.4	44.8	42.2	38.9	34.5
Aspects of Job Noted as Very Satisfactory or Satisfactory (4)												
salary and fringe benefits	44.5	42.4	51.7	44.3	51.3	39.0	40.2	43.2	37.5	37.2	52.1	42.0
oppty for scholarly pursuits	45.4	46.0	43.2	53.3	62.4	38.1	38.8	40.3	34.8	38.9	43.6	32.7
teaching load	50.3	50.6	49.1	58.3	63.5	42.2	45.2	46.0	43.6	44.9	49.3	43.3
quality of students	37.5	39.7	29.9	38.0	58.6	32.2	43.3	43.1	40.9	44.9	30.2	24.7
working conditions	64.6	64.8	63.9	66.4	74.8	58.0	66.2	66.5	65.4	66.0	63.9	62.7
autonomy and independence	82.9	83.5	80.8	85.0	89.1	80.0	83.8	82.6	85.3	84.7	80.6	84.9
relationships with other faculty	75.1	73.7	80.1	69.0	74.3	73.9	79.7	77.2	80.4	82.9	80.0	81.6
competency of colleagues	68.4	67.6	71.1	64.6	75.0	63.3	74.4	72.8	73.7	77.0	71.2	69.0
visibility for jobs	43.1	43.5	41.9	45.5	58.8	38.3	39.5	39.3	38.7	40.0	42.0	38.5
job security	74.6	73.4	79.1	73.5	73.8	75.4	69.9	66.6	72.6	73.1	79.2	70.5
undergraduate course assignments	77.5	77.7	78.2	76.8	79.5	75.4	79.7	79.5	79.0	80.3	78.0	78.0
graduate course assignments	72.3	73.7	42.1	75.1	78.0	71.0	68.2	68.6	70.4	65.3	41.3	71.6
relationships with admin	51.8	51.4	53.0	48.4	53.1	49.0	58.2	55.9	58.4	61.5	52.8	57.3
overall job satisfaction	69.2	67.7	74.4	65.6	74.8	64.9	71.4	70.0	72.5	72.7	74.4	73.6

ALL FACULTY

	ALL			Universities		Four-year Colleges					Two-year Colleges	
	Insts	4-yr	2-yr	Pub	Priv	Pub	All Priv	Nons	Cath	Prot	Pub	Priv
Sources of Stress												
household responsibilities	63.7	63.3	65.1	62.1	61.9	61.9	67.8	67.6	68.1	67.8	64.9	69.4
child care	28.9	28.7	29.7	28.2	30.2	27.3	30.6	29.8	30.8	31.5	29.2	41.0
care of elderly parent	26.3	25.8	28.1	25.3	22.3	27.1	26.5	25.8	26.6	27.6	28.0	30.9
my physical health	37.9	37.2	40.5	36.3	35.8	38.3	37.7	37.4	40.2	36.9	40.6	36.4
review/promotion process	45.7	48.7	35.3	52.1	43.5	50.1	44.7	46.7	46.9	40.6	34.9	44.7
subtle discriminiation	29.2	29.6	27.5	28.6	25.3	33.4	27.9	29.6	27.7	25.4	27.6	25.7
long-distance commuting	16.8	15.9	19.7	12.8	16.2	18.5	16.4	18.1	16.9	13.6	19.8	18.4
committee work	57.5	58.2	55.3	59.1	49.5	61.1	57.1	55.4	58.7	58.7	54.4	74.8
faculty meetings	49.6	50.0	48.0	51.3	43.0	52.3	48.3	46.7	52.5	48.3	47.3	65.0
colleagues	54.2	55.6	49.4	57.9	50.6	56.7	53.3	55.0	52.0	51.7	49.5	45.1
students	50.4	49.3	54.2	47.6	44.7	49.4	53.8	53.5	52.7	54.8	53.8	63.1
research or publishing demands	50.4	61.2	12.3	72.7	71.4	57.4	45.0	50.2	48.0	36.0	12.3	12.3
fund-raising expectations	20.8	23.0	13.1	30.7	24.8	20.5	14.5	14.6	15.6	13.8	12.9	16.8
teaching load	65.0	64.7	66.0	59.0	57.7	68.8	70.6	68.5	71.8	72.9	65.8	69.9
children's problems	31.5	30.6	34.5	30.6	29.0	30.6	31.4	31.1	28.7	33.2	34.5	35.3
marital friction	23.8	23.7	23.8	23.7	25.4	23.5	23.2	24.1	21.6	22.7	23.9	22.2
time pressures	83.5	84.9	79.0	85.2	85.1	83.0	87.1	85.7	87.7	88.8	78.8	82.3
lack of personal life	79.8	80.6	76.7	80.3	80.5	79.2	83.4	81.9	85.0	84.5	76.5	81.4
Still Want to Be College Professor?												
definitely yes	44.7	45.0	43.4	41.5	50.6	44.0	48.7	47.5	51.4	49.0	43.6	37.8
probably yes	34.8	34.6	35.4	35.9	31.5	34.5	34.4	34.0	33.7	35.3	35.2	38.9
not sure	12.1	12.1	12.0	13.1	12.1	11.9	10.8	11.5	10.1	10.0	11.9	14.6
probably no	6.6	6.5	7.0	7.3	4.3	7.4	5.0	5.6	3.9	4.8	7.1	5.1
definitely no	1.9	1.9	2.2	2.2	1.5	2.1	1.1	1.4	0.8	0.8	2.2	3.5
Field of Highest Degree Held												
agriculture	1.2	1.2	1.0	2.6	1.0	0.8	0.2	0.4	0.0	0.2	1.0	0.9
architecture or urban planning	0.5	0.5	0.2	1.0	0.7	0.2	0.2	0.4	0.0	0.0	0.2	0.0
bacteriology, molecular biology	0.8	0.9	0.8	0.9	1.2	0.6	0.9	0.8	0.9	0.9	0.8	0.9
biochemistry	0.6	0.7	0.2	0.9	1.2	0.3	0.6	0.7	0.5	0.6	0.2	0.0
biophysics	0.1	0.2	0.0	0.2	0.4	0.1	0.1	0.1	0.1	0.1	0.0	0.0
botany	0.8	1.0	0.4	1.0	0.4	1.2	0.9	0.8	0.7	1.1	0.3	0.0
marine life sciences	0.1	0.2	0.1	0.8	0.0	0.2	0.1	0.1	0.1	0.1	0.1	0.0
physiology, anatomy	0.7	0.7	0.7	0.8	0.5	0.2	0.6	0.4	1.0	0.8	0.7	0.0
zoology	1.5	1.6	1.1	1.5	1.1	1.8	1.5	1.4	1.5	1.7	1.2	0.0
general, other biological science	1.4	1.3	1.9	1.6	1.3	1.0	1.3	1.4	1.6	1.1	1.8	4.5
accounting	1.6	1.6	1.6	1.4	1.2	1.9	1.7	1.5	2.2	1.8	1.7	0.0
finance	0.7	0.8	0.4	0.7	0.9	1.0	0.8	0.8	1.1	0.6	0.4	0.0
marketing	0.9	0.9	0.9	0.9	1.2	1.1	0.6	0.4	1.3	0.4	1.0	0.0
management	2.0	1.9	2.6	1.5	1.6	2.2	2.0	2.1	2.6	1.5	2.6	0.9
secretarial studies	0.1	0.0	0.5	0.0	0.0	0.0	0.0	0.1	0.0	0.0	0.5	0.0
general, other business	1.0	0.9	1.4	0.8	0.8	1.0	1.0	0.6	1.5	1.2	1.2	4.5
computer science	0.9	0.9	0.8	0.8	0.8	1.0	1.0	1.0	1.5	0.7	0.8	0.0

ALL FACULTY

Field of Degree (continued)

	ALL			Universities		Four-year Colleges					Two-year Colleges	
	Insts	4-yr	2-yr	Pub	Priv	Pub	All Priv	Nons	Cath	Prot	Pub	Priv
business education	1.3	0.7	3.7	0.3	0.0	1.4	0.5	0.5	0.6	0.5	3.7	4.5
elementary education	1.0	1.1	0.8	0.7	0.1	1.8	1.2	0.9	1.0	1.7	0.7	2.7
educational administration	1.8	1.5	3.0	0.9	0.4	2.0	1.9	1.8	1.7	2.2	2.9	3.7
educational psych, counseling	1.3	1.1	2.0	1.0	0.6	1.4	1.0	0.8	1.0	1.2	2.0	0.9
music or art education	0.5	0.5	0.5	0.4	0.1	0.8	0.5	0.4	0.2	0.9	0.5	0.0
physical or health education	2.8	2.7	3.1	2.3	0.4	3.6	3.1	2.7	1.7	4.4	3.1	2.7
secondary education	1.2	1.1	1.7	0.9	0.3	1.4	1.3	1.4	1.2	1.3	1.6	5.4
special education	0.6	0.6	0.5	0.5	0.0	0.8	0.7	0.8	1.0	0.4	0.5	0.9
general, other education fields	4.5	3.7	7.4	3.6	0.9	4.9	3.5	3.5	3.5	3.4	7.5	5.4
aeronautical, astronautical eng	0.1	0.2	0.1	0.3	0.1	0.1	0.0	0.0	0.1	0.0	0.1	0.0
chemical engineering	0.4	0.5	0.1	0.6	1.2	0.4	0.1	0.2	0.1	0.1	0.1	0.0
civil engineering	0.8	0.9	0.4	1.6	1.1	0.6	0.2	0.3	0.2	0.1	0.4	0.0
electrical engineering	1.5	1.5	1.2	2.2	2.7	1.1	0.6	0.9	0.5	0.1	1.3	0.0
industrial engineering	0.4	0.4	0.7	0.8	0.1	0.4	0.2	0.2	0.0	0.1	0.2	0.0
mechanical engineering	0.9	1.0	0.0	1.4	1.4	0.9	0.4	0.6	0.2	0.3	0.7	0.0
nuclear engineering	0.1	0.1	0.0	0.1	0.0	0.1	0.0	0.0	0.1	0.0	0.0	0.0
general, other engineering field	1.0	1.1	0.5	1.8	1.4	0.8	0.3	0.6	0.1	0.0	0.6	0.0
ethnic studies	0.1	0.1	0.0	0.1	0.1	0.1	0.1	0.1	0.2	0.0	0.0	0.0
art	2.4	2.3	2.7	2.2	1.3	2.6	2.5	2.7	1.9	2.7	2.6	4.5
dramatics or speech	2.0	2.0	2.1	2.0	1.0	2.1	2.6	2.2	2.6	3.1	2.1	2.8
music	2.8	3.2	1.7	3.0	1.5	3.3	4.0	3.3	2.3	5.8	1.5	6.4
other fine arts	0.6	0.6	0.5	0.8	0.4	0.5	0.6	0.8	0.5	0.3	0.5	0.0
forestry	0.2	0.3	0.1	0.5	0.1	0.3	0.0	0.0	0.0	0.0	0.1	0.0
geology	0.7	0.8	0.4	0.9	0.2	1.2	0.3	0.4	0.0	0.3	0.5	0.0
dentistry	0.1	0.1	0.4	0.0	0.2	0.1	0.0	0.1	0.0	0.0	0.4	0.0
health technology	0.1	0.0	0.3	0.0	0.1	0.1	0.0	0.0	0.0	0.0	0.4	0.0
medicine or surgery	0.2	0.2	0.1	0.4	0.7	0.3	0.0	0.0	0.0	0.0	0.1	1.8
nursing	2.8	1.9	5.9	1.4	0.0	2.6	2.4	1.2	3.8	3.2	6.1	2.7
pharmacy, pharmacology	0.4	0.4	0.1	0.9	0.3	0.2	0.2	0.2	0.2	0.2	0.1	0.9
therapy (speech,physical,occup)	0.4	0.5	0.3	0.5	0.1	0.7	0.3	0.2	0.7	0.2	0.3	0.9
veterinary medicine	0.2	0.2	0.2	0.4	0.3	0.1	0.1	0.3	0.0	0.0	0.2	0.0
general, other health fields	0.6	0.5	1.2	0.4	0.1	0.7	0.4	0.6	0.3	0.2	1.3	0.0
home economics	0.7	0.7	0.5	1.1	0.2	0.8	0.4	0.5	0.7	0.2	0.5	0.0
English language & literature	6.8	6.3	8.5	5.7	5.7	5.9	8.0	8.3	7.3	7.9	8.3	12.8
foreign languages & literature	0.5	0.5	0.3	0.7	0.6	0.3	0.7	0.9	0.5	0.9	0.3	0.9
French	0.8	1.0	0.3	0.9	1.6	0.7	1.2	1.4	1.1	1.1	0.3	0.9
German	0.6	0.7	0.2	0.7	1.0	0.5	0.8	1.0	0.3	0.9	0.2	0.0
Spanish	1.0	1.1	0.5	0.9	1.5	0.8	1.5	1.5	1.4	1.5	0.5	0.9
other foreign languages	0.8	1.0	0.1	1.3	2.0	0.4	0.7	1.0	0.6	0.5	0.1	0.0

ALL FACULTY

Field of Degree (continued)

	ALL			Universities		Four-year Colleges						Two-year Colleges	
	Insts	4-yr	2-yr	Pub	Priv	Pub	All Priv	Nons	Cath	Prot	Pub	Priv
history	4.1	4.4	3.0	4.0	6.3	3.9	4.6	4.8	4.7	4.3	3.0	4.6
linguistics	0.7	0.8	0.3	1.0	1.5	0.4	0.4	0.5	0.5	0.3	0.3	0.9
philosophy	1.6	1.8	0.8	1.4	3.3	1.3	2.3	1.7	4.5	1.8	0.8	0.0
religion & theology	1.3	1.5	0.5	0.4	2.3	0.6	4.1	2.8	4.9	5.7	0.4	4.7
general, other humanities fields	1.0	1.1	0.6	1.2	2.0	0.8	1.0	1.1	0.6	1.1	0.6	0.9
journalism	0.5	0.5	0.4	0.7	0.4	0.6	0.4	0.4	0.3	0.3	0.4	0.0
law	0.7	0.7	0.8	0.6	0.7	0.8	0.6	0.6	0.9	0.3	0.8	0.0
law enforcement	0.2	0.1	0.4	0.1	0.1	0.2	0.0	0.0	0.1	0.0	0.4	0.0
library science	0.2	0.3	0.2	0.2	0.0	0.4	0.3	0.2	0.3	0.4	0.2	0.0
mathematics and/or statistics	5.6	5.4	6.3	4.6	6.3	5.5	6.0	5.9	6.1	6.2	6.4	4.5
military science	0.0	0.0	0.0	0.0	0.0	0.0	0.0	0.0	0.0	0.0	0.0	0.0
astronomy	0.2	0.2	0.1	0.2	0.2	0.2	0.2	0.3	0.1	0.2	0.1	0.0
atmospheric sciences	0.1	0.1	0.1	0.3	0.0	0.1	0.1	0.0	0.0	0.1	0.1	0.0
chemistry	3.0	3.1	2.4	2.8	3.4	2.7	4.1	4.3	3.7	4.0	2.4	1.8
earth sciences	1.1	1.2	0.6	1.6	1.6	1.2	0.6	0.9	0.2	0.5	0.5	1.8
marine sciences	0.1	0.1	0.1	0.1	0.2	0.1	0.0	0.1	0.0	0.0	0.1	0.0
physics	2.2	2.4	1.5	2.2	3.9	2.1	2.4	2.6	2.4	2.1	1.6	0.0
general, other physical sciences	0.1	0.1	0.3	0.0	0.1	0.1	0.0	0.0	0.0	0.1	0.3	0.0
clinical psychology	0.6	0.7	0.3	0.7	0.6	0.7	0.9	0.8	1.1	0.9	0.3	0.0
counseling & guidance	0.7	0.4	1.8	0.2	0.1	0.6	0.7	0.7	0.9	0.5	1.8	1.8
experimental psychology	1.2	1.5	0.5	1.5	1.6	1.4	1.5	1.6	1.4	1.4	0.5	0.0
social psychology	0.6	0.7	0.2	0.5	2.0	0.5	0.6	0.7	0.8	0.3	0.2	0.0
general, other psychology	1.1	1.0	1.1	0.9	1.0	1.1	1.3	1.3	1.2	1.3	1.2	0.0
anthropology	1.0	1.2	0.4	1.4	2.1	1.0	0.8	1.0	0.4	0.6	0.4	0.0
archaeology	0.2	0.2	0.0	0.2	0.8	0.1	0.1	0.1	0.0	0.0	0.0	0.0
economics	2.8	3.2	1.2	3.6	5.3	2.6	3.4	4.1	3.4	2.6	1.2	1.8
political science, government	2.4	2.7	1.0	2.6	4.6	2.4	2.5	3.0	2.0	2.0	1.1	0.0
sociology	2.3	2.6	1.3	3.1	3.0	2.4	2.2	2.1	2.2	2.4	1.3	1.8
general, other social sciences	0.6	0.6	0.4	0.8	0.7	0.6	0.4	0.5	0.5	0.4	0.4	0.0
social work, social welfare	0.5	0.5	0.5	0.2	0.4	0.8	0.7	0.5	0.9	0.9	0.5	0.9
building trades	0.1	0.0	0.3	0.0	0.0	0.1	0.0	0.0	0.0	0.0	0.3	0.0
data processing, computer prog	0.1	0.1	0.2	0.0	0.0	0.1	0.1	0.2	0.0	0.0	0.2	0.0
drafting/design	0.1	0.0	0.3	0.1	0.0	0.0	0.0	0.0	0.0	0.0	0.3	0.0
electronics	0.1	0.1	0.4	0.1	0.0	0.2	0.0	0.0	0.0	0.0	0.4	0.0
industrial arts	0.3	0.3	0.6	0.1	0.0	0.6	0.1	0.1	0.0	0.1	0.6	0.0
mechanics	0.2	0.0	0.6	0.0	0.0	0.0	0.1	0.1	0.0	0.0	0.7	0.0
other technical	0.4	0.2	1.1	0.1	0.0	0.4	0.0	0.1	0.0	0.0	1.1	0.9
other vocational	0.4	0.2	1.3	0.2	0.0	0.3	0.1	0.2	0.0	0.0	1.3	0.0
women's studies	0.0	0.0	0.0	0.0	0.0	0.1	0.0	0.0	0.0	0.0	0.0	0.0
all other fields	1.5	1.5	1.3	1.8	1.0	1.6	1.3	1.6	1.5	0.9	1.3	0.9

ALL FACULTY

Department of Current Faculty Appointment	ALL			Universities		Four-year Colleges					Two-year Colleges	
	Insts	4-yr	2-yr	Pub	Priv	Pub	All Priv	Nons	Cath	Prot	Pub	Priv
agriculture..................	1.3	1.5	0.8	2.9	1.6	1.0	0.1	0.3	0.0	0.0	0.8	0.9
architecture or urban planning..	0.4	0.5	0.1	1.1	0.3	0.2	0.2	0.4	0.0	0.0	0.1	0.0
bacteriology, molecular biology.	0.6	0.6	0.5	0.7	1.1	0.5	0.3	0.3	0.4	0.4	0.4	0.9
biophysics...................	0.2	0.2	0.0	0.5	0.4	0.0	0.0	0.1	0.0	0.0	0.0	0.0
botany.......................	0.1	0.1	0.0	0.6	0.7	0.0	0.0	0.0	0.0	0.0	0.0	0.0
marine life sciences.........	0.2	0.3	0.1	0.6	0.2	0.1	0.0	0.0	0.0	0.3	0.1	0.0
physiology, anatomy..........	0.3	0.2	0.0	0.2	0.3	0.1	0.2	0.1	0.4	0.2	0.6	1.0
zoology......................	0.4	0.4	0.1	0.8	0.3	0.2	0.3	0.2	0.3	0.3	0.1	0.0
general, other biological science	3.8	4.0	3.5	3.0	2.9	4.7	4.8	4.5	5.1	5.1	3.5	3.7
accounting...................	2.2	2.1	2.8	1.7	1.5	2.6	2.0	1.7	3.2	1.7	2.9	1.9
finance......................	0.8	1.0	0.1	0.9	1.2	1.2	0.7	0.6	1.2	0.5	0.1	0.0
marketing....................	1.1	1.1	1.0	1.0	1.3	1.3	0.8	0.9	1.1	0.3	1.0	0.0
management...................	2.1	2.4	1.3	2.3	1.9	2.4	2.7	3.1	3.9	1.5	1.3	0.9
secretarial studies..........	0.6	0.1	2.2	0.0	0.0	0.1	0.3	0.2	0.2	0.3	2.3	0.9
general, other business......	1.8	1.6	2.8	1.0	1.0	1.9	2.2	1.6	2.6	2.7	2.7	6.6
computer science.............	1.9	1.8	2.1	1.4	2.0	2.0	1.9	1.9	2.5	1.5	2.1	1.9
business education...........	0.6	0.3	1.7	0.1	0.2	0.6	0.2	0.1	0.2	2.5	1.6	2.8
elementary education.........	1.2	1.5	0.1	0.9	0.2	2.4	1.7	1.1	1.6	2.5	0.0	0.9
educational administration...	0.2	0.3	0.1	0.3	0.1	0.4	0.2	0.2	0.1	0.2	0.1	0.0
educational psych, counseling.	0.5	0.5	0.3	0.7	0.3	0.5	0.3	0.2	0.2	0.4	0.3	0.0
music or art education........	0.2	0.2	0.1	0.2	0.1	0.3	0.2	0.1	0.1	0.4	0.1	0.9
physical or health education..	3.1	3.1	2.9	2.8	0.6	4.1	3.5	3.2	1.6	5.0	2.8	3.7
secondary education..........	0.6	0.7	0.3	0.5	0.2	0.9	0.8	0.5	0.8	1.1	0.1	0.0
special education............	0.5	0.5	0.3	0.6	0.0	0.8	0.3	0.2	0.7	0.2	0.3	0.0
general, other education fields..	1.8	1.8	1.7	1.8	0.8	2.0	2.0	2.1	2.0	1.9	1.6	4.7
aeronautical, astronautical eng.	0.1	0.1	0.1	0.3	0.0	0.0	0.0	0.0	0.0	0.0	0.0	0.0
chemical engineering.........	0.4	0.4	0.0	0.5	1.5	0.3	0.1	0.1	0.0	0.0	0.0	0.0
civil engineering............	0.7	0.8	0.5	1.5	1.1	0.6	0.1	0.1	0.3	0.0	0.5	0.0
electrical engineering........	1.3	1.4	0.6	2.3	2.5	0.8	0.6	1.0	0.5	0.2	0.6	0.0
industrial engineering........	0.4	0.4	0.2	0.7	0.2	0.3	0.2	0.3	0.0	0.0	0.2	0.0
mechanical engineering........	1.0	1.1	0.5	1.5	2.1	0.9	0.4	0.7	0.3	0.0	0.6	0.0
nuclear engineering..........	0.1	0.1	0.0	0.2	0.1	0.0	0.0	0.0	0.0	0.0	0.0	0.0
general, other engineering field.	1.1	1.2	0.6	2.0	1.5	0.9	0.3	0.5	0.0	0.2	0.6	0.0
ethnic studies...............	0.1	0.2	0.0	0.2	0.1	0.2	0.1	0.2	0.1	0.1	0.0	0.0
art..........................	2.5	2.6	2.2	2.7	1.5	2.9	2.7	2.9	1.9	2.8	2.1	3.8
dramatics or speech..........	2.0	2.1	1.8	2.1	1.1	2.2	2.5	2.2	2.5	3.1	1.8	2.9
music........................	3.0	3.4	1.8	3.3	1.6	3.7	4.1	3.3	2.1	6.3	1.6	6.7
other fine arts..............	0.6	0.6	0.5	0.7	0.5	0.6	0.6	0.9	0.6	0.1	0.6	0.0
forestry.....................	0.3	0.3	0.1	0.6	0.0	0.3	0.0	0.0	0.0	0.0	0.1	0.0

ALL FACULTY

Current Department (contuned)

	ALL			Universities		Four-year Colleges					Two-year Colleges	
	Insts	4-yr	2-yr	Pub	Priv	Pub	All Priv	Nons	Cath	Prot	Pub	Priv
geology	0.6	0.8	0.2	1.0	0.3	1.1	0.2	0.2	0.1	0.3	0.2	0.0
dentistry	0.2	0.1	0.8	0.0	0.2	0.1	0.0	0.0	0.0	0.0	0.9	0.0
health technology	0.4	0.2	1.2	0.1	0.1	0.3	0.2	0.3	0.0	0.0	1.2	0.0
medicine or surgery	0.2	0.3	0.0	0.5	0.0	0.4	0.0	0.0	0.7	0.0	0.0	0.0
nursing	3.5	2.5	6.9	1.9	0.9	3.4	2.9	1.5	4.7	3.9	7.1	1.9
pharmacy, pharmacology	0.4	0.4	0.1	0.9	0.3	0.2	0.2	0.1	0.1	0.3	0.1	0.0
therapy (speech,physical,occup)	0.6	0.6	0.5	0.6	0.3	0.8	0.4	0.3	1.2	0.1	0.5	1.9
veterinary medicine	0.1	0.2	0.1	0.4	0.2	0.0	0.0	0.0	0.0	0.0	0.1	0.0
general, other health fields	0.9	0.5	2.4	0.5	0.2	0.7	0.3	0.4	0.4	0.1	2.5	0.0
home economics	1.0	1.1	0.5	1.8	0.3	1.2	0.4	0.3	0.8	0.3	0.5	0.9
English language & literature	7.4	6.7	10.1	6.0	5.6	6.3	8.7	9.0	7.6	9.0	9.9	14.2
foreign languages & literature	1.7	2.0	0.4	1.7	3.3	1.4	2.8	3.2	2.3	2.5	0.5	0.0
French	0.5	0.6	0.2	0.7	0.7	0.3	0.4	0.6	0.2	0.5	0.2	0.9
German	0.3	0.4	0.0	0.5	0.6	0.1	0.4	0.5	0.2	0.4	0.1	0.0
Spanish	0.6	0.7	0.5	0.8	0.6	0.5	0.8	0.7	0.6	1.0	0.4	1.9
other foreign languages	0.7	0.9	0.1	1.5	1.7	0.2	0.7	1.0	0.3	0.4	0.1	0.0
history	3.6	4.0	1.9	3.9	5.3	3.6	4.2	4.1	3.9	4.5	1.9	2.8
linguistics	0.2	0.3	0.0	0.4	1.1	0.2	0.1	0.1	0.0	0.0	0.0	0.0
philosophy	1.5	1.7	0.7	1.3	3.2	1.2	2.2	1.6	4.2	1.8	0.8	0.0
religion & theology	1.2	1.4	0.3	0.2	2.4	0.4	4.1	2.4	5.2	5.8	0.1	4.8
general, other humanities fields	1.3	1.3	1.3	0.8	2.7	1.0	1.5	1.9	1.3	1.1	1.4	1.0
journalism	0.6	0.7	0.3	0.9	0.7	0.7	0.4	0.5	0.5	0.2	0.3	0.0
law	0.1	0.1	0.1	0.1	0.1	0.1	0.1	0.1	0.1	0.0	0.1	0.0
law enforcement	0.4	0.3	0.6	0.1	0.3	0.7	0.1	0.0	0.3	0.0	0.7	0.0
library science	0.2	0.2	0.2	0.1	0.0	0.3	0.3	0.3	0.2	0.5	0.3	0.0
mathematics and/or statistics	6.1	5.7	7.6	5.2	5.4	5.9	6.3	6.1	6.3	6.6	7.6	8.4
military science	0.1	0.1	0.0	0.0	0.1	0.1	0.1	0.0	0.2	0.0	0.0	0.0
astronomy	0.1	0.1	0.0	0.1	0.4	0.0	0.1	0.1	0.0	0.0	0.0	0.0
atmospheric sciences	0.1	0.1	0.1	0.2	0.1	0.0	0.0	0.0	0.0	0.0	0.1	0.0
chemistry	3.0	3.1	2.6	2.5	2.8	2.9	4.2	4.4	3.9	4.2	2.6	2.9
earth sciences	1.1	1.3	0.4	1.7	1.9	1.3	0.6	0.9	0.1	0.6	0.4	0.0
marine sciences	0.0	0.0	0.1	0.0	0.0	0.1	0.0	0.0	0.0	0.0	0.1	0.0
physics	2.0	2.2	1.3	1.8	2.9	2.2	2.2	2.4	2.0	2.1	1.3	0.9
general,other physical sciences	0.4	0.3	1.0	0.2	0.1	0.4	0.3	0.2	0.5	0.3	1.0	0.0

ALL FACULTY

Current Department (contuned)

	ALL			Universities		Four-year Colleges					Two-year Colleges	
	Insts	4-yr	2-yr	Pub	Priv	Pub	All Priv	Nons	Cath	Prot	Pub	Priv
clinical psychology	0.3	0.4	0.1	0.4	0.4	0.4	0.4	0.5	0.5	0.1	0.1	0.0
counseling & guidance	0.3	0.2	0.9	0.1	0.0	0.2	0.2	0.2	0.3	0.2	0.9	0.9
experimental psychology	0.7	0.9	0.1	1.0	1.4	0.6	0.7	0.7	0.5	0.7	0.1	0.0
social psychology	0.3	0.4	0.1	0.3	1.7	0.1	0.2	0.2	0.2	0.1	0.1	0.0
general, other psychology	2.2	2.1	2.5	1.5	1.4	2.4	3.1	2.9	2.9	3.3	2.4	5.6
anthropology	0.9	1.0	0.3	1.4	1.8	0.8	0.5	0.7	0.3	0.3	0.3	0.0
archaeology	0.0	0.0	0.0	0.0	0.1	0.0	0.0	0.0	0.0	0.0	0.0	0.0
economics	2.3	2.7	0.9	2.4	4.6	2.2	2.9	3.7	2.3	2.2	1.0	0.0
political science, government	2.1	2.5	0.8	2.5	4.2	2.0	2.3	2.9	2.0	1.8	0.8	1.9
sociology	2.2	2.5	1.3	2.9	2.5	2.1	2.3	2.3	2.0	2.5	1.2	1.0
general, other social sciences	1.5	1.2	2.5	1.0	1.3	1.5	1.2	1.5	1.4	0.6	2.6	1.0
social work, social welfare	0.4	0.5	0.3	0.2	0.4	0.7	0.5	0.3	0.9	0.7	0.3	0.9
building trades	0.2	0.0	1.0	0.0	0.0	0.1	0.0	0.0	0.0	0.0	1.0	0.0
data processing, computer prog.	0.3	0.1	1.0	0.1	0.0	0.1	0.3	0.4	0.4	0.1	1.1	0.0
drafting/design	0.3	0.1	0.9	0.1	0.0	0.1	0.1	0.2	0.0	0.0	0.9	0.0
electronics	0.5	0.1	2.0	0.1	0.0	0.1	0.1	0.2	0.0	0.0	2.0	0.0
industrial arts	0.3	0.2	0.3	0.2	0.0	0.5	0.1	0.1	0.0	0.1	0.3	0.0
mechanics	0.4	0.1	1.3	0.0	0.0	0.0	0.2	0.3	0.0	0.0	1.4	0.0
other technical	0.8	0.4	2.1	0.3	0.0	0.9	0.1	0.3	0.0	0.0	2.2	0.9
other vocational	0.5	0.1	2.1	0.1	0.0	0.1	0.1	0.3	0.0	0.0	2.2	0.0
women's studies	0.1	0.1	0.0	0.0	0.1	0.2	0.1	0.1	0.0	0.0	0.0	0.0
all other fields	2.3	2.3	2.4	2.5	2.4	2.4	2.0	2.5	2.5	1.0	2.5	0.9

Notes

1. Percentages will sum to more than 100 if any respondents checked more than one category.

2. Recategorization of this item from a longer list is shown in the American College Teacher.

3. Nine-month salaries converted to twelve-month.

4. Respondents marking "not applicable" are not included in tabulations.

52

National Normative Data for

the 1989-90 HERI Faculty Survey

Male Faculty

MALE FACULTY

	ALL			Universities		Four-year Colleges					Two-year Colleges	
	Insts	4-yr	2-yr	Pub	Priv	Pub	All Priv	Nons	Cath	Prot	Pub	Priv
Age as of December 31, 1989												
less than 30	1.4	1.4	1.3	1.2	1.6	1.0	2.3	2.0	2.2	2.8	1.3	1.7
30 - 34	7.3	7.9	4.8	8.0	10.5	6.1	8.7	8.8	7.3	9.2	4.5	11.8
35 - 39	11.9	12.4	9.6	11.5	14.1	11.7	14.1	14.0	15.6	13.6	9.3	17.0
40 - 44	16.3	15.9	17.8	15.3	16.3	15.6	17.5	17.3	19.4	16.7	17.8	17.0
45 - 49	19.2	18.5	22.3	18.0	15.9	20.8	17.1	16.2	17.4	18.1	22.4	20.2
50 - 54	16.6	16.1	19.1	15.9	12.0	18.5	15.0	15.7	13.4	14.8	19.5	8.5
55 - 59	14.3	14.3	14.5	15.2	11.9	14.6	13.6	14.3	11.9	13.3	14.6	12.0
60 - 64	9.2	9.6	7.6	10.5	11.5	8.5	8.6	8.4	8.2	9.0	7.7	6.7
65 - 69	3.3	3.5	2.4	3.8	5.8	2.7	2.7	2.8	3.8	2.1	2.4	3.5
70 or more	0.5	0.5	0.6	0.6	0.5	0.5	0.5	0.5	0.8	0.4	0.6	1.7
Academic Rank												
professor	40.7	43.2	29.8	47.4	47.6	41.0	37.0	38.1	27.2	40.2	29.7	31.3
associate professor	26.7	29.1	16.8	27.5	25.6	31.2	30.3	29.3	37.3	28.4	16.9	14.8
assistant professor	20.3	22.3	11.8	20.5	22.7	22.4	24.7	22.8	30.7	24.5	11.6	16.5
lecturer	1.2	1.3	0.4	2.1	1.4	1.0	0.6	0.7	0.6	0.4	0.4	0.0
instructor	9.3	3.1	35.8	2.1	0.8	3.1	6.3	7.5	3.5	5.8	36.3	22.2
other	1.9	1.0	5.5	0.4	1.9	1.3	1.2	1.6	0.8	0.8	5.1	15.3
Administrative Title												
not applicable	77.6	77.8	76.9	83.1	81.4	77.2	67.7	70.5	68.6	63.3	77.6	57.0
director or coordinator	8.7	8.9	7.8	8.4	7.8	9.7	9.2	9.7	9.5	8.2	7.4	18.9
department chair	9.3	9.0	10.9	3.9	7.0	8.7	19.0	16.1	18.2	23.5	10.6	20.7
dean	0.2	0.4	0.1	0.1	0.2	0.3	0.3	0.5	0.2	0.7	0.2	1.7
associate or assistant dean	0.4	0.4	0.0	0.4	0.5	0.0	0.6	0.5	0.4	0.8	0.1	0.0
vice-pres, provost, vice-chanc	0.1	0.1	0.0	0.1	0.1	0.0	0.1	0.0	0.1	0.1	0.0	0.0
president, chancellor	0.0	0.0	0.0	0.0	0.0	0.0	0.0	0.0	0.1	0.0	0.0	0.0
other	3.7	3.7	3.9	4.1	3.0	3.8	3.1	3.1	2.9	3.4	4.0	1.7
Principal Activity												
administration	3.3	3.4	3.0	3.2	3.8	3.7	3.0	3.0	2.5	3.4	2.8	6.6
teaching	88.9	87.4	95.4	80.8	76.8	93.2	95.7	95.6	96.4	95.7	95.5	91.7
research	6.8	8.4	0.1	15.1	18.9	2.2	0.6	0.9	0.4	0.3	0.1	0.0
services to clients and patients	0.5	0.4	0.7	0.6	0.1	0.5	0.2	0.2	0.2	0.1	0.8	0.0
other	0.4	0.4	0.8	0.3	0.3	0.4	0.4	0.3	0.5	0.5	0.7	1.7
Racial Background (1)												
White/Caucasian	91.1	90.7	92.6	91.7	93.4	87.5	92.4	90.1	95.7	94.1	92.4	98.4
Black/Negro/Afro-American	2.9	2.9	2.6	1.1	1.6	5.3	3.1	3.8	0.7	3.3	2.6	1.6
American Indian	0.9	0.7	1.5	0.7	0.4	0.8	0.7	0.8	0.5	0.7	1.6	0.0
Asian-American	3.5	3.8	2.0	4.4	3.1	4.5	2.2	2.8	1.7	1.6	2.1	0.0
Mexican-American/Chicano	0.7	0.5	1.7	0.6	0.1	0.6	0.4	0.4	0.5	0.3	1.8	0.0
Puerto Rican-American	0.3	0.4	0.0	0.4	0.1	0.1	0.9	1.7	0.1	0.2	0.0	0.0
Other	2.3	2.4	2.0	2.7	2.2	2.4	1.9	2.2	2.0	1.4	2.1	0.0

55

MALE FACULTY

	ALL			Universities		Four-year Colleges					Two-year Colleges	
	Insts	4-yr	2-yr	Pub	Priv	Pub	All Priv	Nons	Cath	Prot	Pub	Priv
Highest Degree Earned												
bachelor's (B.A., B.S., etc.)	2.6	1.0	9.3	0.9	0.4	1.0	1.6	2.1	1.2	1.1	9.6	1.6
master's (M.A., M.S., etc.)	22.5	14.5	57.5	9.5	6.3	17.7	22.9	20.5	25.0	25.4	57.3	63.1
LL.B., J.D.	0.7	0.7	0.8	0.5	0.6	0.9	0.7	0.9	0.9	0.5	0.9	0.0
M.D., D.D.S. (or equivalent)	0.4	0.4	0.5	0.6	0.2	0.6	0.2	0.2	0.1	0.2	0.4	1.6
other first professional	0.6	0.7	0.5	0.8	0.3	0.9	0.8	0.9	0.7	0.8	0.5	0.0
Ed.D.	4.4	4.5	3.7	3.2	0.9	7.9	3.7	3.4	2.2	4.8	3.7	5.1
Ph.D.	63.1	73.8	16.1	80.7	88.4	66.7	64.5	66.4	64.3	61.9	15.9	21.9
other degree	3.9	3.5	6.0	3.0	2.2	3.9	4.2	4.1	4.2	4.5	6.0	5.0
none	1.8	0.9	5.7	0.7	0.8	0.8	1.3	1.5	1.3	0.9	5.8	1.6
Field of Highest Degree (2)												
agriculture or forestry	1.9	1.9	1.8	3.6	1.2	1.3	0.3	0.5	0.0	0.2	1.8	1.7
biological sciences	6.9	7.1	6.3	7.9	7.1	6.6	6.5	5.7	6.7	7.4	6.2	7.0
business	7.0	6.7	8.3	5.3	6.2	8.1	7.0	6.5	11.4	5.6	8.4	3.5
education	11.4	10.0	17.7	8.3	2.3	14.8	10.1	9.2	7.1	12.9	17.9	14.0
engineering	6.9	7.3	5.1	10.9	9.8	5.5	2.6	3.8	2.1	1.1	5.3	0.0
English	5.9	5.5	7.4	4.9	5.2	5.4	6.9	7.1	6.9	6.8	7.1	15.8
health related	1.7	1.6	2.1	2.5	1.0	1.6	0.7	0.9	0.5	0.6	2.1	3.5
history or political science	7.7	8.3	5.3	7.4	11.3	7.8	8.7	9.2	8.8	7.8	5.3	7.0
humanities	8.0	8.9	3.8	8.0	13.3	5.4	13.3	11.4	16.1	14.8	3.4	14.2
fine arts	8.6	8.7	8.1	9.2	4.8	8.7	10.0	9.7	6.3	12.2	7.7	19.3
mathematics or statistics	6.4	6.2	7.4	5.3	7.3	6.0	6.9	6.9	6.4	7.2	7.6	3.5
physical sciences	8.8	9.0	7.5	8.7	11.4	8.2	9.5	10.3	8.7	8.8	7.5	7.0
social sciences	13.0	14.4	8.5	13.3	16.0	14.1	13.5	14.2	14.4	12.0	8.7	3.5
other technical	1.7	1.3	3.3	1.1	0.9	1.6	1.3	1.7	1.4	0.8	3.4	0.0
other non-technical	4.3	3.5	7.4	3.5	2.2	4.8	2.5	2.9	3.0	1.8	7.6	
Year Highest Degree Earned												
1951 or earlier	2.7	2.5	3.7	2.5	4.3	1.9	2.2	2.3	2.4	2.1	3.7	3.3
1952 – 1956	3.9	4.2	2.6	5.0	7.6	3.0	2.7	3.4	2.2	2.1	2.7	1.7
1957 – 1961	6.9	7.2	5.4	9.0	8.5	5.5	6.1	6.7	6.7	5.1	5.4	1.7
1962 – 1966	13.5	13.4	13.9	15.6	13.3	12.4	11.3	12.5	9.0	10.6	13.9	13.5
1967 – 1971	20.3	19.7	22.9	20.2	15.4	22.6	17.2	17.4	14.3	18.2	22.9	21.9
1972 – 1976	18.4	17.7	21.2	16.1	15.5	19.4	19.1	17.7	22.1	19.8	21.7	6.9
1977 – 1981	13.7	13.5	14.2	11.8	12.3	14.2	16.2	15.2	19.8	15.8	14.1	17.1
1982 – 1986	13.8	14.6	10.5	13.1	16.7	14.1	16.3	16.4	16.0	16.3	9.9	27.1
1987 – 1989	6.9	7.2	5.8	6.7	6.3	6.9	8.8	8.4	7.4	10.0	5.8	6.7
Degree Currently Working Toward												
bachelor's (B.A., B.S., etc.)	1.7	0.5	6.7	0.2	1.0	0.5	0.8	1.6	0.1	0.1	7.1	0.0
master's (M.A., M.S., etc.)	3.5	1.4	12.2	0.7	0.7	1.9	2.2	2.3	1.5	2.2	12.6	5.2
LL.B., J.D.	0.3	0.3	0.1	0.0	0.2	0.1	0.4	0.7	0.0	0.1	0.1	0.0
M.D., D.D.S. (or equivalent)	0.2	0.1	0.3	0.5	0.1	0.2	0.1	0.2	0.0	0.2	0.2	2.6
other first professional	0.2	0.2	0.4	0.1	0.1	0.1	0.5	0.4	0.8	0.2	0.3	2.7
Ed.D.	2.4	1.7	5.7	0.6	0.7	3.1	2.2	2.1	2.0	2.5	5.6	7.9
Ph.D.	9.5	8.4	14.5	4.8	2.7	10.5	14.0	12.6	16.6	14.7	14.5	15.8
other degree	1.8	1.2	4.4	1.0	0.9	1.2	1.7	1.8	1.7	1.6	4.4	5.2
none	80.4	86.3	55.6	92.2	94.4	82.4	78.1	78.3	77.2	78.1	55.3	60.7

MALE FACULTY

Department of Current Faculty Appointment (2)	ALL			Universities		Four-year Colleges					Two-year Colleges	
	Insts	4-yr	2-yr	Pub	Priv	Pub	All Priv	Nons	Cath	Prot	Pub	Priv
agriculture or forestry	2.0	2.2	1.3	4.1	2.0	1.5	0.2	0.4	0.0	0.1	1.3	1.8
biological sciences	6.4	6.5	5.9	6.6	6.7	6.5	6.2	5.4	6.7	7.2	5.9	5.5
business	8.8	8.6	9.9	6.8	7.3	10.5	9.5	9.1	14.9	7.3	10.0	7.4
education	6.5	7.0	4.6	6.8	1.9	9.3	6.6	5.5	4.2	9.3	4.7	3.6
engineering	6.6	7.2	4.0	10.9	10.9	4.9	2.3	3.6	1.6	0.9	4.1	0.0
English	6.3	5.7	8.7	5.1	5.1	5.5	7.4	7.5	7.1	7.4	8.4	18.5
health related	1.9	1.8	2.6	2.8	1.3	1.6	0.6	0.5	0.9	0.5	2.7	0.0
history or political science	6.9	7.6	3.7	7.2	10.3	6.8	8.1	8.3	8.0	7.8	3.7	3.7
humanities	7.9	8.7	4.1	7.5	13.4	5.2	13.3	11.5	15.7	14.8	3.7	14.9
fine arts	9.0	9.2	7.9	9.9	4.6	9.7	10.2	9.7	6.5	12.8	7.5	20.4
mathematics or statistics	6.5	6.1	8.4	5.4	6.3	6.2	6.9	6.8	6.2	7.4	8.5	3.7
physical sciences	8.6	8.8	7.8	7.9	9.8	8.8	9.5	10.1	8.8	9.0	7.8	7.4
social sciences	12.6	13.2	10.0	12.5	14.3	13.7	13.1	14.2	12.8	11.6	10.0	9.3
other technical	4.1	2.6	10.6	2.0	2.2	3.2	3.1	4.0	2.9	1.9	10.9	1.8
other non-technical	5.8	4.8	10.5	4.5	3.8	6.6	3.0	3.4	3.7	1.9	10.8	1.8
Year Appointed to Current Position												
1951 or earlier	2.0	2.0	1.7	2.0	2.3	1.8	2.3	2.2	3.0	2.0	1.7	1.7
1952 - 1956	1.5	1.7	0.4	2.0	3.2	0.8	1.9	2.0	1.9	1.9	0.4	0.0
1957 - 1961	4.0	4.6	1.7	4.9	6.4	3.3	4.9	4.8	5.2	4.9	1.8	0.0
1962 - 1966	11.9	12.3	10.0	13.0	12.2	12.6	10.6	11.7	8.2	10.3	9.8	17.3
1967 - 1971	21.3	19.9	27.7	21.7	15.4	22.9	14.9	15.9	12.1	14.7	28.0	18.8
1972 - 1976	13.4	12.3	17.7	13.1	12.0	12.9	10.4	9.9	10.9	10.8	18.0	12.2
1977 - 1981	13.4	13.1	14.4	12.1	13.9	12.8	14.8	13.5	18.9	14.9	14.3	17.2
1982 - 1986	17.0	17.7	14.2	16.5	18.4	17.5	19.4	19.4	20.0	19.1	14.1	15.5
1987 - 1989	15.6	16.4	12.1	14.8	16.1	15.4	20.7	20.5	19.7	21.5	11.9	17.3
Tenured?												
yes	72.5	71.8	75.5	75.9	71.0	73.5	62.7	63.0	61.5	62.7	76.1	58.6
no	27.5	28.2	24.5	24.1	29.0	26.5	37.3	37.0	38.5	37.3	23.9	41.4
Year Received Tenure												
1951 or earlier	0.4	0.4	0.4	0.5	0.1	0.3	0.5	0.5	1.0	0.3	0.4	0.0
1952 - 1956	0.4	0.5	0.2	0.7	0.8	0.2	0.5	0.6	0.5	0.5	0.2	0.0
1957 - 1961	2.1	2.4	0.4	2.7	4.6	1.4	2.3	2.6	2.0	1.9	0.4	0.0
1962 - 1966	6.8	7.5	3.9	8.1	10.1	5.8	7.3	7.8	6.0	7.2	3.8	6.4
1967 - 1971	19.6	19.3	20.9	20.6	18.7	19.5	17.0	18.3	13.9	16.4	21.1	12.5
1972 - 1976	25.5	24.5	29.4	24.8	20.0	27.2	22.3	23.6	20.1	21.6	29.4	31.0
1977 - 1981	17.7	17.6	18.5	18.1	18.0	17.6	16.0	14.8	16.3	17.6	18.6	12.6
1982 - 1986	16.7	17.0	15.6	15.6	17.7	16.8	19.8	18.3	22.1	21.0	15.7	12.5
1987 - 1989	10.7	10.8	10.6	9.0	10.0	11.2	14.2	13.5	18.0	13.4	10.2	25.0
Primary Interest												
very heavily in teaching	33.0	24.9	68.3	14.6	10.1	31.8	39.9	34.1	42.4	47.0	68.4	64.8
leaning toward teaching	35.8	38.4	24.6	33.7	32.1	43.1	42.8	43.8	43.9	40.9	24.7	21.9
leaning toward research	26.9	31.6	6.6	44.4	46.1	22.2	16.2	20.6	12.8	11.4	6.4	11.7
very heavily in research	4.2	5.1	0.4	7.2	11.7	2.8	1.1	1.5	0.9	0.7	0.4	1.6

MALE FACULTY

	ALL			Universities		Four-year Colleges					Two-year Colleges	
	Insts	4-yr	2-yr	Pub	Priv	Pub	All Priv	Nons	Cath	Prot	Pub	Priv
Marital Status												
married (currently)	82.1	82.0	82.6	83.6	80.0	81.7	81.2	80.1	73.7	86.3	82.3	88.4
separated	1.4	1.4	1.3	1.5	0.9	1.5	1.3	1.3	1.9	0.8	1.3	0.0
single (never married)	7.7	8.0	6.2	6.3	10.1	7.5	10.4	9.6	17.7	8.0	6.1	6.6
single (with partner)	1.7	1.7	1.5	1.7	3.6	1.3	1.3	1.7	1.3	0.6	1.6	0.0
single (divorced)	6.5	6.2	7.7	6.2	4.7	7.4	5.4	6.6	5.1	3.9	7.9	3.3
single (widowed)	0.6	0.6	0.8	0.7	0.7	0.6	0.5	0.6	0.3	0.4	0.8	1.6
Spouse's or Partner's Education												
8th grade or less	0.2	0.1	0.2	0.1	0.1	0.2	0.1	0.1	0.1	0.1	0.2	0.0
some high school	0.4	0.3	0.7	0.3	0.2	0.6	0.3	0.2	0.4	0.3	0.7	0.0
completed high school	4.7	4.0	7.9	4.1	2.9	4.3	4.1	4.6	5.1	2.9	8.1	1.8
some college	14.1	12.2	22.5	12.5	8.9	12.8	12.6	12.1	11.5	13.9	22.5	21.7
graduated from college	21.8	21.2	24.3	20.4	19.8	21.2	23.3	22.2	20.8	26.2	24.3	25.2
attended grad/prof school	11.4	11.7	10.0	12.2	11.7	11.0	11.8	12.2	10.2	11.8	9.7	18.2
attained advanced degree	37.8	40.7	25.6	42.0	45.8	39.7	36.7	38.0	34.5	35.8	25.4	29.4
does not apply	9.6	9.8	8.9	8.4	10.6	10.3	11.1	10.5	17.3	9.0	9.1	3.6
Father's Education												
8th grade or less	21.3	20.3	25.7	20.0	16.2	22.9	19.4	18.4	22.6	19.3	25.9	20.7
some high school	11.4	10.6	15.1	9.9	10.5	11.1	11.1	10.8	11.9	11.1	15.3	10.3
completed high school	22.5	21.8	25.9	21.8	19.3	22.4	22.1	22.4	23.6	21.0	25.6	36.1
some college	12.9	13.3	11.6	13.0	12.6	13.6	13.5	12.9	12.5	14.8	11.7	8.8
graduated from college	12.7	13.4	9.5	13.8	15.9	12.0	13.3	13.7	13.7	12.5	9.4	10.5
attended grad/prof school	4.7	5.1	3.2	5.6	5.4	4.7	4.7	4.5	3.9	5.3	3.3	0.0
attained advanced degree	14.4	15.6	9.0	15.9	20.0	13.4	16.0	17.2	11.7	16.1	8.8	13.7
Mother's Education												
8th grade or less	15.8	15.3	17.7	15.1	11.6	17.4	14.6	14.6	16.8	13.6	17.9	12.2
some high school	11.1	10.6	13.5	9.5	9.4	11.8	11.4	11.2	12.5	11.0	13.6	10.2
completed high school	33.9	33.2	37.2	34.1	30.9	32.7	33.9	33.5	34.6	34.0	37.0	41.2
some college	15.7	15.8	14.9	15.7	17.0	15.6	15.8	14.4	16.4	17.4	14.9	15.5
graduated from college	14.2	15.0	10.7	15.5	17.7	13.7	14.6	15.6	11.9	14.3	10.6	13.8
attended grad/prof school	3.4	3.7	2.4	3.5	5.4	3.2	3.8	3.9	3.5	3.7	2.3	3.5
attained advanced degree	5.8	6.3	3.6	6.6	8.1	5.5	6.1	6.7	4.2	6.0	3.7	3.5
Base Institutional Salary in Thousands (3)												
less than 20	0.4	0.2	0.9	0.0	0.1	0.1	0.9	0.9	0.9	0.9	0.9	0.0
20 – 29	4.9	4.3	7.8	2.5	1.5	2.5	12.6	11.0	9.4	16.6	7.1	25.5
30 – 39	12.9	11.8	18.0	7.5	5.8	11.1	23.5	19.0	27.7	28.1	17.2	39.9
40 – 49	26.1	24.8	31.8	20.8	16.9	29.9	28.2	23.1	35.0	32.4	31.8	32.9
50 – 59	21.4	21.7	20.3	20.6	19.6	26.5	17.3	19.1	17.0	14.9	21.0	1.7
60 – 69	17.9	18.2	16.9	20.9	22.2	18.6	10.6	15.1	8.2	5.2	17.5	0.0
70 – 79	7.6	8.6	3.1	11.2	9.9	8.6	3.5	5.7	1.7	1.2	3.2	0.0
80 – 89	4.9	5.9	1.0	9.5	11.7	1.9	2.4	4.4	0.0	0.5	1.0	0.0
90 – 98	1.5	1.9	0.2	2.9	5.0	0.3	0.6	1.1	0.0	0.1	0.2	0.0
99 or more	2.2	2.7	0.1	4.5	7.3	0.5	0.3	0.6	0.0	0.0	0.1	0.0

MALE FACULTY

	ALL			Universities		Four-year Colleges					Two-year Colleges	
	Insts	4-yr	2-yr	Pub	Priv	Pub	All Priv	Nons	Cath	Prot	Pub	Priv
General Activities												
held academic admin position....	42.4	44.4	34.1	41.1	45.6	45.2	47.9	47.3	49.8	47.7	33.9	40.7
award for outstanding teaching..	31.8	31.3	33.7	31.1	26.1	33.5	31.6	31.3	29.4	33.1	33.6	36.8
spouse or partner an academic...	32.9	31.9	37.5	29.8	27.8	34.6	33.5	32.0	28.2	38.1	37.3	44.1
commute a long distance to work.	17.1	15.8	22.8	13.3	16.1	18.5	15.8	17.2	17.8	11.2	23.3	8.5
research/writing on women/gender	13.6	15.1	7.0	15.3	16.9	13.7	15.8	15.2	18.4	15.3	7.2	3.3
research/writing on race/ethncty	17.3	18.8	11.0	18.5	17.5	20.0	18.2	18.8	18.4	17.2	11.1	8.3
have dependent children.........	58.3	57.9	60.2	58.2	55.0	58.4	58.2	57.2	55.7	60.8	59.9	67.7
am a U.S. citizen...............	94.1	93.4	97.5	92.8	89.1	94.2	95.5	94.5	96.5	96.6	97.5	98.4
interrupted career for hlth/fam.	3.6	3.6	3.6	3.1	3.6	4.0	3.9	3.8	4.5	3.8	3.6	3.3
considered career in acad admin.	40.7	40.8	40.3	41.5	33.0	43.8	39.8	38.9	38.7	41.6	40.3	40.2
plan working beyond age 70......	36.6	38.4	29.2	38.8	44.0	35.6	38.7	39.4	42.2	36.0	28.8	40.0
General Activities in the Last Two Years												
had one or more firm job offers.	31.7	30.8	35.4	29.0	30.9	31.0	33.4	33.4	31.4	34.4	35.5	31.7
part in fac development program.	48.4	42.9	72.3	29.8	27.2	50.5	61.9	56.8	65.4	67.6	72.3	71.9
developed a new course.........	68.5	70.0	62.0	66.1	73.3	68.8	76.1	76.1	78.7	74.7	62.4	51.4
considered early retirement.....	31.3	29.3	40.0	30.9	21.9	33.3	25.1	25.7	23.9	24.8	40.2	33.3
considered leaving academe......	36.3	35.7	38.7	36.4	29.2	38.0	35.1	35.7	35.9	33.8	38.5	43.3
Teaching Activities in the Last Two Years												
taught honors course............	19.7	21.4	12.0	21.8	32.3	16.9	20.7	22.1	20.3	18.8	11.7	20.9
taught interdisciplinary course.	35.3	37.6	25.1	34.4	42.1	34.7	44.4	46.7	37.9	44.4	25.3	19.0
taught general education course.	46.2	46.1	46.6	35.7	32.8	55.4	56.3	52.5	48.1	65.5	46.6	46.3
taught develop/remedial course..	12.5	9.0	27.1	6.5	4.3	11.8	11.9	12.0	11.5	11.9	27.3	21.0
taught ethnic studies course....	5.8	6.3	3.3	4.7	6.0	7.1	8.1	8.9	6.1	7.9	3.3	3.9
taught women's studies course...	2.1	2.2	1.7	1.7	2.6	1.7	3.6	3.5	3.7	3.7	1.7	1.9
team-taught a course............	33.6	35.6	24.7	37.6	39.0	31.3	36.9	37.6	28.6	39.8	24.5	27.9
worked w/students on resrch proj	66.7	73.1	36.9	79.4	79.9	70.0	63.0	65.8	61.6	59.6	36.8	37.6
attd racial/cultural workshop...	22.1	19.9	31.8	15.3	14.1	23.7	25.2	25.5	31.1	21.7	32.4	14.9
attd women's/minorities workshop	14.3	12.9	20.0	10.0	10.5	13.5	18.5	20.3	23.6	13.4	20.4	7.3
held faculty senate/council ofc.	26.1	25.3	29.7	22.4	23.3	27.4	28.1	28.0	29.2	27.6	29.7	31.3
used funds for research.........	46.8	53.9	13.7	64.5	67.8	44.3	41.8	46.1	38.1	37.3	13.4	24.1
served as a paid consultant.....	49.1	51.6	38.5	54.4	57.6	51.9	42.4	44.9	42.5	38.6	39.0	23.2
Research Working Environment												
work essentially alone..........	68.7	68.1	71.5	62.5	65.2	69.9	76.5	75.0	74.4	79.6	70.9	86.0
work with one or two colleagues.	24.9	26.4	18.2	31.0	28.9	25.3	18.9	20.4	21.4	15.6	18.5	10.4
member of larger group..........	6.3	5.5	10.3	6.5	5.8	4.7	4.6	4.6	4.2	4.8	10.5	3.6

MALE FACULTY

	ALL			Universities		Four-year Colleges					Two-year Colleges	
HOURS PER WEEK SPENT ON:	Insts	4-yr	2-yr	Pub	Priv	Pub	All Priv	Nons	Cath	Prot	Pub	Priv
Scheduled Teaching												
none	0.4	0.4	0.3	0.7	0.6	0.2	0.1	0.1	0.1	0.1	0.3	0.0
1 – 4	7.6	9.1	1.4	12.8	19.8	4.8	2.9	3.4	2.1	2.6	1.2	7.2
5 – 8	28.0	33.4	4.3	49.1	52.8	20.0	16.4	20.7	14.4	11.2	4.2	7.2
9 – 12	32.5	36.6	14.6	26.1	21.4	46.1	48.6	46.9	56.2	47.4	14.3	23.5
13 – 16	16.5	12.6	33.2	6.2	3.4	18.1	20.6	17.2	19.4	26.1	32.9	41.9
17 – 20	9.0	5.3	25.1	3.8	1.0	7.2	7.7	7.4	6.2	8.7	25.4	16.5
21 – 34	5.4	2.2	19.4	1.2	0.9	3.0	3.2	3.6	1.6	3.5	19.9	3.7
35 – 44	0.5	0.2	1.4	0.1	0.1	0.4	0.3	0.5	0.2	0.1	1.4	0.0
45 or more	0.1	0.1	0.3	0.0	0.0	0.1	0.1	0.1	0.0	0.2	0.3	0.0
Preparing for Teaching												
none	0.3	0.3	0.3	0.5	0.6	0.2	0.1	0.1	0.1	0.0	0.3	0.0
1 – 4	9.1	9.1	9.0	11.4	11.7	7.8	5.7	6.1	5.4	5.4	8.8	14.6
5 – 8	23.7	23.7	23.4	26.9	27.5	22.3	18.3	19.8	16.9	16.8	23.1	30.8
9 – 12	25.3	25.3	25.7	25.5	27.7	25.3	23.2	23.7	23.8	22.2	25.9	18.3
13 – 16	17.2	17.1	17.5	16.3	15.2	14.9	19.1	18.6	18.7	20.1	17.6	14.6
17 – 20	13.4	13.4	13.6	11.3	10.1	9.9	16.6	16.5	16.6	16.7	13.7	10.9
21 – 34	8.9	9.0	8.6	6.6	5.9	4.9	13.4	11.9	14.7	14.9	8.5	10.7
35 – 44	1.6	1.6	1.4	0.9	0.8	1.8	2.9	2.5	3.2	3.2	1.5	0.0
45 or more	0.5	0.6	0.5	0.5	0.5	0.5	0.7	0.7	0.7	0.7	0.5	0.0
Advising/Counseling of Students												
none	2.8	2.7	3.3	3.4	1.8	2.9	1.7	1.7	2.0	1.7	3.4	1.8
1 – 4	58.1	57.3	61.6	60.7	61.6	53.5	54.7	53.7	53.5	56.8	61.2	74.5
5 – 8	28.6	29.2	26.3	26.5	26.5	31.2	31.9	33.4	32.8	29.3	26.8	12.7
9 – 12	7.6	7.9	6.4	6.7	7.5	8.9	8.5	8.2	9.2	8.5	6.3	9.2
13 – 16	1.8	1.9	1.3	1.5	1.7	2.2	2.1	2.1	1.4	2.2	1.3	1.9
17 – 20	0.7	0.8	0.5	0.8	0.7	0.8	0.8	0.8	0.7	1.0	0.5	0.0
21 – 34	0.3	0.3	0.3	0.3	0.1	0.3	0.2	0.1	0.2	0.4	0.3	0.0
35 – 44	0.1	0.1	0.2	0.0	0.0	0.1	0.0	0.0	0.1	0.1	0.2	0.0
45 or more	0.0	0.0	0.0	0.0	0.0	0.0	0.0	0.0	0.1	0.0	0.0	0.0
Committee Work and Meetings												
none	4.9	4.2	8.0	4.0	5.9	3.4	4.8	4.9	5.1	4.6	8.2	1.8
1 – 4	69.0	67.8	74.6	65.0	69.8	67.3	71.8	70.9	71.2	73.5	74.5	76.5
5 – 8	20.5	22.4	13.7	23.9	19.0	22.9	19.5	20.0	19.9	18.6	13.6	14.6
9 – 12	4.1	4.4	2.8	5.1	3.9	4.8	2.8	3.0	2.7	2.5	2.7	7.2
13 – 16	1.1	1.2	0.6	1.6	1.1	1.1	0.8	0.9	0.9	0.5	0.6	0.0
17 – 20	0.3	0.3	0.2	0.4	0.1	0.3	0.2	0.2	0.1	0.2	0.2	0.0
21 – 34	0.1	0.1	0.0	0.1	0.1	0.1	0.0	0.1	0.1	0.2	0.0	0.0
35 – 44	0.0	0.0	0.0	0.0	0.0	0.0	0.0	0.0	0.1	0.0	0.0	0.0
45 or more	0.0	0.0	0.0	0.0	0.0	0.0	0.0	0.0	0.0	0.0	0.0	0.0

MALE FACULTY

HOURS PER WEEK SPENT ON:

	ALL			Universities		Four-year Colleges					Two-year Colleges	
	Insts	4-yr	2-yr	Pub	Priv	Pub	All Priv	Nons	Cath	Prot	Pub	Priv
Other Administration												
none	36.3	35.1	41.6	35.6	31.5	37.5	32.9	33.5	36.9	30.2	42.1	28.3
1 – 4	38.6	39.0	37.0	40.5	43.4	36.7	37.3	37.7	36.3	37.1	37.0	37.7
5 – 8	11.5	11.8	10.5	11.6	12.8	11.6	13.6	12.7	12.0	15.6	10.3	15.2
9 – 12	5.8	6.0	4.7	5.3	5.6	6.1	7.3	7.5	7.6	6.9	4.7	5.6
13 – 16	3.1	3.3	2.3	2.7	3.2	3.8	3.4	3.1	2.7	4.1	2.3	3.8
17 – 20	2.4	2.5	1.9	2.2	2.0	2.7	3.0	2.9	2.2	3.4	1.8	3.3
21 – 34	1.8	1.9	1.4	1.6	1.3	2.3	2.1	2.0	1.9	2.2	1.3	3.7
35 – 44	0.3	0.3	0.4	0.4	0.2	0.3	0.3	0.3	0.2	0.3	0.3	1.9
45 or more	0.2	0.2	0.2	0.1	0.0	0.3	0.2	0.2	0.2	0.3	0.2	0.0
Research and Scholarly Writing												
none	16.7	9.9	48.3	4.3	3.0	11.6	21.1	18.4	18.8	26.1	48.5	43.3
1 – 4	25.9	24.7	31.4	15.9	13.5	31.3	36.6	32.8	39.0	41.0	31.2	37.9
5 – 8	16.9	18.2	10.8	16.5	15.6	20.1	19.8	20.2	22.5	18.1	10.9	7.5
9 – 12	13.5	15.2	5.5	17.7	16.9	14.6	10.7	13.2	9.7	7.7	5.4	7.5
13 – 16	8.3	9.8	1.7	12.5	12.6	8.7	5.1	6.5	4.5	3.4	1.6	3.8
17 – 20	7.8	9.2	1.5	13.0	13.9	6.7	3.4	4.4	3.2	2.1	1.5	0.0
21 – 34	7.6	9.1	0.7	13.9	16.0	5.4	2.5	3.4	2.0	1.3	0.7	0.0
35 – 44	2.0	2.5	0.1	3.9	5.3	0.9	0.5	0.8	0.3	0.2	0.1	0.0
45 or more	1.2	1.4	0.2	2.3	3.2	0.5	0.2	0.3	0.1	0.1	0.2	0.0
Consultation with Clients or Patients												
none	68.7	68.1	71.0	65.7	69.8	66.5	73.3	72.3	71.3	75.7	70.8	78.9
1 – 4	20.6	21.1	18.4	22.8	19.3	22.1	18.0	18.6	17.9	17.1	18.6	12.7
5 – 8	6.5	6.7	5.8	7.1	6.7	7.2	5.1	5.2	6.1	4.6	5.8	6.3
9 – 12	2.3	2.2	2.5	2.2	2.8	2.2	1.8	2.3	1.4	1.3	2.6	0.0
13 – 16	0.8	0.8	0.8	0.8	0.7	0.8	0.7	0.7	1.3	0.4	0.8	0.0
17 – 20	0.6	0.6	0.5	0.5	0.3	0.5	0.6	0.8	0.7	0.3	0.5	0.0
21 – 34	0.4	0.3	0.2	0.1	0.1	0.1	0.3	0.1	0.8	0.5	0.1	2.0
35 – 44	0.1	0.1		0.0	0.3		0.1	0.0	0.6	0.0		
45 or more	0.1	0.1	0.2	0.0	0.0	0.2	0.0	0.0	0.0	0.0	0.3	0.0
Number of Days Spent Off-Campus for Professional Activities												
none	12.3	10.7	19.1	9.8	8.0	11.3	12.8	13.0	16.2	11.1	19.0	21.5
1 – 2	13.7	11.5	23.3	8.5	8.2	13.2	15.7	13.7	19.0	17.0	23.5	20.0
3 – 4	22.5	21.3	27.4	17.3	17.2	23.3	27.4	26.1	25.6	30.1	27.4	28.3
5 – 10	29.7	31.7	21.4	33.4	27.8	32.7	29.6	30.7	25.2	30.0	21.4	21.8
11 – 20	14.2	16.1	6.2	19.3	23.9	13.6	10.0	11.0	9.5	8.8	6.2	6.6
21 – 50	5.8	6.7	1.7	8.8	12.6	4.3	3.4	4.1	3.4	2.3	1.7	1.7
50+	1.8	2.0	0.8	3.0	2.2	1.5	1.2	1.4	1.1	0.8	0.9	0.0

61

MALE FACULTY

NUMBER OF:	ALL			Universities		Four-year Colleges					Two-year Colleges	
	Insts	4-yr	2-yr	Pub	Priv	Pub	All Priv	Nons	Cath	Prot	Pub	Priv
Articles in Academic or Professional Journals												
none	22.9	15.1	56.3	8.0	5.4	18.7	27.0	24.1	26.9	31.4	55.8	68.3
1-2	17.2	15.6	24.1	9.7	7.9	20.2	22.9	20.0	25.3	26.1	24.2	21.7
3-4	13.1	13.9	9.8	10.6	11.0	16.8	16.7	16.8	19.0	15.4	10.0	5.0
5-10	16.2	18.5	6.3	19.0	17.8	19.3	16.8	19.0	15.7	14.3	6.4	5.0
11-20	12.5	14.9	2.0	19.2	19.5	12.1	9.4	11.0	8.6	7.5	2.1	0.0
21-50	11.9	14.4	1.2	21.2	22.5	9.9	5.2	6.5	3.6	4.2	1.3	0.0
50+	6.2	7.6	0.2	12.2	16.0	3.1	1.8	2.6	0.9	1.1	0.2	0.0
Chapters in Edited Volumes												
none	61.9	55.5	89.4	44.1	33.7	65.8	71.4	66.0	75.7	77.2	89.4	90.0
1-2	18.6	21.4	6.9	23.9	23.2	20.2	17.9	19.5	16.9	15.9	6.8	8.4
3-4	9.5	11.5	1.2	15.0	20.4	7.4	6.4	8.6	4.8	4.0	1.2	1.6
5-10	6.6	7.9	0.9	11.4	14.7	4.8	3.1	4.1	2.1	2.1	1.0	0.0
11-20	2.3	2.6	0.5	4.0	5.7	1.2	0.8	0.6	0.4	0.6	0.9	0.0
21-50	0.8	0.9	0.1	1.3	1.9	0.4	0.3	0.1	0.0	0.2	0.5	0.0
50+	0.2	0.3	0.1	0.3	0.4	0.3	0.1	0.1	0.0	0.2	0.1	0.0
Books, Manuals, Monographs												
none	49.0	46.0	62.0	39.6	36.0	49.6	57.1	54.5	58.1	60.4	61.2	84.9
1-2	30.6	31.8	25.6	32.9	34.4	31.3	29.1	29.6	29.9	28.1	26.1	13.5
3-4	11.0	11.8	7.7	14.2	13.0	11.1	8.3	9.3	8.2	6.8	8.0	1.6
5-10	6.6	7.4	3.0	9.3	11.8	5.9	4.0	4.8	2.6	3.5	3.1	0.0
11-20	1.9	2.1	1.1	2.9	3.8	1.4	1.0	1.2	0.7	0.7	1.2	0.0
21-50	0.5	0.6	0.2	0.7	0.9	0.5	0.4	0.5	0.3	0.4	0.2	0.0
50+	0.3	0.3	0.3	0.4	0.1	0.2	0.1	0.2	0.2	0.0	0.3	0.0
Professional Writings Accepted or Published in Last Two Years												
none	40.9	31.8	80.0	19.6	14.0	40.5	49.2	43.7	50.5	56.3	79.8	84.6
1-2	26.1	28.7	15.2	26.7	25.1	31.4	30.0	30.6	31.0	28.6	15.3	13.7
3-4	17.4	20.7	3.4	26.1	28.5	16.4	13.5	16.1	12.8	10.0	3.5	1.7
5-10	12.4	15.1	0.9	22.0	25.9	9.5	6.0	7.8	4.5	4.1	1.0	0.0
11-20	2.4	2.9	0.3	4.5	5.0	1.7	1.0	1.2	0.9	0.7	0.3	0.0
21-50	0.6	0.7	0.1	1.0	1.5	0.3	0.3	0.4	0.1	0.1	0.1	0.0
50+	0.1	0.1	0.1	0.1	0.0	0.1	0.1	0.1	0.1	0.1	0.1	0.0
Professional Goals Noted as Very Important or Essential												
engage in research	61.1	69.2	25.7	79.6	84.8	60.9	55.4	60.3	52.5	49.6	25.7	25.1
engage in outside activities	49.8	49.3	52.0	46.8	47.9	51.6	50.8	51.7	50.7	49.4	51.9	56.0
provide services to the cmty	39.9	38.1	47.8	34.3	31.3	42.9	41.0	40.0	42.5	41.7	48.0	41.7
participate in comm/admin work	25.7	24.5	30.9	21.7	18.1	27.5	28.2	26.7	30.6	29.2	31.1	25.1
be a good colleague	77.4	76.6	80.7	74.6	73.6	77.1	81.2	80.3	78.5	83.7	80.6	81.6
be a good teacher	98.1	97.9	99.1	97.4	96.0	98.2	99.1	99.1	99.0	99.3	99.0	100.0

MALE FACULTY

	ALL			Universities		Four-year Colleges					Two-year Colleges	
	Insts	4-yr	2-yr	Pub	Priv	Pub	All Priv	Nons	Cath	Prot	Pub	Priv
Evaluation Methods Used in Most or All Undergaduate Courses												
multiple-choice mid-terms/finals	30.8	26.9	47.3	25.5	15.6	33.2	26.2	22.8	28.6	30.0	47.3	47.3
essay mid-terms/finals	41.3	44.0	29.4	42.5	50.3	40.8	47.8	47.6	49.3	47.4	29.0	40.5
short-answer mid-terms/finals	34.9	35.3	33.6	36.0	36.4	33.2	36.5	35.8	36.8	37.4	33.3	42.1
multiple-choice quizzes	14.8	11.5	29.3	9.6	5.5	14.8	12.9	10.8	14.1	15.3	29.2	31.0
short-answer quizzes	23.4	21.4	31.9	18.6	15.9	23.8	25.6	23.5	26.3	28.3	31.6	42.4
weekly essay assignments	12.6	12.0	15.1	11.0	12.3	12.5	12.8	14.0	12.2	11.5	15.3	11.8
student presentation	21.7	22.9	16.6	22.0	18.8	23.8	25.4	26.9	24.5	23.6	16.4	24.0
term/research papers	30.9	33.7	18.7	33.9	36.9	31.1	35.7	37.5	34.0	33.9	18.5	25.3
stdnt evals of each others' work	7.8	7.9	7.3	8.0	4.9	8.8	8.2	8.8	7.9	7.4	7.3	8.4
grading on a curve	26.2	27.9	19.0	31.7	30.8	26.3	22.7	24.2	21.3	21.1	18.6	31.9
competency-based grading	51.8	51.1	54.8	53.2	52.8	49.4	49.3	52.3	46.2	46.5	55.4	37.8
student evaluations of teaching	82.4	85.5	69.0	90.7	88.6	82.3	80.4	81.9	85.1	76.0	68.4	86.2
Instructional Methods Used in Most or All Undergrad Courses												
class discussions	66.7	66.3	68.6	62.1	65.2	68.8	69.9	72.6	68.0	67.0	68.8	63.2
computer/machine-aided instruct.	12.0	11.1	16.2	10.8	10.1	12.0	10.6	12.0	9.3	9.3	16.2	17.2
cooperative learning	20.5	20.1	22.4	18.9	16.2	21.7	21.9	22.5	22.5	20.8	22.6	17.2
experiential learning/field stud	15.9	15.8	16.2	16.1	12.8	17.3	15.0	15.9	12.9	14.8	16.3	12.1
graduate teaching assistants	9.8	11.9	0.7	18.8	29.3	4.8	1.0	1.7	0.7	0.2	0.7	1.8
undergrad teaching assistants	3.1	3.4	1.8	2.8	3.9	2.4	5.5	7.0	2.8	4.6	1.7	5.2
group projects	13.3	13.4	13.1	13.5	10.2	14.4	13.4	14.6	14.3	11.1	13.1	13.8
independent projects	31.4	32.0	29.1	32.0	30.5	32.5	32.0	34.2	29.8	29.9	29.4	22.1
extensive lecturing	61.1	61.8	58.2	66.2	67.9	59.5	54.4	51.4	59.5	56.3	57.6	74.2
multiple drafts of written work	10.6	10.9	9.5	10.0	10.3	11.1	12.5	14.0	13.0	10.1	9.4	12.3
readings on racial/ethnic issues	8.5	9.2	5.3	8.1	8.9	9.5	10.6	11.1	10.3	9.9	5.2	10.4
readings on women/gender issues	7.5	8.1	4.8	7.1	8.9	7.9	9.7	10.4	10.2	8.5	4.6	10.4
student-developed activities	13.6	12.8	16.9	10.9	9.4	15.9	13.3	13.8	15.8	11.3	16.7	20.8
student-selected topics	7.2	7.2	7.3	6.9	7.0	7.9	7.0	7.1	8.1	6.3	7.3	5.2
Goals for Undergraduates Noted as Very Important or Essential												
develop ability to think clearly	99.3	99.4	98.8	99.3	99.6	99.5	99.5	99.4	99.8	99.6	98.9	96.7
increase self-directed learning	91.6	92.0	89.6	91.6	90.0	92.8	92.9	93.5	92.3	92.3	89.6	88.2
prepare for employment	58.4	55.1	72.4	54.2	42.5	61.9	53.9	52.0	53.6	56.8	73.3	48.4
prepare for graduate education	50.6	52.6	41.8	48.9	53.8	53.3	57.1	54.8	54.5	61.6	42.0	36.5
develop moral character	54.0	52.4	61.1	46.0	47.0	52.2	66.6	61.9	66.4	73.4	60.3	83.5
provide for emotional development	35.5	33.4	44.7	27.5	26.7	35.0	44.7	42.2	43.7	48.7	44.3	55.1
prepare for family living	16.1	14.1	24.6	9.7	8.3	15.8	22.0	19.3	19.0	27.3	24.3	31.8
teach stdnts classics west civ	36.3	37.9	29.5	33.9	36.9	37.9	45.0	41.4	48.5	48.4	28.9	45.2
help develop personal values	60.4	59.2	65.2	53.3	51.6	60.8	71.2	66.9	70.7	77.5	64.8	76.8
enhance out-of-class experience	38.9	37.7	43.8	33.4	28.2	41.4	44.8	45.3	42.2	45.4	43.5	50.0
enhance self-understanding	63.5	62.6	67.5	57.1	55.8	66.0	70.4	68.8	69.8	73.1	67.4	70.0

MALE FACULTY

	ALL			Universities		Four-year Colleges						Two-year Colleges	
	Insts	4-yr	2-yr	Pub	Priv	Pub	All Priv	Nons	Cath	Prot	Pub	Priv
NUMBER OF COURSES TAUGHT IN:												
General Education												
none	56.9	59.0	47.9	70.4	69.0	51.2	48.3	51.0	55.7	41.1	48.0	45.1
one	21.5	23.5	13.1	21.3	22.5	23.9	27.1	27.2	17.9	31.1	12.8	21.5
two	10.6	10.8	10.1	5.9	6.3	14.7	14.4	12.5	14.4	17.1	10.2	7.9
three	5.7	4.7	9.9	1.8	1.8	7.1	6.9	6.5	7.8	7.0	9.9	7.9
four	2.7	1.4	8.2	0.3	0.3	2.3	2.5	1.9	3.4	2.8	8.5	1.9
five or more	2.5	0.6	10.8	0.3	0.0	0.9	0.9	0.9	0.8	0.9	10.6	15.8
Other BA or BS Undergraduate Credit Courses												
none	9.8	6.4	26.1	6.8	7.0	6.4	5.6	6.5	4.3	4.9	26.3	21.3
one	30.7	34.9	10.5	45.4	52.9	27.1	18.5	19.6	16.2	18.0	10.0	12.7
two	27.8	30.4	15.2	31.1	30.3	29.8	30.2	32.8	27.0	27.9	15.0	19.3
three	17.6	17.8	16.5	13.0	7.4	21.7	26.0	24.2	29.2	26.9	16.4	19.2
four	8.8	7.4	15.4	2.3	1.7	10.9	14.0	11.3	17.8	16.0	15.3	19.0
five or more	5.3	3.1	16.2	1.4	0.8	4.1	5.8	5.6	5.5	6.2	16.5	8.6
Non-BA Credit Courses (developmental or remedial)												
none	89.7	95.1	69.3	96.6	96.1	93.5	94.6	93.5	95.9	95.6	68.9	80.1
one	4.9	3.3	11.0	2.4	3.1	4.2	3.3	3.7	2.7	3.1	11.0	9.8
two	2.1	0.9	6.8	0.5	0.6	1.2	1.1	1.6	0.9	0.6	6.9	2.6
three	1.5	0.4	5.8	0.3	0.0	0.6	0.3	0.5	0.4	0.1	5.7	7.5
four	0.8	0.1	3.4	0.1	0.1	0.1	0.2	0.3	0.0	0.2	3.5	0.0
five or more	1.0	0.2	3.8	0.1	0.1	0.3	0.4	0.4	0.2	0.4	3.9	0.0
Graduate Courses												
none	60.5	53.7	98.2	39.7	36.3	61.2	83.0	80.5	76.7	89.9	98.1	100.0
one	33.0	38.8	1.0	50.9	56.7	31.1	13.1	15.3	17.2	7.8	1.1	0.0
two	5.1	6.0	0.3	7.4	6.4	5.9	2.8	3.3	4.2	1.5	0.3	0.0
three	1.0	1.0	0.1	1.4	0.3	1.4	0.7	0.6	1.5	0.5	0.1	0.0
four	0.3	0.3	0.1	0.3	0.2	0.3	0.2	0.2	0.1	0.3	0.1	0.0
five or more	0.2	0.1	0.3	0.1	0.0	0.2	0.1	0.1	0.3	0.0	0.4	0.0
Political Orientation												
far left	4.9	5.4	2.5	5.7	8.2	4.1	5.2	6.3	5.6	3.4	2.6	1.7
liberal	35.6	37.9	25.7	39.8	45.7	34.6	35.2	37.7	36.5	30.9	25.6	29.0
moderate	39.8	39.2	42.7	39.7	31.2	41.8	39.1	37.8	40.8	40.1	42.8	40.7
conservative	19.2	17.1	28.4	14.5	14.2	18.5	20.2	17.9	16.6	25.3	28.5	26.9
far right	0.5	0.5	0.6	0.4	0.7	0.5	0.3	0.3	0.4	0.3	0.6	1.7
Agrees Strongly or Somewhat												
abolish death penalty	43.3	46.4	29.8	47.0	56.6	41.7	46.5	48.8	51.0	41.1	29.6	34.0
national health care plan needed	79.8	80.9	75.2	81.7	83.9	79.8	79.4	82.0	81.6	74.6	75.4	69.6
abortion should be legalized	75.4	77.0	68.5	81.9	81.4	77.0	66.2	74.1	56.2	59.7	69.0	56.1
grading in college too easy	77.4	78.5	72.7	78.5	78.7	77.8	77.8	76.2	83.3	77.6	72.6	76.4
wealthy should pay more taxes	82.3	83.1	78.9	83.5	82.3	82.6	83.8	84.8	84.2	82.2	78.8	81.2
college can ban extreme speakers	19.6	17.7	27.8	13.1	15.8	17.6	26.7	22.1	25.4	33.8	27.5	37.4
college increases earning power	24.8	21.4	39.2	20.7	15.0	26.7	18.4	20.3	18.2	15.7	39.8	23.4
racial discrim no longer problem	7.7	7.3	9.6	7.3	6.8	8.1	6.1	6.6	6.1	5.4	9.6	8.5

MALE FACULTY

	ALL			Universities		Four-year Colleges					Two-year Colleges	
	Insts	4-yr	2-yr	Pub	Priv	Pub	All Priv	Nons	Cath	Prot	Pub	Priv
Agrees Strongly or Somewhat												
fac interested in students' prob	71.9	69.0	84.2	57.8	60.4	71.4	88.8	84.1	91.3	94.7	83.8	94.9
fac sensitive to minority issues	69.5	68.8	72.7	66.4	67.5	67.9	74.7	74.2	75.6	75.1	72.9	66.7
curriculum overspecialized......	29.8	32.8	16.9	42.7	38.1	28.0	20.9	22.1	21.0	19.1	17.1	10.0
many students don't "fit in"....	25.8	27.6	18.2	29.1	32.9	26.5	23.9	27.6	17.7	21.5	18.2	18.3
fac committed to welfare of coll	75.2	73.8	81.1	67.8	75.1	71.2	86.9	83.7	88.2	91.0	80.8	90.0
courses incl minority perspect.	34.6	33.9	37.4	33.0	28.2	35.8	36.0	40.2	31.3	32.1	38.1	18.8
admin consider student concerns.	59.3	58.5	62.4	52.8	57.4	56.9	71.1	70.0	70.6	73.0	62.0	73.5
fac interest in stdnts acad prob	75.3	73.2	84.6	62.0	67.1	76.3	90.4	88.7	90.3	92.9	84.3	91.7
a lot of racial conflict here..	11.0	12.4	4.7	18.8	10.0	9.4	7.9	9.2	6.6	6.5	4.7	10.1
students resent required courses	42.8	41.4	48.7	41.3	27.5	47.5	40.7	38.8	45.4	41.0	48.9	43.2
ethnic groups communicate well.	59.3	56.9	69.4	51.9	53.2	59.5	63.1	60.8	63.1	66.4	69.1	76.8
admin care little about students	24.8	25.0	23.7	30.4	21.7	27.8	13.8	15.9	13.1	11.0	24.0	16.6
low trust btwn minorities/admin.	28.2	30.9	16.9	40.1	35.0	27.1	19.4	22.1	17.4	16.5	17.1	10.0
fac positive about gen ed pgm...	71.6	68.8	83.4	63.8	75.8	65.2	78.4	74.4	80.7	83.0	83.4	84.9
courses incl feminist perspect.	29.8	29.2	32.4	29.6	30.1	26.3	32.6	37.3	35.5	24.5	32.9	18.3
oppty for fac/stdnt socializing.	39.3	39.2	39.4	29.8	40.7	36.3	58.2	54.3	54.4	65.6	49.6	68.4
admin consider faculty concerns.	50.3	50.5	49.7	47.7	53.2	45.3	61.8	58.7	59.2	67.5	49.6	51.5
stdnts well prep academically..	26.6	28.6	18.0	23.3	49.7	20.8	36.6	35.4	30.6	41.2	18.1	16.5
Stdnt Aff staff supported by fac	56.7	56.0	59.7	53.3	53.2	53.3	65.7	64.3	62.2	69.4	59.1	76.8
research interferes w/teaching..	26.9	31.8	6.0	43.0	32.3	30.8	14.5	17.4	18.1	8.5	6.1	3.3
unionization enhances teaching..	30.3	27.0	43.9	26.1	18.4	31.8	26.1	30.4	25.7	20.1	44.2	35.6
tenure is an outmoded concept...	33.7	32.8	37.3	32.3	31.4	32.1	35.8	35.2	38.0	35.7	37.2	39.5
Issues Noted as Being of High or Highest Priority												
promote intellectual development	75.5	75.6	75.0	70.5	84.2	71.6	85.0	83.3	86.0	87.1	74.9	78.3
help students understand values.	45.6	44.9	48.7	31.4	47.5	41.4	70.8	63.2	78.2	78.3	47.7	76.8
increase minorities in fac/admin	46.1	47.3	40.8	51.7	41.7	51.0	37.9	44.4	34.7	30.1	41.4	23.3
devel community among stdnts/fac	38.7	37.0	46.2	25.4	34.9	36.4	58.2	54.1	61.5	62.7	45.5	63.2
devel leadership abil in stdnts.	35.5	34.4	39.9	25.4	30.5	35.0	50.8	48.8	49.6	54.3	39.3	56.9
conduct basic & applied research	47.0	55.3	11.1	81.0	75.1	40.5	24.3	31.1	19.6	16.5	11.4	5.1
raise money for the institution.	57.2	62.0	36.6	62.5	76.4	50.8	69.8	71.3	66.1	69.4	35.3	71.5
devel leadership abil in faculty	22.0	20.9	26.3	19.4	21.0	20.8	23.6	23.5	23.0	24.1	26.0	33.1
increase women in fac/admin.....	40.9	42.8	33.1	47.4	39.8	43.6	35.7	42.4	35.1	26.2	33.4	24.8
facilitate comm svcs involvement	21.2	21.2	21.6	12.4	22.8	19.3	37.3	33.6	44.2	39.4	21.4	28.1
teach students how to change soc	19.4	19.1	20.9	13.8	15.1	19.6	29.2	28.7	30.5	29.4	21.0	18.3
help solve soc/environ problems.	25.9	26.5	23.7	27.0	25.6	24.1	29.8	30.0	30.2	29.4	24.1	13.5
allow airing of diff opinions...	53.4	53.8	52.0	54.9	57.6	48.4	57.8	59.5	58.1	55.2	52.4	40.1
increase/maintain inst prestige.	75.0	77.2	65.6	80.4	86.5	70.3	77.0	78.9	73.6	75.8	65.2	74.8
devel apprec of multi-cultul soc	44.5	45.6	39.8	44.3	39.9	44.5	53.0	55.4	49.8	50.9	40.0	36.3
hire faculty "stars"...........	26.9	31.0	9.3	48.6	46.8	19.2	11.2	13.4	6.5	10.2	9.3	11.6
economize and cut costs........	53.0	53.5	50.7	56.8	55.5	52.6	48.3	49.8	47.2	46.8	50.6	54.8
recruit more minority students..	45.8	48.0	36.4	50.4	44.4	50.4	42.5	47.7	41.1	35.6	36.5	33.0
enhance inst's national image...	62.6	69.0	34.8	78.7	84.0	56.6	63.5	68.9	52.7	60.7	34.2	52.9
create positive undergrad exp...	68.0	67.0	72.3	53.0	71.8	68.1	85.4	82.8	87.4	88.2	72.0	80.1
create multi-cultural environ...	38.2	39.3	33.7	38.2	36.1	40.2	41.6	46.9	37.5	35.7	34.0	24.7
enhance stdnt's out-of-class exp	27.2	26.7	29.6	16.5	26.7	27.0	42.7	43.2	39.5	43.6	29.3	38.3

MALE FACULTY

	ALL			Universities		Four-year Colleges					Two-year Colleges	
	Insts	4-yr	2-yr	Pub	Priv	Pub	All Priv	Nons	Cath	Prot	Pub	Priv
Attributes Noted as Being Very Descriptive of Institution												
easy to see fac outside ofc hour	33.6	31.8	40.9	21.0	26.8	31.0	54.0	50.7	55.2	58.1	40.6	48.9
great conformity among students.	25.1	26.9	17.5	26.0	23.2	23.3	36.3	32.3	42.0	39.4	17.1	27.1
most students very bright.	9.0	10.6	1.9	6.8	35.6	3.3	13.4	17.8	4.6	11.2	1.9	0.0
admin open about policies.	11.5	10.4	15.9	7.7	8.9	9.5	17.3	16.4	13.1	20.6	15.9	16.5
keen competition for grades.	20.5	23.4	8.4	25.6	48.7	13.2	20.2	21.3	19.4	19.1	8.7	0.0
courses more theoret than pract.	9.3	10.7	3.5	10.0	20.6	6.7	12.2	15.5	7.1	9.8	3.5	3.3
fac rewarded for advising skills	1.9	1.9	1.5	1.4	1.9	1.5	3.6	4.0	2.8	3.4	1.6	0.0
little std contact out-of-class.	11.4	9.5	19.3	11.2	4.5	13.9	3.0	3.3	4.9	1.6	20.0	1.6
faculty at odds with admin.	19.1	19.0	19.5	19.7	15.0	22.1	15.2	19.0	14.6	9.9	19.5	20.1
intercoll sports overemphasized.	17.1	19.7	6.1	33.2	6.2	16.6	10.5	10.3	7.7	12.1	5.5	23.4
classes usually informal.	19.8	19.7	25.1	14.8	16.8	19.7	24.2	27.2	20.4	21.8	25.4	15.2
faculty respect each other.	30.1	28.5	37.2	23.3	34.3	23.0	42.1	38.3	40.0	48.7	36.8	49.7
most stdnts treated like numbers	6.3	7.1	3.2	12.1	3.5	6.9	1.5	2.1	1.2	0.6	3.2	1.7
social activities overemphasized	7.1	8.2	2.4	7.8	5.5	6.9	12.3	13.5	7.4	13.0	1.8	18.2
little student/faculty contact.	5.5	5.8	4.1	7.6	5.7	6.2	2.1	3.3	1.5	0.7	4.2	1.6
student body apathetic.	18.3	15.5	30.4	13.8	7.5	23.9	9.7	10.7	9.9	8.2	31.1	11.7
stdnts don't socialize regularly	5.8	4.7	10.6	4.4	1.7	8.1	1.5	1.9	1.8	0.9	11.0	0.0
fac rewarded for good teaching.	9.6	10.0	7.8	6.5	10.7	7.5	19.3	20.3	15.7	19.7	7.6	13.2
student services well supported.	18.6	18.0	21.2	16.3	18.5	15.0	25.1	28.0	22.8	21.9	21.0	25.1
Personal Goals Noted as Very Important or Essential												
become authority in own field...	66.4	68.3	57.8	74.9	79.6	63.4	58.5	62.1	54.1	55.5	57.9	56.0
influence political structure...	18.8	18.9	18.8	18.4	18.9	19.5	18.5	19.7	19.2	16.4	18.6	25.1
influence social values.	42.6	42.0	45.4	38.3	38.0	42.5	49.7	47.9	52.8	50.9	44.9	60.2
raise a family.	77.0	77.0	77.3	77.5	76.1	76.4	77.5	77.0	72.1	80.8	77.1	83.3
have admin responsibility.	12.4	12.2	13.3	11.4	9.9	13.2	13.3	13.4	11.7	13.8	13.2	15.2
be very well-off financially.	36.3	34.9	42.2	37.0	32.0	37.4	29.5	33.3	29.1	24.2	42.7	28.4
help others in difficulty.	64.4	63.6	68.1	60.9	57.7	64.0	71.0	69.8	72.7	72.0	67.9	73.4
be involved in environ clean-up.	42.4	41.4	46.7	39.5	34.5	45.6	42.3	43.2	41.5	41.3	46.5	53.3
develop philosophy of life.	78.6	78.2	80.4	76.3	70.8	79.5	83.8	81.8	86.0	85.7	80.2	86.4
promote racial understanding.	57.0	57.6	54.5	54.7	56.4	58.4	61.8	61.7	63.7	61.1	54.0	68.4
obtain recog from colleagues.	53.3	57.2	36.7	64.9	68.4	51.9	46.2	50.0	44.7	41.3	36.9	30.1
Aspects of Job Noted as Very Satisfactory or Satisfactory (4)												
salary and fringe benefits.	44.3	43.1	49.7	45.2	51.8	38.8	40.9	43.9	39.4	37.3	49.8	46.7
oppty for scholarly pursuits.	48.4	49.4	44.2	56.9	65.5	40.4	41.1	43.0	36.2	40.6	44.6	33.9
teaching load.	51.3	52.0	48.3	59.9	65.7	42.8	44.9	46.0	42.4	44.5	48.5	41.6
quality of students.	35.5	37.6	26.5	35.4	58.6	30.0	40.4	40.5	37.0	41.0	26.6	23.7
working conditions.	65.7	66.0	64.2	67.9	76.7	59.4	66.7	66.8	66.2	66.6	64.2	63.0
autonomy and independence.	83.3	83.9	81.0	85.6	89.7	80.0	83.5	82.7	85.6	83.8	80.9	81.6
relationships with other faculty	74.5	73.5	79.0	69.4	75.1	73.2	79.7	77.4	80.1	82.8	78.9	83.3
competency of colleagues.	68.1	67.7	69.9	64.9	77.0	63.1	73.9	72.6	71.5	76.8	69.9	69.9
visibility for jobs.	43.7	44.3	41.0	46.3	61.3	38.2	39.3	39.6	37.3	39.8	41.3	34.0
job security.	77.7	77.2	80.0	78.1	78.0	78.4	73.3	70.4	77.6	75.6	80.2	74.9
undergraduate course assignments	77.8	77.9	76.9	77.8	79.5	76.3	79.8	79.6	80.0	80.0	77.1	71.6
graduate course assignments.	73.9	75.1	44.7	76.1	79.0	72.8	69.2	69.2	73.7	65.3	43.9	66.9
relationships with admin.	50.7	50.4	52.2	47.6	51.3	48.1	57.8	55.7	57.1	61.2	52.1	54.6
overall job satisfaction.	69.0	68.0	73.1	66.5	75.3	64.5	71.6	70.9	71.9	72.5	73.2	69.9

MALE FACULTY

	ALL			Universities		Four-year Colleges					Two-year Colleges	
	Insts	4-yr	2-yr	Pub	Priv	Pub	All Priv	Nons	Cath	Prot	Pub	Priv
Sources of Stress												
household responsibilities	59.8	59.9	59.5	58.1	59.5	59.0	64.4	63.6	66.2	64.7	59.4	62.2
child care	29.0	28.9	29.5	28.1	29.9	28.2	30.5	29.1	32.0	31.9	29.0	44.7
care of elderly parent	25.5	25.3	26.4	25.0	22.0	26.4	26.0	25.7	24.3	27.4	26.4	25.5
my physical health	36.0	35.3	39.3	34.0	34.5	36.8	35.6	35.2	38.4	34.9	39.4	35.8
review/promotion process	43.8	46.3	33.2	49.1	41.5	48.2	41.6	43.4	44.7	37.6	32.8	44.1
subtle discrimination	21.6	22.0	20.2	21.4	16.8	26.0	19.6	21.1	20.4	17.1	20.0	23.8
long-distance commuting	14.3	13.3	18.5	11.0	14.0	15.8	13.0	14.6	13.3	10.6	18.6	15.1
committee work	55.8	56.6	52.2	57.9	49.5	58.8	55.3	53.0	56.5	58.1	51.3	77.0
faculty meetings	48.5	49.0	46.3	50.2	42.0	51.8	46.8	44.6	51.1	48.0	45.6	65.2
colleagues	53.0	54.4	46.8	56.6	49.7	56.3	50.8	52.9	48.4	48.9	47.1	40.7
students	48.2	47.5	51.6	45.5	43.6	47.9	52.4	52.4	51.5	52.7	51.3	59.9
research or publishing demands	51.4	60.2	13.5	71.5	69.7	54.9	43.9	48.3	40.3	35.3	13.5	15.0
fund-raising expectations	21.9	23.9	13.3	32.1	26.6	20.8	13.5	13.7	14.4	12.8	13.0	20.2
teaching load	62.1	61.8	63.8	55.7	54.4	67.0	68.3	66.2	69.2	71.0	63.4	66.2
children's problems	32.5	32.2	33.8	31.9	30.5	32.7	32.8	31.8	31.7	34.7	33.9	32.2
marital friction	24.7	24.5	25.4	24.1	24.7	25.2	23.9	24.2	24.0	23.3	25.3	28.8
time pressures	80.7	82.4	73.7	83.0	83.2	80.0	84.6	83.0	85.0	86.8	73.6	78.1
lack of personal life	76.2	77.5	70.5	77.9	77.4	75.6	79.9	78.6	80.2	81.7	70.4	73.0
Still Want to Be College Professor?												
definitely yes	45.9	46.6	42.6	43.7	51.3	45.4	50.4	49.5	54.3	49.9	42.9	34.9
probably yes	33.7	33.4	34.8	34.6	30.9	33.0	33.5	33.2	32.2	34.6	34.6	40.1
not sure	11.7	11.6	12.1	12.5	11.9	11.7	9.8	10.3	8.8	9.5	12.1	13.3
probably no	6.7	6.4	7.8	6.9	4.6	7.6	5.1	5.6	3.6	5.0	7.9	4.9
definitely no	2.1	1.9	2.6	2.3	1.4	2.2	1.2	1.4	1.0	0.9	2.5	6.8
Field of Highest Degree Held												
agriculture	1.5	1.5	1.6	3.0	1.1	0.9	0.3	0.5	0.0	0.2	1.6	1.7
architecture or urban planning	0.6	0.6	0.3	1.1	0.8	0.3	0.2	0.5	0.0	0.0	0.3	0.0
bacteriology, molecular biology	0.8	0.9	0.8	0.9	1.3	0.7	0.7	0.5	0.6	1.1	0.7	1.7
biochemistry	0.7	0.8	0.3	1.0	1.4	0.4	0.7	0.8	0.4	0.7	0.3	0.0
biophysics	0.2	0.2	0.0	0.3	0.5	0.1	0.1	0.0	0.1	0.2	0.0	0.0
botany	1.0	1.1	0.5	1.2	0.5	1.5	1.0	0.9	0.5	1.2	0.5	1.8
marine life sciences	0.7	0.7	0.1	0.2	0.1	0.2	0.1	0.1	0.1	0.1	0.1	0.0
physiology, anatomy	0.7	0.7	0.8	0.9	0.6	0.6	0.6	0.3	1.3	0.9	0.8	0.0
zoology	1.8	1.9	1.5	1.8	1.3	2.2	1.8	1.7	1.8	2.1	1.5	0.0
general, other biological science	1.5	1.4	2.3	1.6	1.5	1.0	1.4	1.4	1.8	1.1	2.2	3.5
accounting	1.8	1.7	2.0	1.5	1.2	2.1	1.8	1.6	2.6	1.8	2.1	0.0
finance	0.9	1.0	0.5	0.8	1.0	1.2	1.0	1.0	1.5	0.6	0.5	0.0
marketing	1.0	1.0	1.2	0.9	1.2	0.9	0.6	0.4	1.6	0.5	1.2	0.0
management	2.2	2.0	3.2	1.2	1.7	2.5	2.5	2.8	3.6	1.6	3.4	0.0
secretarial studies	0.0	0.0	0.1	0.0	0.0	0.0	0.0	0.1	0.0	0.0	0.1	0.0
general, other business	1.0	1.0	1.3	0.9	0.9	1.1	1.0	0.6	2.1	1.0	1.2	3.5
computer science	1.0	1.0	0.9	0.9	0.9	1.2	1.1	1.2	1.4	0.8	0.9	0.0

MALE FACULTY

Field of Degree (continued)

	ALL			Universities		Four-year Colleges					Two-year Colleges	
	Insts	4-yr	2-yr	Pub	Priv	Pub	All Priv	Nons	Cath	Prot	Pub	Priv
business education	0.7	0.4	2.1	0.1	0.0	0.9	0.2	0.1	0.4	0.2	2.1	1.8
elementary education	0.6	0.6	0.3	0.5	0.1	1.0	0.5	0.3	0.1	0.9	0.3	0.0
educational administration	1.7	1.4	3.2	0.8	0.4	2.0	1.9	1.9	1.0	2.5	3.1	7.0
educational psych, counseling	1.0	0.9	1.5	0.9	0.5	1.2	0.8	0.6	1.0	1.1	1.6	0.0
music or art education	0.5	0.5	0.5	0.5	0.0	0.8	0.5	0.3	0.3	0.9	0.6	0.0
physical or health education	2.2	2.1	2.7	1.8	0.3	2.9	2.7	2.2	1.5	3.9	2.7	3.5
secondary education	1.0	0.9	1.3	0.8	0.2	1.3	1.0	1.2	0.8	0.9	1.3	1.8
special education	0.3	0.3	0.2	0.4	0.2	0.5	0.2	0.2	0.3	0.1	0.2	0.0
general, other education fields	3.3	2.8	5.8	2.5	0.8	4.1	2.3	2.4	1.8	2.4	6.0	0.0
aeronautical, astronautical eng.	0.2	0.2	0.1	0.4	0.1	0.1	0.1	0.1	0.2	0.0	0.1	0.0
chemical engineering	0.5	0.6	0.1	0.7	1.5	0.5	0.2	0.2	0.2	0.1	0.2	0.0
civil engineering	1.0	1.1	0.6	1.9	1.3	0.7	0.3	0.4	0.3	0.2	0.6	0.0
electrical engineering	2.0	2.0	1.9	2.8	3.4	1.5	0.8	1.3	0.7	0.3	2.0	0.0
industrial engineering	0.5	0.5	0.3	1.0	0.1	0.4	0.2	0.3	0.1	0.3	0.3	0.0
mechanical engineering	1.3	1.3	1.1	1.7	1.6	1.2	0.6	0.9	0.3	0.4	1.2	0.0
nuclear engineering	0.1	0.1	0.0	0.2	0.1	0.1	0.0	0.0	0.1	0.0	0.0	0.0
general, other engineering field	1.3	1.4	0.8	2.2	1.7	1.0	0.4	0.7	0.2	0.0	0.8	0.0
ethnic studies	0.0	0.0	0.0	0.0	0.1	0.1	0.1	0.0	0.1	0.1	0.0	0.0
art	2.2	2.1	2.8	2.1	1.2	2.2	2.5	2.6	1.6	2.7	2.9	1.8
dramatics or speech	2.1	2.1	2.3	2.0	0.9	2.2	2.7	2.5	2.7	3.1	2.2	5.2
music	3.2	3.4	2.4	3.3	1.6	3.7	4.2	3.7	1.9	6.2	2.0	12.3
other fine arts	0.4	0.4	0.3	0.6	0.3	0.3	0.3	0.4	0.1	0.3	0.3	0.0
forestry	0.3	0.4	0.2	0.7	0.1	0.4	0.0	0.0	0.0	0.0	0.2	0.0
geology	0.9	1.0	0.5	1.1	0.2	1.6	0.3	0.5	0.0	0.3	0.6	0.0
dentistry	0.1	0.1	0.4	0.0	0.2	0.1	0.0	0.1	0.0	0.0	0.4	0.0
health technology	0.1	0.0	0.2	0.0	0.1	0.1	0.0	0.0	0.0	0.0	0.2	0.0
medicine or surgery	0.2	0.2	0.1	0.4	0.0	0.2	0.0	0.0	0.0	0.0	0.0	3.5
nursing	0.1	0.1	0.2	0.1	0.0	0.1	0.1	0.1	0.1	0.0	0.2	0.0
pharmacy, pharmacology	0.4	0.5	0.1	0.9	0.3	0.2	0.1	0.2	0.1	0.3	0.1	0.0
therapy (speech,physical,occup)	0.3	0.3	0.3	0.4	0.1	0.5	0.1	0.1	0.2	0.1	0.3	0.0
veterinary medicine	0.2	0.2	0.3	0.4	0.3	0.0	0.1	0.2	0.1	0.0	0.3	0.0
general, other health fields	0.3	0.2	0.8	0.2	0.1	0.4	0.1	0.3	0.0	0.0	0.8	0.0
home economics	0.1	0.1	0.0	0.2	0.0	0.1	0.1	0.1	0.1	0.0	0.0	0.0
English language & literature	5.9	5.5	7.4	4.9	5.2	5.4	6.9	7.1	6.9	6.8	7.1	15.8
foreign languages & literature	0.4	0.4	0.3	0.6	1.0	0.2	0.6	0.6	0.6	0.5	0.3	0.0
French	0.6	0.6	0.2	0.6	1.0	0.4	0.7	0.8	1.0	0.6	0.2	0.0
German	0.6	0.7	0.2	0.7	0.8	0.6	0.9	1.0	0.3	0.9	0.2	0.0
Spanish	0.8	0.9	0.4	0.9	0.8	0.7	1.1	1.3	0.8	0.9	0.4	1.8
other foreign languages	0.7	0.9	0.1	1.3	1.6	0.3	0.7	0.9	0.8	0.5	0.1	0.0

MALE FACULTY

Field of Degree (continued)	ALL			Universities		Four-year Colleges					Two-year Colleges	
	Insts	4-yr	2-yr	Pub	Priv	Pub	All Priv	Nons	Cath	Prot	Pub	Priv
history	4.9	5.1	3.9	4.4	6.5	4.8	5.7	5.7	6.0	5.4	3.8	7.0
linguistics	0.6	0.7	0.2	1.0	1.4	0.3	0.3	0.3	0.5	0.3	0.2	0.0
philosophy	1.9	2.1	1.2	1.6	3.7	1.6	2.8	2.0	6.1	2.4	1.2	1.7
religion & theology	1.6	1.8	0.8	0.5	2.4	0.7	5.3	3.5	5.6	7.7	0.5	8.9
general, other humanities fields	0.8	0.9	0.4	0.9	1.3	0.6	0.9	0.9	0.5	1.1	0.4	1.8
journalism	0.5	0.6	0.3	0.8	0.4	0.6	0.4	0.5	0.2	0.3	0.3	0.0
law	0.7	0.7	0.8	0.6	0.8	0.9	0.7	0.8	1.0	0.3	0.8	0.0
law enforcement	0.2	0.1	0.6	0.1	0.1	0.2	0.0	0.0	0.2	0.0	0.6	0.0
library science	0.1	0.1	0.1	0.1	0.0	0.2	0.1	0.1	0.1	0.1	0.1	0.0
mathematics and/or statistics	6.4	6.2	7.4	5.3	7.3	6.0	6.9	6.9	6.4	7.2	7.6	3.5
military science	0.0	0.0	0.0	0.0	0.0	0.0	0.0	0.0	0.0	0.0	0.0	0.0
astronomy	0.2	0.2	0.1	0.2	0.3	0.1	0.2	0.3	0.1	0.2	0.1	0.0
atmospheric sciences	0.2	0.2	0.2	0.4	0.0	0.1	0.0	0.0	0.1	0.1	0.2	0.0
chemistry	3.7	3.8	3.3	3.4	3.8	3.2	5.1	5.3	4.5	5.0	3.3	3.5
earth sciences	1.4	1.6	0.9	1.8	2.0	1.6	0.8	1.1	0.2	0.6	0.8	3.5
marine sciences	0.1	0.1	0.2	0.1	0.2	0.2	0.1	0.1	0.1	0.0	0.2	0.0
physics	3.0	3.1	2.5	2.7	4.8	2.8	3.3	3.5	3.8	2.7	2.6	0.0
general, other physical sciences	0.2	0.1	0.4	0.0	0.1	0.2	0.1	0.0	0.0	0.1	0.4	0.0
clinical psychology	0.7	0.7	0.4	0.7	0.6	0.7	0.9	0.8	1.3	0.8	0.4	0.0
counseling & guidance	0.6	0.4	1.6	0.2	0.1	0.5	0.7	0.7	0.9	0.5	1.6	0.0
experimental psychology	1.4	1.6	0.6	1.6	1.8	1.6	1.6	1.7	1.7	1.5	0.6	0.0
social psychology	0.5	0.6	0.2	0.5	1.1	0.6	0.5	0.5	0.8	0.3	0.2	0.0
general, other psychology	1.0	1.0	1.1	0.8	0.9	1.1	1.0	0.9	1.3	1.2	1.1	0.0
anthropology	1.0	1.2	0.4	1.3	2.1	1.0	0.8	1.1	0.4	0.6	0.4	0.0
archaeology	0.1	0.1	0.0	0.2	0.2	0.1	0.1	0.1	0.0	0.1	0.0	0.0
economics	3.4	3.7	1.7	3.4	5.1	3.2	4.3	5.0	4.2	3.4	1.7	0.0
political science, government	2.9	3.2	1.4	3.0	4.7	2.9	3.0	3.4	2.8	2.5	1.5	1.7
sociology	2.4	2.6	1.3	2.7	3.2	2.6	2.2	2.1	2.5	2.4	1.3	0.0
general, other social sciences	0.6	0.6	0.5	0.7	0.7	0.7	0.4	0.5	0.3	0.3	0.5	1.8
social work, social welfare	0.3	0.3	0.3	0.2	0.1	0.5	0.5	0.4	0.9	0.5	0.3	0.0
building trades	0.1	0.0	0.5	0.0	0.0	0.1	0.0	0.0	0.0	0.0	0.5	0.0
data processing, computer prog	0.1	0.1	0.2	0.0	0.0	0.1	0.2	0.3	0.0	0.0	0.2	0.0
drafting/design	0.1	0.0	0.4	0.1	0.0	0.1	0.0	0.0	0.0	0.0	0.4	0.0
electronics	0.2	0.1	0.6	0.1	0.0	0.3	0.0	0.0	0.0	0.0	0.7	0.0
industrial arts	0.4	0.3	0.9	0.2	0.0	0.8	0.1	0.1	0.0	0.1	1.0	0.0
mechanics	0.2	0.0	1.0	0.0	0.0	0.0	0.1	0.2	0.0	0.0	1.1	0.0
other technical	0.5	0.2	1.7	0.1	0.0	0.5	0.0	0.1	0.0	0.0	1.8	0.0
other vocational	0.4	0.2	1.3	0.2	0.0	0.4	0.1	0.2	0.0	0.0	1.3	0.0
women's studies	0.0	0.0	0.0	0.0	0.0	0.1	0.2	0.2	0.0	0.0	0.0	0.0
all other fields	1.1	1.1	1.1	1.4	0.8	0.9	1.1	1.1	1.3	0.9	1.2	0.0

MALE FACULTY

Department of Current Faculty Appointment	ALL			Universities		Four-year Colleges					Two-year Colleges	
	Insts	4-yr	2-yr	Pub	Priv	Pub	All Priv	Nons	Cath	Prot	Pub	Priv
agriculture	1.7	1.8	1.2	3.3	1.9	1.2	0.2	0.4	0.0	0.1	1.2	1.8
architecture or urban planning	0.5	0.6	0.2	1.2	0.3	0.2	0.3	0.5	0.0	0.0	0.2	0.0
bacteriology, molecular biology	0.6	0.6	0.6	0.7	1.1	0.6	0.3	0.3	0.3	0.3	0.5	1.8
biochemistry	0.3	0.3	0.0	0.7	0.5	0.0	0.1	0.1	0.1	0.0	0.0	0.0
biophysics	0.1	0.1	0.0	0.0	0.9	0.1	0.0	0.0	0.0	0.0	0.0	0.0
botany	0.3	0.3	0.2	0.6	0.3	0.1	0.2	0.0	0.1	0.4	0.1	1.9
marine life sciences	0.0	0.0	0.0	0.0	0.0	0.0	0.0	0.0	0.1	0.0	0.0	0.0
physiology, anatomy	0.3	0.2	0.7	0.3	0.3	0.1	0.2	0.2	0.5	0.1	0.7	0.0
zoology	0.5	0.5	0.2	1.0	0.3	0.2	0.3	0.2	0.5	0.4	0.2	0.0
general, other biological science	4.3	4.3	4.1	3.4	3.3	5.3	5.1	4.5	5.3	6.0	4.2	1.8
accounting	2.4	2.2	3.5	1.8	1.6	2.7	2.2	2.0	4.2	1.7	3.6	1.8
finance	1.0	1.2	0.2	1.1	1.4	1.5	0.8	0.8	1.4	0.5	0.2	0.0
marketing	1.2	1.2	1.1	1.1	1.3	1.5	0.8	0.7	1.7	0.4	1.9	0.0
management	2.3	2.4	1.8	1.9	1.9	2.6	3.3	3.9	4.7	1.7	0.4	0.0
secretarial studies	0.1	0.0	0.4	0.0	0.0	0.0	0.0	0.0	0.0	0.1	0.4	0.0
general, other business	1.8	1.6	2.9	0.9	1.1	2.1	2.3	1.7	3.0	3.0	2.8	5.5
computer science	2.1	2.1	2.3	1.6	2.1	2.5	2.2	2.3	2.8	1.8	2.3	1.8
business education	0.2	0.1	0.6	0.1	0.0	0.3	0.1	0.1	0.1	0.0	0.6	0.0
elementary education	0.8	0.9	0.0	0.7	0.1	1.7	0.8	0.5	0.2	1.4	0.0	0.0
educational administration	0.3	0.3	0.1	0.3	0.1	0.5	0.3	0.3	0.1	0.3	0.1	0.0
educational psych, counseling	0.5	0.5	0.2	0.7	0.3	0.5	0.3	0.1	0.3	0.5	0.2	0.0
music or art education	0.1	0.2	0.1	0.2	0.0	0.2	0.1	0.1	0.0	0.3	0.1	0.0
physical or health education	2.5	2.5	2.7	2.2	0.5	3.2	3.0	2.7	1.4	4.3	2.7	3.6
secondary education	0.5	0.6	0.1	0.5	0.0	0.8	0.8	0.5	0.9	1.1	0.1	0.0
special education	0.3	0.3	0.2	0.4	0.0	0.5	0.1	0.1	0.4	0.1	0.2	0.0
general, other education fields	1.3	1.4	0.7	1.7	0.8	1.6	1.1	1.1	0.9	1.3	0.7	0.0
aeronautical, astronautical eng	0.1	0.1	0.1	0.3	0.0	0.1	0.0	0.0	0.0	0.1	0.2	0.0
chemical engineering	0.5	0.6	0.0	0.6	1.8	0.4	0.1	0.2	0.1	0.0	0.0	0.0
civil engineering	1.0	1.0	0.7	1.7	1.3	0.7	0.2	0.2	0.3	0.2	0.8	0.0
electrical engineering	1.7	1.9	1.0	2.8	3.2	1.0	0.8	1.3	0.7	0.2	1.0	0.0
industrial engineering	0.5	0.3	0.3	0.9	0.3	0.3	0.2	0.4	0.1	0.0	0.3	0.0
mechanical engineering	1.4	1.5	0.9	1.8	2.4	1.3	0.6	0.9	0.4	0.2	0.9	0.0
nuclear engineering	0.1	0.1	0.0	0.2	0.1	0.0	0.0	0.0	0.0	0.0	0.0	0.0
general, other engineering field	1.4	1.5	0.9	2.5	1.8	1.1	0.4	0.6	0.0	0.3	0.9	0.0
ethnic studies	0.1	0.1	0.1	0.1	0.1	0.2	0.2	0.2	0.1	0.1	0.1	0.0
art	2.4	2.4	2.5	2.6	1.2	2.6	2.6	2.7	2.0	2.7	2.5	1.9
dramatics or speech	2.1	2.1	2.2	2.0	1.0	2.3	2.6	2.2	2.6	3.1	2.1	5.5
music	3.5	3.7	2.5	3.6	1.7	4.1	4.4	3.7	1.7	6.8	2.1	13.0
other fine arts	0.5	0.4	0.5	0.5	0.3	0.6	0.3	0.5	0.2	0.2	0.5	0.0
forestry	0.3	0.4	0.1	0.8	0.1	0.4	0.0	0.0	0.0	0.0	0.1	0.0

MALE FACULTY

Current Department (contuned)	ALL			Universities		Four-year Colleges					Two-year Colleges	
	Insts	4-yr	2-yr	Pub	Priv	Pub	All Priv	Nons	Cath	Prot	Pub	Priv
geology	0.8	1.0	0.2	1.2	0.3	1.4	0.3	0.3	0.1	0.3	0.2	0.0
dentistry	0.1	0.0	0.2	0.0	0.2	0.0	0.0	0.0	0.0	0.0	0.2	0.0
health technology	0.2	0.1	0.6	0.0	0.1	0.2	0.1	0.3	0.1	0.0	0.6	0.0
medicine or surgery	0.2	0.3	0.0	0.5	0.1	0.3	0.0	0.0	0.1	0.0	0.0	0.0
nursing	0.1	0.5	0.1	0.1	0.4	0.1	0.1	0.1	0.0	0.1	0.2	0.0
pharmacy, pharmacology	0.4	0.4	0.4	1.0	0.4	0.2	0.2	0.1	0.0	0.3	0.1	0.0
therapy (speech,physical,occup)	0.4	0.4	0.4	0.4	0.3	0.5	0.2	0.1	0.5	0.1	0.4	0.0
veterinary medicine	0.2	0.2	0.0	0.5	0.2	0.0	0.0	0.0	0.1	0.0	0.0	0.0
general, other health fields	0.5	0.3	1.6	0.3	0.1	0.5	0.2	0.2	0.2	0.1	1.7	0.0
home economics	0.3	0.3	0.1	0.6	0.1	0.2	0.1	0.1	0.1	0.0	0.1	0.0
English language & literature	6.3	5.7	8.7	5.1	5.1	5.5	7.4	7.5	7.1	7.4	8.4	18.5
foreign languages & literature	1.4	1.7	0.3	1.5	2.5	1.2	2.3	2.6	2.0	1.9	0.3	0.0
French	0.3	0.4	0.1	0.6	0.4	0.2	0.3	0.4	0.2	0.2	0.1	0.0
German	0.3	0.4	0.0	0.5	0.7	0.1	0.5	0.6	0.2	0.5	0.0	0.0
Spanish	0.5	0.5	0.6	0.7	0.2	0.4	0.5	0.4	0.5	0.5	0.4	3.7
other foreign languages	0.7	0.8	0.0	1.4	1.0	0.2	0.6	0.8	0.3	0.3	0.0	0.0
history	4.3	4.7	2.5	4.3	5.9	4.4	5.2	4.9	5.2	5.6	2.5	3.7
linguistics	0.3	0.3	0.0	0.4	1.3	0.1	0.1	0.1	0.0	0.0	0.0	0.0
philosophy	1.8	2.0	1.1	1.5	3.6	1.4	2.7	1.9	5.5	2.4	1.1	0.0
religion & theology	1.4	1.6	0.4	0.2	2.3	0.5	5.3	3.1	6.3	7.9	0.1	9.3
general, other humanities fields	1.1	1.0	1.6	0.7	1.3	1.0	1.3	1.5	1.0	1.1	1.6	1.9
journalism	0.6	0.7	0.2	0.9	0.8	0.8	0.4	0.4	0.6	0.2	0.3	0.0
law	0.1	0.1	0.0	0.1	0.1	0.2	0.1	0.2	0.0	0.1	0.0	0.0
law enforcement	0.5	0.4	0.9	0.1	0.3	0.9	0.1	0.1	0.5	0.1	0.9	0.0
library science	0.2	0.2	0.2	0.1	0.0	0.3	0.2	0.2	0.1	0.3	0.2	0.0
mathematics and/or statistics	6.5	6.1	8.4	5.4	6.3	6.2	6.9	6.8	6.2	7.4	8.5	3.7
military science	0.1	0.1	0.0	0.1	0.1	0.2	0.1	0.0	0.4	0.1	0.0	0.0
astronomy	0.1	0.1	0.1	0.1	0.4	0.0	0.1	0.2	0.0	0.0	0.1	0.0
atmospheric sciences	0.1	0.1	0.1	0.3	0.1	0.0	0.0	0.0	0.0	0.0	0.1	0.0
chemistry	3.6	3.6	3.5	3.1	3.1	3.5	5.2	5.4	4.6	5.2	3.5	5.5
earth sciences	1.5	1.7	0.5	2.0	2.3	1.7	0.8	1.1	0.2	0.7	0.5	0.0
marine sciences	0.1	0.1	0.1	0.0	0.0	0.1	0.0	0.0	0.0	0.0	0.1	0.0
physics	2.7	2.8	2.1	2.2	3.7	3.0	3.0	3.1	3.2	2.8	2.1	1.8
general,other physical sciences	0.5	0.3	1.4	0.2	0.1	0.5	0.4	0.3	0.8	0.4	1.5	0.0

MALE FACULTY

Current Department (contued)

	ALL			Universities		Four-year Colleges					Two-year Colleges	
	Insts	4-yr	2-yr	Pub	Priv	Pub	All Priv	Nons	Cath	Prot	Pub	Priv
clinical psychology..........	0.4	0.4	0.2	0.4	0.3	0.4	0.5	0.7	0.6	0.1	0.2	0.0
counseling & guidance.........	0.2	0.2	0.6	0.1	0.0	0.2	0.2	0.2	0.3	0.2	0.5	1.8
experimental psychology.......	0.8	1.0	0.1	1.1	1.3	0.7	0.8	0.8	0.6	0.8	0.1	0.0
social psychology............	0.2	0.3	0.1	0.3	0.5	0.1	0.2	0.2	0.2	0.1	0.1	0.0
general,other psychology......	2.2	2.1	2.8	1.5	1.5	2.6	2.8	2.4	3.0	3.3	2.8	3.7
anthropology.................	0.9	1.1	0.4	1.4	2.0	0.8	0.5	0.6	0.3	0.4	0.4	0.0
archaeology..................	0.0	0.0	0.0	0.0	0.1	0.0	0.0	0.1	0.0	0.0	0.0	0.0
economics....................	2.7	3.1	1.2	2.7	4.0	2.7	3.7	4.5	3.0	2.9	1.2	0.0
political science, government.	2.6	2.9	1.2	2.9	4.4	2.4	2.9	3.4	2.8	2.2	1.2	1.9
sociology....................	2.2	2.4	1.1	2.6	2.7	2.3	2.4	2.3	2.5	2.3	1.1	1.9
general,other social sciences	1.6	1.3	3.1	1.0	1.3	1.7	1.2	1.5	1.2	0.6	3.2	1.9
social work, social welfare..	0.3	0.3	0.1	0.1	0.1	0.6	0.4	0.2	0.9	0.4	0.1	0.0
building trades..............	0.3	0.0	1.6	0.0	0.0	0.1	0.0	0.0	0.0	0.0	1.6	0.0
data processing,computer prog.	0.3	0.1	1.2	0.0	0.0	0.1	0.3	0.5	0.1	0.0	1.2	0.0
drafting/design..............	0.3	0.1	1.2	0.1	0.1	0.1	0.1	0.2	0.0	0.0	1.2	0.0
electronics..................	0.7	0.1	3.1	0.1	0.0	0.2	0.2	0.3	0.0	0.0	3.3	0.0
industrial arts..............	0.3	0.3	0.4	0.2	0.0	0.7	0.1	0.1	0.0	0.1	0.5	0.0
mechanics....................	0.5	0.1	2.2	0.0	0.0	0.2	0.2	0.5	0.0	0.0	2.3	0.0
other technical..............	1.0	0.5	3.1	0.4	0.0	1.2	0.1	0.2	0.0	0.0	3.2	0.0
other vocational.............	0.5	0.1	2.4	0.1	0.0	0.1	0.1	0.2	0.1	0.0	2.5	0.0
women's studies..............	0.0	0.0	0.0	0.0	0.0	0.0	0.0	0.0	0.0	0.0	0.0	0.0
all other fields.............	1.9	2.0	1.5	2.0	2.3	2.0	1.7	1.9	2.0	1.1	1.4	1.8

Notes

1. Percentages will sum to more than 100 if any respondents checked more than one category.

2. Recategorization of this item from a longer list is shown in the American College Teacher.

3. Nine-month salaries converted to twelve-month.

4. Respondents marking "not applicable" are not included in tabulations.

National Normative Data for the 1989-90 HERI Faculty Survey

Female Faculty

FEMALE FACULTY

	ALL			Universities		Four-year Colleges					Two-year Colleges	
	Insts	4-yr	2-yr	Pub	Priv	Pub	All Priv	Nons	Cath	Prot	Pub	Priv
Age as of December 31, 1989												
less than 30	4.1	4.8	2.5	4.5	10.7	3.3	4.9	4.9	2.3	6.8	2.2	7.1
30 − 34	9.9	11.6	6.0	11.1	17.9	10.0	12.2	12.9	11.3	11.9	6.0	5.4
35 − 39	17.1	17.8	15.6	19.5	18.0	15.8	18.7	20.4	15.9	18.5	15.2	23.2
40 − 44	19.8	19.6	20.5	21.8	20.5	17.9	19.3	20.6	17.5	18.6	20.5	21.4
45 − 49	18.2	17.0	20.7	16.1	13.8	18.2	17.4	17.5	16.6	17.9	21.1	12.5
50 − 54	13.5	12.1	16.7	11.3	7.2	14.5	11.4	11.4	12.3	10.6	16.9	14.3
55 − 59	9.1	9.0	9.3	8.2	5.8	11.5	7.6	5.5	11.5	7.7	9.7	1.8
60 − 64	6.1	5.9	6.4	4.9	4.2	7.2	5.7	4.9	7.3	5.7	6.3	8.9
65 − 69	1.8	1.8	1.9	2.2	1.9	1.3	2.1	1.4	3.6	1.9	1.9	1.8
70 or more	0.4	0.4	0.4	0.3	0.0	0.2	0.7	0.4	1.7	0.4	0.2	3.6
Academic Rank												
professor	16.4	15.8	17.9	15.0	14.1	17.7	14.6	14.9	13.0	15.4	18.5	5.4
associate professor	23.2	26.9	14.7	28.2	28.0	26.9	25.4	26.6	27.7	21.9	14.8	12.5
assistant professor	30.9	38.5	13.5	33.9	40.0	39.1	41.8	40.1	42.5	43.5	13.0	23.2
lecturer	3.3	4.4	0.7	7.2	12.6	2.3	1.8	2.2	1.5	1.4	0.7	1.8
instructor	22.7	11.5	48.3	9.2	4.5	12.3	15.0	14.6	13.1	16.9	48.5	44.6
other	3.5	2.9	5.0	6.6	0.9	1.7	1.5	1.5	2.0	0.9	4.6	12.5
Administrative Title												
not applicable	77.3	77.8	76.2	81.5	82.0	80.2	69.6	70.9	65.3	71.0	77.1	58.2
director or coordinator	10.6	10.3	11.3	9.4	8.7	9.5	12.6	12.6	13.2	12.1	11.1	16.4
department chair	6.9	6.2	8.4	2.5	2.8	4.8	12.7	12.6	15.1	11.0	7.7	21.8
dean	0.1	0.2	0.0	0.0	0.2	0.1	0.4	0.4	0.3	0.6	0.0	0.0
associate or assistant dean	0.3	0.4	0.1	0.7	0.0	0.2	0.4	0.2	0.4	0.7	0.1	0.0
vice-pres, provost, vice-chanc	0.0	0.0	0.0	0.0	0.0	0.0	0.1	0.1	0.1	0.3	0.0	0.0
president, chancellor	0.0	0.0	0.0	0.0	0.0	0.0	0.0	0.0	0.0	0.0	0.0	0.0
other	4.8	5.1	4.0	5.8	6.2	5.1	4.1	3.2	5.7	4.3	4.0	3.6
Principal Activity												
administration	3.1	3.2	2.9	2.9	1.1	3.3	4.1	4.0	4.9	3.6	2.9	3.6
teaching	92.2	90.9	95.1	86.8	82.0	93.5	94.4	94.4	93.7	94.7	95.1	96.4
research	3.1	4.4	0.0	8.4	16.5	1.6	0.4	0.6	0.1	0.2	0.0	0.0
services to clients and patients	0.9	0.7	1.4	1.0	0.4	0.6	0.5	0.2	0.8	0.7	1.4	0.0
other	0.7	0.8	0.5	0.9	0.0	1.0	0.7	0.8	0.4	0.8	0.6	0.0
Racial Background (1)												
White/Caucasian	88.8	88.7	89.1	91.2	92.6	84.8	90.1	85.4	96.9	91.8	88.7	96.4
Black/Negro/Afro-American	6.6	6.9	6.2	2.5	3.6	11.5	6.0	8.5	0.9	6.2	6.3	3.6
American Indian	1.0	1.1	0.8	1.5	0.8	1.3	0.5	0.5	0.5	0.4	0.8	0.0
Asian-American	2.4	2.3	2.5	3.8	1.6	1.8	1.8	2.3	1.6	1.3	2.6	0.0
Mexican-American/Chicano	0.9	0.6	1.6	1.4	0.3	0.4	0.2	0.0	0.5	0.3	1.7	0.0
Puerto Rican-American	0.7	0.7	0.5	0.5	0.2	0.4	1.5	3.2	0.2	0.0	0.5	0.0
Other	1.7	1.9	1.3	2.3	2.8	1.7	1.4	1.7	1.4	1.0	1.3	0.0

FEMALE FACULTY

	ALL			Universities		Four-year Colleges					Two-year Colleges	
	Insts	4-yr	2-yr	Pub	Priv	Pub	All Priv	Nons	Cath	Prot	Pub	Priv
Highest Degree Earned												
bachelor's (B.A., B.S., etc.)	4.6	1.9	10.8	1.4	1.1	1.6	3.1	4.0	2.0	2.7	11.0	7.1
master's (M.A., M.S., etc.)	42.0	31.6	65.7	24.1	16.1	34.4	40.8	35.1	43.4	46.9	65.2	76.8
LL.B., J.D.	0.6	0.5	0.9	0.7	0.2	0.5	0.3	0.2	0.5	0.3	0.9	0.0
M.D., D.D.S. (or equivalent)	0.4	0.4	0.3	0.3	0.2	0.8	0.2	0.2	0.1	0.1	0.3	0.0
other first professional	0.5	0.7	0.3	0.5	0.2	1.0	0.6	0.6	0.7	0.4	0.3	0.0
Ed.D.	5.6	6.6	3.3	5.7	1.4	9.5	5.5	5.8	3.1	6.6	3.5	0.0
Ph.D.	39.3	52.9	7.9	62.7	77.6	46.6	43.4	48.4	44.7	35.5	7.9	8.9
other degree	4.3	3.5	5.9	3.4	2.6	3.4	4.2	3.9	3.5	5.1	6.0	5.4
none	2.7	1.8	4.9	1.3	0.6	2.3	2.0	1.7	2.0	2.4	5.1	1.8
Field of Highest Degree (2)												
agriculture or forestry	0.4	0.5	0.2	1.1	0.4	0.3	0.1	0.1	0.0	0.2	0.2	0.0
biological sciences	4.1	4.2	3.6	4.2	3.1	4.0	5.0	5.3	5.6	3.9	3.5	5.7
business	5.2	4.8	6.0	5.5	4.0	4.9	4.2	3.2	4.7	5.2	5.9	7.5
education	23.9	21.4	29.7	19.0	5.2	26.8	21.9	21.6	19.4	23.9	29.2	39.6
engineering	0.7	0.9	0.3	1.4	1.3	0.7	0.4	0.7	0.3	0.0	0.3	0.0
English	9.0	8.5	10.2	8.5	7.4	7.4	10.2	11.4	7.9	10.4	10.2	9.4
health related	12.4	10.0	17.8	9.3	4.4	12.3	9.5	6.4	12.1	11.8	18.3	7.5
history or political science	3.3	3.8	2.2	3.8	9.5	2.6	3.6	4.3	3.3	2.7	2.2	1.9
humanities	8.6	10.9	3.5	10.5	25.8	6.5	11.9	13.2	11.8	10.3	3.6	1.9
fine arts	7.7	8.6	5.5	8.6	5.5	8.6	9.6	9.0	9.0	10.9	5.4	7.5
mathematics or statistics	3.7	3.2	4.7	1.7	2.3	4.0	4.0	3.4	5.6	3.7	4.6	5.7
physical sciences	2.0	2.3	1.3	1.9	2.1	2.4	2.7	2.7	2.8	2.5	1.4	0.0
social sciences	11.4	13.1	7.5	14.5	24.6	10.5	11.5	12.4	10.6	10.9	7.4	9.4
other technical	1.0	0.7	1.8	0.5	0.9	0.6	0.9	0.8	1.8	0.5	1.9	0.8
other non-technical	6.7	7.2	5.7	9.6	3.6	8.3	4.6	5.4	5.1	3.1	5.8	3.8
Year Highest Degree Earned												
1951 or earlier	2.4	1.9	3.5	1.7	0.6	2.4	1.9	2.3	1.9	1.2	3.6	1.8
1952 - 1956	1.4	1.5	1.3	1.6	2.1	1.3	1.4	1.1	2.0	1.5	1.4	0.0
1957 - 1961	2.9	2.6	3.5	2.3	2.6	2.7	2.7	2.4	4.1	2.1	3.7	0.0
1962 - 1966	6.0	5.7	6.8	4.8	2.6	6.6	5.7	5.7	6.6	5.0	6.7	7.1
1967 - 1971	11.6	10.9	13.1	12.0	9.3	11.9	9.2	8.4	10.1	9.5	13.0	14.3
1972 - 1976	17.2	16.6	18.6	16.3	13.5	17.2	17.2	16.6	17.7	17.7	18.3	23.2
1977 - 1981	20.5	20.2	21.1	21.1	23.3	18.9	20.0	20.6	19.2	19.9	21.0	23.2
1982 - 1986	23.2	23.8	21.9	22.9	19.7	23.7	26.0	26.4	24.0	27.0	22.1	17.9
1987 - 1989	14.8	16.8	10.3	17.3	24.3	15.3	15.9	16.5	14.4	16.0	10.1	12.5
Degree Currently Working Toward												
bachelor's (B.A., B.S., etc.)	1.8	0.3	5.3	0.1	0.7	0.3	0.3	0.5	0.2	0.0	5.6	0.0
master's (M.A., M.S., etc.)	7.7	3.3	17.9	2.0	0.7	3.0	5.5	6.0	4.2	5.9	18.0	15.4
LL.B., J.D.	0.2	0.1	0.3	0.0	0.0	0.2	0.1	0.0	0.0	0.4	0.3	0.0
M.D., D.D.S. (or equivalent)	0.2	0.2	0.2	0.0	0.0	0.1	0.3	0.4	0.5	0.1	0.0	0.0
other first professional	0.2	0.2	0.0	0.0	0.0	0.2	0.3	0.3	0.4	0.2	0.0	0.0
Ed.D.	5.8	5.0	7.5	2.8	0.9	5.6	7.5	7.6	5.6	8.7	7.5	7.7
Ph.D.	19.3	21.4	14.3	15.1	16.8	24.1	24.4	24.3	23.1	25.2	14.7	7.7
other degree	3.2	2.9	3.8	1.4	0.2	4.0	3.7	3.4	2.4	4.9	3.5	7.7
none	61.8	66.5	50.8	78.5	80.7	62.3	57.9	57.4	63.7	54.5	50.1	61.5

FEMALE FACULTY

Department of Current Faculty Appointment (2)	ALL			Universities		Four-year Colleges					Two-year Colleges	
	Insts	4-yr	2-yr	Pub	Priv	Pub	All Priv	Nons	Cath	Prot	Pub	Priv
agriculture or forestry	0.5	0.7	0.2	1.5	0.2	0.6	0.0	0.0	0.0	0.0	0.2	0.0
biological sciences	3.5	3.7	3.3	3.2	2.2	3.4	4.9	5.3	5.5	4.1	3.1	5.8
business	8.1	7.0	10.7	7.5	5.2	7.2	6.7	6.7	8.2	6.3	10.5	13.5
education	13.5	14.5	11.1	11.7	3.4	19.3	14.7	13.7	12.1	18.0	10.5	23.1
engineering	0.7	0.9	0.2	1.4	1.2	0.9	0.3	0.4	0.3	0.0	0.3	0.0
English	10.2	9.4	12.1	9.2	7.6	8.3	11.7	12.7	8.4	12.7	12.2	9.6
health related	15.8	12.5	23.6	12.2	5.8	15.5	10.9	7.1	15.1	13.2	24.5	7.7
history or political science	2.7	3.3	1.3	3.5	6.5	2.5	3.2	3.9	2.7	2.7	1.3	1.9
humanities	8.3	10.7	2.9	9.1	29.2	5.8	12.3	13.9	11.9	10.4	3.0	1.9
fine arts	7.7	9.2	4.3	9.7	6.6	9.0	9.7	9.4	8.0	11.4	4.2	5.8
mathematics or statistics	5.1	4.6	6.4	4.2	1.8	5.3	4.8	4.3	6.4	4.5	6.1	13.5
physical sciences	2.1	2.2	1.8	1.7	1.9	2.1	2.8	2.9	3.1	2.5	1.9	0.0
social sciences	10.8	11.9	8.1	12.2	22.4	9.8	10.8	11.7	9.3	10.7	7.9	11.5
other technical	2.6	1.4	5.4	1.0	2.0	1.4	1.7	1.8	3.0	0.6	5.5	1.9
other non-technical	8.3	8.2	8.5	11.8	4.0	8.7	5.4	6.8	6.1	3.0	8.8	3.8
Year Appointed to Current Position												
1951 or earlier	1.8	1.8	1.8	1.7	1.2	1.7	2.2	2.5	2.9	1.2	1.9	0.0
1952 – 1956	0.4	0.5	0.2	0.3	0.1	0.7	0.7	0.5	1.3	0.7	0.1	1.9
1957 – 1961	1.3	1.6	0.6	1.5	0.9	1.6	2.1	1.2	3.4	2.3	0.5	1.9
1962 – 1966	4.7	5.1	3.9	4.2	4.0	6.3	4.6	5.2	4.6	3.8	3.7	7.4
1967 – 1971	12.5	10.9	16.1	9.2	8.4	14.9	8.0	8.0	9.6	6.9	16.5	9.3
1972 – 1976	14.4	11.9	20.1	12.6	12.1	12.8	10.0	10.0	9.6	10.4	20.4	13.0
1977 – 1981	15.6	14.4	18.2	15.7	12.3	13.3	15.5	15.6	15.6	15.2	18.2	16.7
1982 – 1986	23.0	24.0	20.5	24.6	23.3	22.4	25.9	25.8	22.0	29.0	20.1	29.6
1987 – 1989	26.3	29.7	18.6	30.1	37.6	26.3	30.9	31.1	31.1	30.5	18.6	20.4
Tenured?												
yes	52.9	48.3	63.3	48.5	43.8	53.2	43.0	44.8	42.1	41.2	63.9	51.8
no	47.1	51.7	36.7	51.5	56.2	46.8	57.0	55.2	57.9	58.8	36.1	48.2
Year Received Tenure												
1951 or earlier	0.6	0.2	1.4	0.2	0.0	0.1	0.4	0.4	1.0	0.0	1.4	*0.0*
1952 – 1956	0.1	0.2	0.0	0.1	0.2	0.1	0.3	0.1	0.8	0.1	0.0	*0.0*
1957 – 1961	0.7	0.9	0.3	1.1	0.4	0.7	1.3	1.2	2.1	1.0	0.3	*0.0*
1962 – 1966	2.1	2.8	0.8	2.6	2.2	2.9	3.1	1.9	3.7	4.4	0.8	*0.0*
1967 – 1971	10.9	10.6	11.3	7.6	7.3	13.8	9.8	9.3	9.4	10.9	11.1	*16.7*
1972 – 1976	22.5	21.1	24.8	18.0	20.7	25.0	18.1	19.6	19.4	14.9	25.3	*12.5*
1977 – 1981	21.7	21.5	22.2	24.8	23.7	21.0	17.6	17.1	18.6	17.6	22.5	*12.5*
1982 – 1986	25.7	25.5	26.0	27.5	24.3	22.9	28.4	30.5	23.7	28.9	26.0	*25.0*
1987 – 1989	15.8	17.1	13.3	18.0	21.2	13.6	20.9	19.9	21.4	22.2	12.6	*33.3*
Primary Interest												
very heavily in teaching	45.8	34.1	72.4	23.4	13.7	38.1	46.1	40.7	48.9	51.6	71.7	85.7
leaning toward teaching	34.3	39.1	23.6	38.2	32.5	40.5	40.2	40.7	40.9	39.1	24.3	10.7
leaning toward research	16.9	22.7	3.7	32.6	41.3	18.6	12.2	15.7	9.7	9.0	3.7	3.6
very heavily in research	2.9	4.1	0.2	5.8	12.5	2.7	1.5	2.9	0.5	0.4	0.2	0.0

FEMALE FACULTY

	ALL			Universities		Four-year Colleges					Two-year Colleges	
	Insts	4-yr	2-yr	Pub	Priv	Pub	All Priv	Nons	Cath	Prot	Pub	Priv
Marital Status												
married (currently)	60.3	57.6	66.5	57.6	60.8	55.3	59.4	61.7	50.7	62.7	66.3	69.6
separated	1.2	1.4	0.9	1.0	1.0	1.6	1.7	1.9	1.8	1.2	0.9	0.0
single (never married)	19.0	21.8	12.9	21.6	17.7	21.6	23.5	17.1	36.4	23.2	12.5	19.6
single (with partner)	4.0	4.5	2.9	4.5	10.0	3.9	3.5	5.7	1.3	1.9	3.0	1.8
single (divorced)	12.8	12.3	13.9	12.7	9.4	14.6	9.9	11.3	8.7	8.7	14.3	7.1
single (widowed)	2.6	2.5	3.0	2.6	1.1	3.1	2.0	2.3	1.2	2.3	3.1	1.8
Spouse's or Partner's Education												
8th grade or less	0.2	0.2	0.3	0.2	0.3	0.2	0.1	0.1	0.0	0.2	0.3	0.0
some high school	0.6	0.3	1.1	0.3	0.1	0.5	0.3	0.3	0.5	0.3	1.1	1.9
completed high school	3.4	2.1	6.2	1.2	1.2	3.1	2.1	2.0	1.8	2.4	6.4	1.9
some college	8.2	6.3	12.6	6.3	2.3	7.2	6.6	6.2	6.0	7.5	12.9	7.7
graduated from college	13.1	10.4	19.1	10.7	7.3	10.0	11.7	13.4	9.6	10.8	18.8	26.9
attended grad/prof school	8.3	8.2	8.5	7.0	10.8	8.1	8.5	8.3	7.9	9.1	8.6	7.7
attained advanced degree	42.5	46.3	34.0	48.9	57.5	42.3	45.0	48.3	38.6	44.9	33.9	34.6
does not apply	23.7	26.2	18.1	25.6	20.4	28.6	25.7	21.4	35.6	24.8	18.1	19.2
Father's Education												
8th grade or less	16.4	14.6	20.5	11.4	7.7	18.8	14.4	12.9	18.4	13.8	20.2	26.4
some high school	9.8	8.8	12.1	8.9	5.9	9.8	8.5	7.4	9.6	9.4	12.4	7.5
completed high school	22.8	21.8	25.1	22.5	17.8	22.0	22.3	20.5	24.5	23.1	25.4	18.9
some college	15.5	15.0	16.7	13.9	17.4	15.7	14.3	13.6	14.6	15.0	16.6	18.9
graduated from college	13.6	14.6	11.4	15.8	13.4	13.2	15.6	17.0	14.1	14.7	11.1	17.0
attended grad/prof school	5.5	6.3	3.6	6.1	9.9	5.6	6.2	6.9	5.1	5.9	3.4	7.5
attained advanced degree	16.4	18.9	10.5	21.4	27.9	14.9	18.8	21.6	13.8	18.3	10.9	3.8
Mother's Education												
8th grade or less	10.8	9.6	13.7	7.3	5.8	11.6	10.3	9.9	13.3	8.8	13.5	17.0
some high school	10.7	9.8	12.6	7.3	12.2	12.0	8.5	7.7	8.4	9.8	12.6	13.2
completed high school	31.8	30.7	34.5	32.7	26.4	29.9	31.1	30.0	33.6	31.0	35.0	24.5
some college	18.1	18.2	18.1	18.3	16.7	17.7	19.1	18.4	19.3	19.9	17.7	24.5
graduated from college	16.0	17.2	13.0	18.7	20.9	16.2	15.9	16.5	14.5	16.1	13.0	13.2
attended grad/prof school	5.3	5.6	4.5	5.6	7.1	4.8	6.2	6.9	4.9	6.2	4.3	7.5
attained advanced degree	7.4	9.0	3.7	10.0	10.9	7.8	8.8	10.7	6.0	8.1	3.8	0.0
Base Institutional Salary in Thousands (3)												
less than 20	1.0	0.9	1.4	0.2	0.1	0.3	2.6	2.7	1.9	2.9	1.1	7.7
20 - 29	13.0	12.8	13.6	7.8	8.7	9.2	24.0	20.2	22.7	30.3	13.1	23.1
30 - 39	27.2	27.3	27.0	24.8	18.7	24.6	36.3	32.0	42.8	37.6	25.5	55.8
40 - 49	31.6	32.2	30.3	32.3	33.1	38.0	23.9	25.8	22.8	22.0	31.2	13.5
50 - 59	15.2	14.6	16.4	16.3	16.3	17.1	9.1	12.4	8.1	5.2	17.2	0.0
60 - 69	8.5	7.9	9.9	12.0	12.6	7.5	2.9	4.6	1.3	1.7	10.4	0.0
70 - 79	2.1	2.5	1.3	3.1	5.3	2.7	0.7	1.2	0.3	0.1	1.4	0.0
80 - 89	0.8	1.0	0.1	2.1	1.3	0.6	0.4	0.9	0.0	0.2	0.0	0.0
90 - 98	0.3	0.5	0.0	0.9	2.2	0.0	0.1	0.1	0.0	0.0	0.0	0.0
99 or more	0.2	0.4	0.0	0.6	1.7	0.0	0.0	0.1	0.0	0.0	0.0	0.0

FEMALE FACULTY

	ALL			Universities		Four-year Colleges					Two-year Colleges	
	Insts	4-yr	2-yr	Pub	Priv	Pub	All Priv	Nons	Cath	Prot	Pub	Priv
General Activities												
held academic admin position....	30.1	32.1	25.6	30.0	28.6	30.0	38.2	37.7	46.3	33.1	25.3	31.5
award for outstanding teaching..	28.5	27.8	29.9	28.9	21.2	29.5	26.7	24.3	28.9	28.5	30.1	27.8
spouse or partner an academic...	33.7	36.3	28.1	37.5	37.1	35.1	36.5	38.6	31.3	36.9	27.9	31.9
commute a long distance to work.	21.4	20.8	22.8	17.9	18.0	23.6	20.8	23.0	19.8	18.3	22.9	20.4
research/writing on women/gender	31.6	37.2	18.7	40.2	43.9	33.8	36.3	40.9	32.2	32.9	18.8	17.0
research/writing on race/ethncty	20.7	23.6	14.0	26.6	22.2	22.7	22.3	26.5	18.0	19.4	14.5	5.8
have dependent children.........	42.6	39.6	49.4	39.4	36.5	38.0	42.8	44.0	39.2	43.9	49.1	55.6
am a U.S. citizen...............	96.1	95.1	98.4	94.0	89.7	96.7	95.8	94.4	97.1	96.7	98.3	100.0
interrupted career for hlth/fam.	25.4	23.6	29.7	25.8	17.7	23.8	23.2	22.1	23.6	24.6	29.3	25.9
considered career in acad admin.	38.8	39.1	38.1	37.7	36.6	39.7	40.6	43.4	41.8	35.8	37.9	42.6
plan working beyond age 70......	31.8	35.4	23.6	37.0	40.9	31.7	36.9	38.8	39.8	32.0	23.4	25.9
General Activities in the Last Two Years												
had one or more firm job offers.	41.6	42.6	39.3	41.4	48.3	40.3	44.9	44.8	45.2	44.8	39.6	33.3
part in fac development program.	66.3	59.6	81.5	42.3	43.9	66.1	73.2	68.4	78.5	75.9	81.3	85.2
developed a new course..........	70.5	72.4	66.2	71.5	78.4	69.7	75.0	75.2	75.8	74.1	66.0	70.4
considered early retirement......	27.5	25.4	32.5	25.2	16.7	31.0	21.0	21.1	20.0	21.7	32.8	25.9
considered leaving academe......	40.4	41.7	37.4	43.7	39.3	39.5	43.6	44.7	44.6	41.4	37.1	44.4
Teaching Activities in the Last Two Years												
taught honors course............	13.7	15.1	10.4	15.8	23.3	12.3	15.3	17.6	14.8	12.4	10.4	10.6
taught interdisciplinary course.	31.9	35.2	23.6	33.3	41.2	31.7	39.8	45.5	32.6	36.7	23.0	35.4
taught general education course.	42.6	43.5	40.5	33.6	32.0	48.2	50.7	49.4	49.9	53.1	39.9	52.1
taught develop/remedial course..	19.9	14.3	33.1	8.8	7.0	16.3	19.8	22.3	19.0	16.8	33.0	34.7
taught ethnic studies course....	7.4	8.9	3.8	9.3	9.7	7.7	9.9	9.7	9.6	10.3	4.0	0.0
taught women's studies course...	12.5	15.3	5.8	16.4	20.0	12.7	15.8	19.2	13.3	12.7	6.0	2.2
team-taught a course............	40.5	41.1	39.1	42.6	36.0	39.6	43.4	44.0	38.8	45.7	39.7	26.7
worked w/students on resrch proj	52.6	61.5	30.1	69.0	71.1	57.8	55.3	61.5	52.1	48.7	29.7	37.5
attd racial/cultural workshop...	39.1	37.0	43.9	31.6	29.3	40.7	40.1	41.0	45.6	34.9	45.2	37.5
attd women's/minorities workshop	24.5	25.0	23.3	21.5	24.4	24.6	29.3	32.3	33.2	22.1	23.8	18.4
held faculty senate/council ofc.	24.3	22.9	27.6	19.8	21.0	24.4	24.5	23.0	30.8	22.1	27.8	12.8
used funds for research.........	32.3	42.2	7.7	52.6	60.1	37.0	31.9	37.0	29.7	26.3	7.9	24.5
served as a paid consultant.....	39.2	42.5	31.2	46.5	49.2	42.2	36.3	35.5	40.0	34.8	31.9	17.4
Research Working Environment												
work essentially alone..........	64.8	67.8	57.5	65.6	63.7	67.6	71.7	72.1	70.4	72.0	57.1	65.4
work with one or two colleagues.	25.1	25.7	23.9	28.6	31.7	25.3	21.0	20.5	22.7	20.5	24.0	21.2
member of larger group..........	10.1	6.6	18.6	5.8	4.6	7.1	7.4	7.4	6.9	7.6	18.9	13.5

79

FEMALE FACULTY

HOURS PER WEEK SPENT ON:

	ALL			Universities		Four-year Colleges					Two-year Colleges	
	Insts	4-yr	2-yr	Pub	Priv	Pub	All Priv	Nons	Cath	Prot	Pub	Priv
Scheduled Teaching												
none	0.2	0.2	0.2	0.3	0.5	0.2	0.2	0.2	0.2	0.1	0.2	0.0
1 – 4	6.1	7.2	3.6	10.2	13.6	5.4	4.6	4.1	5.6	4.4	3.8	0.0
5 – 8	21.5	28.2	6.1	42.5	54.3	18.5	17.9	22.6	15.0	13.7	6.3	2.0
9 – 12	30.9	37.6	15.4	30.6	24.0	42.3	43.1	40.6	49.0	42.1	15.5	14.0
13 – 16	20.4	16.0	30.5	8.3	4.6	20.0	22.1	20.8	19.7	25.7	29.4	52.0
17 – 20	12.7	6.7	26.5	4.6	2.0	8.8	7.6	6.8	7.1	9.1	26.6	24.0
21 – 34	7.2	3.5	15.8	3.1	0.9	4.1	4.0	4.5	2.6	4.3	16.3	6.0
35 – 44	0.7	0.4	1.5	0.4	0.0	0.5	0.5	0.4	0.4	0.6	1.6	0.0
45 or more	0.2	0.1	0.4	0.0	0.0	0.2	0.1	0.0	0.4	0.0	0.3	2.0
Preparing for Teaching												
none	0.2	0.2	0.1	0.3	0.4	0.1	0.3	0.4	0.3	0.1	0.1	0.0
1 – 4	6.8	6.5	7.6	6.7	7.1	6.9	5.6	6.5	4.2	5.5	7.7	5.9
5 – 8	21.0	20.7	21.6	22.7	21.9	21.5	17.1	17.9	17.4	15.8	21.7	19.6
9 – 12	24.8	24.2	26.3	27.3	20.6	23.9	22.7	22.2	21.5	24.4	26.2	27.5
13 – 16	17.7	18.0	17.0	18.1	23.5	16.4	18.2	19.0	17.4	17.7	16.8	19.6
17 – 20	14.6	14.9	13.7	12.5	13.9	16.1	16.1	14.5	18.2	16.8	14.0	7.8
21 – 34	10.8	11.3	9.6	9.8	9.3	10.4	14.8	13.8	16.3	15.0	9.6	9.8
35 – 44	3.0	3.0	2.9	1.7	3.0	3.4	3.8	4.3	3.5	3.4	2.7	7.8
45 or more	1.1	1.1	1.1	0.8	0.5	1.2	1.4	1.4	1.2	1.5	1.1	2.0
Advising/Counseling of Students												
none	2.0	2.0	2.2	2.5	0.7	2.2	1.6	1.8	1.5	1.5	2.2	2.0
1 – 4	52.9	52.0	55.0	54.2	64.7	49.5	48.6	46.5	49.5	50.8	55.4	46.0
5 – 8	31.5	32.1	30.2	32.7	25.8	32.0	33.9	35.0	34.5	32.0	30.1	34.0
9 – 12	9.1	9.6	7.8	7.3	6.8	11.1	11.0	10.9	10.5	11.6	7.4	16.0
13 – 16	2.4	2.7	1.9	1.7	0.8	3.8	2.8	3.1	2.2	2.7	2.0	2.0
17 – 20	1.2	1.1	1.5	1.0	0.6	0.9	1.6	2.3	1.3	0.8	1.5	0.0
21 – 34	0.7	0.4	1.2	0.5	0.1	0.3	0.4	0.5	0.3	0.3	1.3	0.0
35 – 44	0.2	0.1	0.2	0.0	0.0	0.2	0.2	0.0	0.0	0.3	0.2	0.0
45 or more	0.0	0.0	0.0	0.0	0.0	0.1	0.0	0.0	0.0	0.0	0.0	0.0
Committee Work and Meetings												
none	3.9	4.0	3.8	6.5	4.1	2.1	3.8	4.3	2.4	4.2	3.7	5.9
1 – 4	68.4	64.7	76.9	59.5	74.6	62.5	69.4	67.5	70.7	71.2	76.5	84.3
5 – 8	21.0	23.7	14.8	25.1	16.7	26.5	21.1	21.4	22.2	19.7	15.2	5.9
9 – 12	4.7	5.5	2.8	6.5	3.6	6.4	4.2	4.7	3.0	3.6	2.8	2.0
13 – 16	1.2	1.3	1.0	1.5	0.9	1.5	1.2	1.6	1.1	0.3	0.9	2.0
17 – 20	0.5	0.5	0.2	0.7	0.1	0.6	0.3	0.2	0.6	0.2	0.5	0.0
21 – 34	0.2	0.3	0.0	0.2	0.0	0.4	0.2	0.2	0.0	0.0	0.2	0.0
35 – 44	0.0	0.0	0.0	0.0	0.0	0.0	0.0	0.0	0.0	0.0	0.0	0.0
45 or more	0.0	0.0	0.1	0.0	0.0	0.0	0.0	0.0	0.0	0.0	0.1	0.0

FEMALE FACULTY

HOURS PER WEEK SPENT ON:	ALL			Universities		Four-year Colleges					Two-year Colleges	
	Insts	4-yr	2-yr	Pub	Priv	Pub	All Priv	Nons	Cath	Prot	Pub	Priv
Other Administration												
none	36.8	35.4	40.0	38.0	32.0	35.7	33.6	33.5	30.3	36.2	39.9	43.2
1 – 4	38.5	38.8	37.7	39.8	43.8	37.7	37.5	37.3	38.0	37.3	37.6	38.6
5 – 8	11.4	11.4	11.2	9.7	8.2	12.7	12.6	12.5	14.2	11.8	11.2	11.4
9 – 12	6.0	6.5	4.9	6.0	11.4	5.5	6.7	6.7	7.2	6.4	4.9	4.5
13 – 16	2.9	3.0	2.6	2.2	3.6	3.0	3.6	4.3	3.5	2.8	2.8	0.0
17 – 20	2.2	2.6	1.3	2.2	0.4	3.0	3.1	3.0	3.9	2.7	1.3	2.3
21 – 34	1.6	1.6	1.7	1.1	0.6	1.8	2.2	2.1	2.5	2.2	1.8	0.0
35 – 44	0.5	0.4	0.4	0.8	0.0	0.8	0.5	0.7	0.2	0.4	0.4	0.0
45 or more	0.2	0.2	0.2	0.2	0.0	0.2	0.2	0.0	0.4	0.3	0.2	0.0
Research and Scholarly Writing												
none	29.2	17.8	57.1	9.5	7.1	18.4	29.2	25.5	29.6	34.0	56.6	66.0
1 – 4	33.1	33.5	32.1	24.7	17.1	38.5	41.4	38.1	45.6	43.1	32.3	27.7
5 – 8	15.0	18.1	7.3	18.9	20.7	19.1	15.1	17.3	14.1	12.7	7.3	6.4
9 – 12	9.7	12.8	2.3	20.6	14.7	11.0	6.5	5.3	5.3	5.5	2.4	0.0
13 – 16	4.8	6.4	0.6	8.2	13.1	5.5	3.7	5.3	2.5	2.4	0.6	0.0
17 – 20	4.0	5.5	0.4	9.0	11.6	3.7	2.5	3.5	1.6	1.8	0.4	0.0
21 – 34	2.8	3.9	0.1	6.6	8.5	2.6	1.2	1.9	1.0	0.3	0.2	0.0
35 – 44	1.0	1.4	0.1	1.8	5.9	0.8	0.3	0.4	0.3	0.3	0.1	0.0
45 or more	0.4	0.5	0.1	0.8	1.3	0.5	0.1	0.1	0.0	0.0	0.1	0.0
Consultation with Clients or Patients												
none	69.2	69.8	68.1	68.7	72.0	68.0	72.3	73.7	70.9	71.4	68.0	70.5
1 – 4	21.0	20.7	21.8	21.4	23.4	21.1	18.6	17.0	20.3	19.5	21.7	22.7
5 – 8	5.8	5.4	6.5	4.8	2.7	6.5	5.5	6.1	4.8	5.2	6.5	6.8
9 – 12	1.9	2.0	1.7	2.8	1.7	1.7	1.7	1.6	1.8	2.0	1.7	0.0
13 – 16	0.7	0.9	0.9	1.1	0.1	1.0	0.7	0.8	0.8	0.6	0.6	0.0
17 – 20	0.7	0.7	0.6	0.7	0.1	0.7	0.8	0.7	0.7	1.1	0.4	0.0
21 – 34	0.4	0.5	0.4	0.3	0.0	0.9	0.3	0.1	0.0	0.2	0.2	0.0
35 – 44	0.1	0.1	0.1	0.1	0.0	0.0	0.1	0.1	0.0	0.0	0.1	0.0
45 or more	0.1	0.0	0.1	0.0	0.0	0.1	0.0	0.0	0.0	0.0	0.1	0.0
Number of Days Spent Off-Campus for Professional Activities												
none	12.7	11.6	15.2	11.3	8.7	11.4	13.0	15.1	11.5	11.0	15.0	18.9
1-2	15.7	13.0	22.0	11.0	9.4	12.5	16.7	15.1	18.7	17.5	21.6	30.2
3-4	26.7	24.4	31.9	19.1	19.3	24.9	30.6	27.5	32.0	33.9	31.9	30.2
5-10	29.8	32.4	24.0	35.1	34.8	33.0	28.1	27.9	27.8	28.6	24.5	15.1
11-20	10.9	13.2	5.5	17.9	17.6	12.5	8.3	10.7	6.9	6.1	5.6	3.8
21-50	3.2	4.1	1.1	4.7	8.1	4.1	2.3	2.4	2.5	2.1	1.0	1.9
50+	1.0	1.3	0.3	1.0	2.0	1.6	1.0	1.3	0.6	0.9	0.3	0.0

FEMALE FACULTY

	ALL			Universities		Four-year Colleges					Two-year Colleges	
	Insts	4-yr	2-yr	Pub	Priv	Pub	All Priv	Nons	Cath	Prot	Pub	Priv
NUMBER OF:												
Articles in Academic or Professional Journals												
none	43.3	31.3	70.6	20.5	18.6	33.6	42.9	39.1	44.0	47.4	70.4	74.1
1-2	22.7	24.0	19.8	22.1	17.5	24.4	27.4	25.2	28.5	29.6	19.8	18.5
3-4	12.9	16.0	5.9	14.2	18.1	18.5	13.7	15.0	13.4	12.2	5.9	5.6
5-10	11.3	15.0	2.8	19.9	18.3	14.3	10.0	11.4	9.9	8.1	2.9	0.0
11-20	6.1	8.6	0.5	14.6	16.7	5.6	4.1	6.1	3.2	1.9	0.6	0.0
21-50	3.0	4.3	0.2	6.8	8.6	3.4	1.4	2.4	0.8	0.6	0.2	1.9
50+	0.7	0.9	0.2	1.8	2.2	0.4	0.5	0.8	0.2	0.2	0.3	0.0
Chapters in Edited Volumes												
none	76.1	68.5	93.3	55.6	51.8	73.3	80.4	74.6	82.8	86.9	93.2	96.2
1-2	15.1	19.6	4.7	24.9	28.4	17.8	14.1	17.3	13.7	9.9	4.7	3.8
3-4	4.8	6.5	1.0	10.4	8.0	5.7	3.4	4.6	2.4	2.3	1.0	0.0
5-10	3.0	4.0	0.7	6.9	8.0	2.5	1.8	2.8	1.0	1.0	0.7	0.0
11-20	0.7	1.0	0.1	1.6	2.7	0.7	0.2	0.4	0.0	0.1	0.1	0.0
21-50	0.2	0.3	0.1	0.6	1.0	0.0	0.1	0.2	0.0	0.0	0.1	0.0
50+	0.1	0.1	0.1	0.0	0.0	0.2	0.0	0.1	0.0	0.0	0.1	0.0
Books, Manuals, Monographs												
none	60.9	57.5	68.6	49.8	46.0	59.3	66.5	62.8	69.0	69.9	67.8	84.6
1-2	28.2	30.4	23.1	34.0	36.7	29.9	25.4	26.4	23.7	25.1	23.9	7.7
3-4	7.1	7.7	5.9	10.3	10.5	6.6	5.5	7.4	4.7	3.4	5.9	5.8
5-10	2.9	3.4	1.7	4.8	4.1	3.3	1.9	2.0	2.1	1.5	1.7	1.9
11-20	0.6	0.7	0.4	0.7	1.3	0.6	0.6	1.1	0.4	0.2	0.4	0.0
21-50	0.2	0.2	0.2	0.3	0.8	0.0	0.0	0.1	0.1	0.0	0.2	0.0
50+	0.1	0.1	0.1	0.0	0.6	0.0	0.0	0.1	0.0	0.0	0.0	0.0
Professional Writings Accepted or Published in Last Two Years												
none	56.3	43.5	85.2	28.7	22.9	48.6	58.0	52.8	60.3	63.7	85.2	84.9
1-2	24.5	30.1	11.8	31.1	30.2	30.8	28.3	28.5	29.4	27.2	11.9	9.4
3-4	11.7	16.0	1.8	21.2	27.9	14.3	9.2	12.1	7.6	6.2	1.8	1.9
5-10	6.7	9.3	0.9	17.2	16.2	5.7	4.0	6.0	2.4	2.5	0.9	1.9
11-20	0.6	0.8	0.2	1.2	2.2	0.5	0.2	0.2	0.3	0.2	0.1	1.9
21-50	0.2	0.2	0.1	0.4	0.4	0.0	0.2	0.3	0.0	0.0	0.1	0.0
50+	0.1	0.1	0.1	0.1	0.3	0.1	0.1	0.1	0.0	0.0	0.1	0.0
Professional Goals Noted as Very Important or Essential												
engage in research	52.3	64.5	24.1	74.6	86.8	61.1	51.7	59.6	45.1	45.5	24.2	22.6
engage in outside activities	59.1	58.8	59.6	55.8	49.6	61.7	60.9	60.6	60.7	61.3	59.7	58.5
provide services to the cmty.	52.0	48.9	59.1	41.2	42.4	52.9	53.2	51.4	55.7	54.1	59.3	55.6
participate in comm/admin work	37.9	35.1	44.4	27.8	23.9	39.1	40.7	37.4	46.8	40.8	44.3	46.3
be a good colleague	86.4	84.7	90.2	80.7	79.3	86.4	88.2	86.2	89.9	89.8	90.5	85.2
be a good teacher	98.4	98.0	99.5	98.1	93.3	98.4	98.8	98.8	98.8	98.9	99.6	98.1

FEMALE FACULTY

	ALL			Universities		Four-year Colleges					Two-year Colleges	
	Insts	4-yr	2-yr	Pub	Priv	Pub	All Priv	Nons	Cath	Prot	Pub	Priv
Evaluation Methods Used in Most or All Undergraduate Courses												
multiple-choice mid-terms/finals	40.8	35.1	53.7	34.0	18.5	42.5	31.9	25.7	36.3	37.2	54.5	37.5
essay mid-terms/finals	38.9	43.7	28.0	42.9	50.4	40.7	46.0	47.6	44.7	44.9	27.6	33.9
short-answer mid-terms/finals	31.8	33.5	27.9	32.8	39.5	32.0	34.3	32.7	34.8	36.2	27.9	27.8
multiple-choice quizzes	21.3	15.0	35.7	11.3	7.2	18.5	16.6	15.1	16.8	18.6	36.1	27.3
short-answer quizzes	26.4	24.3	31.2	20.4	21.1	24.0	29.4	29.5	26.3	31.5	30.8	37.5
weekly essay assignments	18.3	16.6	22.0	15.7	11.4	16.8	19.0	19.8	17.1	19.3	22.7	8.9
student presentations	35.0	39.0	26.0	35.5	37.1	38.7	43.5	45.7	41.3	42.0	26.4	19.6
term/research papers	34.4	40.6	20.2	41.9	48.5	38.4	39.7	42.2	36.0	39.1	20.1	21.8
stdnt evals of each others' work	15.6	16.4	13.9	17.9	11.5	15.7	17.4	18.5	17.5	15.9	13.9	12.5
grading on a curve	14.5	17.5	7.7	20.3	26.1	16.1	13.7	16.9	12.1	10.6	7.7	7.1
competency-based grading	53.9	50.8	60.7	52.1	46.3	50.0	51.9	54.0	52.1	49.0	62.0	34.0
student evaluations of teaching	85.4	88.5	78.4	93.0	89.3	85.4	87.9	89.2	90.3	84.4	78.8	71.4
Instructional Methods Used in Most or All Undergrad Courses												
class discussions	76.9	78.4	73.4	79.9	76.1	77.2	79.3	80.7	75.8	80.0	73.9	63.6
computer/machine-aided instruct.	16.0	13.0	22.7	13.7	6.9	14.0	13.0	14.1	12.9	11.5	22.6	25.5
cooperative learning	39.5	39.8	38.9	40.8	28.8	40.6	41.6	42.4	41.5	40.6	39.4	29.1
experiential learning./field stud	26.1	26.6	25.0	27.1	17.3	27.7	27.9	26.5	29.5	28.5	25.4	16.4
graduate teaching assistants	4.7	6.7	0.3	14.1	14.4	3.5	1.0	2.1	0.1	0.2	0.3	0.0
undergrad teaching assistants	2.4	2.5	2.2	2.0	3.2	1.8	3.7	4.8	2.7	2.8	2.3	0.0
group projects	21.5	22.7	18.7	23.4	17.9	23.8	22.2	21.9	23.5	21.8	18.9	14.5
independent projects	40.9	43.7	34.7	43.7	40.1	45.1	42.9	45.2	42.6	40.1	35.1	25.5
extensive lecturing	42.4	40.9	46.1	43.3	46.5	41.8	35.3	33.0	38.5	36.3	45.9	49.1
multiple drafts of written work	16.7	17.1	15.7	16.1	17.3	15.8	19.7	23.2	17.2	16.9	15.8	5.6
readings on racial/ethnic issues	17.6	19.7	12.7	21.4	20.0	18.0	20.3	22.2	18.0	19.5	13.1	7.4
readings on women/gender issues	18.3	20.7	12.6	22.1	26.5	17.7	21.4	24.9	18.6	18.7	12.9	12.7
student-developed activities	19.4	19.0	20.4	17.6	16.0	21.0	18.7	21.2	17.6	16.1	20.8	
student-selected topics	11.5	12.1	10.4	12.7	11.2	12.1	11.7	14.4	10.7	8.8	10.3	10.9
Goals for Undergraduates Noted as Very Important or Essential												
develop ability to think clearly	99.6	99.6	99.7	99.6	98.5	99.7	99.7	99.8	99.7	99.7	99.7	100.0
increase self-directed learning	94.9	95.3	94.0	95.3	94.2	95.0	96.2	96.3	96.7	95.7	94.3	87.0
prepare for employment	70.7	64.8	84.3	59.7	40.5	73.1	67.0	60.8	72.4	72.0	84.4	81.5
prepare for graduate education	51.0	54.7	42.3	48.3	42.6	58.5	60.2	55.8	60.0	66.5	41.5	57.4
develop moral character	61.9	60.0	66.3	51.0	55.1	59.5	71.2	65.6	73.4	77.5	66.1	70.4
provide for emotional developmnt	49.7	46.8	56.5	37.9	41.9	46.5	57.0	52.6	56.3	63.8	55.8	69.8
prepare for family living	25.2	22.0	32.6	15.9	13.6	24.5	27.3	23.5	28.3	32.0	32.1	43.6
teach stdnts classics west civ	33.1	36.1	26.2	29.7	41.3	35.7	40.8	39.0	41.9	42.8	25.9	31.5
help develop personal values	70.6	69.7	72.6	60.8	62.6	70.6	79.5	76.0	81.9	82.6	72.0	84.9
enhance out-of-class experience	48.5	46.5	53.1	42.2	31.5	48.7	52.9	52.7	51.4	54.1	52.9	57.4
enhance self-understanding	76.8	75.2	80.6	71.6	68.0	75.4	80.9	79.3	81.7	82.6	80.2	88.7

FEMALE FACULTY

	ALL			Universities		Four-year Colleges					Two-year Colleges	
	Insts	4-yr	2-yr	Pub	Priv	Pub	All Priv	Nons	Cath	Prot	Pub	Priv
NUMBER OF COURSES TAUGHT IN:												
General Education												
none	60.0	61.2	57.0	72.9	67.2	57.7	53.2	55.0	54.6	50.0	57.4	50.0
one	17.0	19.4	11.5	15.3	22.4	19.3	22.4	21.7	20.1	24.9	11.3	14.3
two	10.0	10.7	8.6	7.3	7.2	11.9	13.2	14.0	12.2	12.9	8.6	7.1
three	6.1	5.3	7.9	3.1	2.1	6.4	6.8	5.2	8.6	7.7	7.9	7.1
four	3.5	2.3	6.2	1.0	0.7	3.1	3.0	2.6	3.8	2.8	6.2	7.1
five or more	3.4	1.1	8.9	0.4	0.3	1.5	1.4	1.4	0.8	1.8	8.6	14.3
Other BA or BS Undergraduate Credit Courses												
none	15.0	8.2	33.0	8.4	5.1	9.0	8.0	9.2	6.5	7.4	33.7	18.6
one	24.3	28.5	13.2	36.2	49.4	24.0	19.3	20.5	17.8	19.0	13.6	4.7
two	26.1	29.5	17.0	32.6	29.4	27.6	28.9	30.6	28.8	26.7	16.9	18.6
three	17.6	19.3	13.1	14.5	13.2	21.9	23.1	21.7	23.4	24.8	12.7	20.9
four	10.6	10.5	11.0	6.3	2.3	13.2	14.0	11.6	18.4	14.1	10.6	18.6
five or more	6.4	4.0	12.7	2.2	0.6	4.3	6.7	6.5	5.1	8.1	12.4	18.6
Non-BA Credit Courses (developmental or remedial)												
none	81.0	90.1	62.5	93.3	95.6	89.1	87.1	84.6	90.1	88.2	62.3	65.7
one	6.6	5.1	9.6	3.5	3.4	5.4	6.7	7.2	5.7	6.7	9.6	8.6
two	4.6	2.3	9.5	1.8	0.4	2.3	3.0	4.1	2.4	2.0	9.5	8.6
three	2.6	1.3	5.4	0.6	0.2	1.8	1.5	2.5	0.7	0.7	5.4	5.7
four	2.7	0.6	6.9	0.4	0.0	0.7	1.0	1.0	0.5	1.3	6.8	8.6
five or more	2.5	0.7	6.2	0.5	0.4	0.7	0.8	0.6	0.6	1.1	6.3	2.9
Graduate Courses												
none	73.7	64.6	99.4	53.1	39.1	65.2	86.7	83.8	84.9	92.1	99.4	100.0
one	20.6	27.7	0.4	37.5	51.3	25.8	10.2	12.3	11.7	6.2	0.4	0.0
two	4.6	6.1	0.2	7.7	8.7	6.6	2.5	3.2	2.6	1.4	0.2	0.0
three	1.0	1.3	0.0	1.2	0.7	2.1	0.4	0.5	0.5	0.3	0.0	0.0
four	0.1	0.1	0.0	0.1	0.1	0.1	0.1	0.0	0.4	0.0	0.0	0.0
five or more	0.1	0.2	0.2	0.3	0.0	0.2	0.1	0.2	0.0	0.1	0.2	0.0
Political Orientation												
far left	5.1	6.5	1.8	9.6	8.1	4.7	5.5	7.7	3.1	4.1	1.8	1.9
liberal	39.7	44.2	29.3	50.8	57.3	38.6	41.0	46.8	39.7	33.7	29.5	24.5
moderate	40.9	37.6	48.7	31.5	28.8	42.8	39.4	33.7	45.6	42.8	48.4	54.7
conservative	14.2	11.6	20.1	8.1	5.7	13.8	14.1	11.9	11.5	19.2	20.1	18.9
far right	0.1	0.1	0.2	0.0	0.0	0.1	0.1	0.0	0.1	0.1	0.2	0.0
Agrees Strongly or Somewhat												
abolish death penalty	45.8	50.7	34.6	54.7	61.5	44.0	52.2	55.5	55.5	45.3	34.2	43.6
national health care plan needed	81.0	82.9	76.6	81.4	90.1	81.7	83.3	87.2	83.9	77.5	76.9	70.9
abortion should be legalized	80.0	82.6	74.1	89.5	91.8	82.5	73.0	84.5	58.7	67.2	74.4	67.3
grading in college too easy	71.7	74.6	64.9	76.8	80.1	74.1	71.3	70.7	75.0	69.6	64.8	66.7
wealthy should pay more taxes	84.7	86.2	81.2	86.8	89.4	85.3	85.7	86.3	85.4	85.1	81.0	85.2
college can ban extreme speakers	19.5	16.8	25.5	10.7	16.6	15.8	24.2	18.0	28.1	30.1	25.1	34.5
college increases earning power	24.3	19.5	35.	18.3	9.5	24.3	17.7	19.0	16.2	17.0	35.3	30.9

FEMALE FACULTY

	ALL			Universities		Four-year Colleges					Two-year Colleges	
	Insts	4-yr	2-yr	Pub	Priv	Pub	All Priv	Nons	Cath	Prot	Pub	Priv
Agrees Strongly or Somewhat												
fac interested in students' prob	78.5	74.6	87.2	60.5	62.5	76.1	90.3	85.6	94.1	94.1	86.6	100.0
fac sensitive to minority issues	68.0	65.6	73.5	58.9	64.8	67.0	70.6	68.7	73.8	70.8	73.1	81.5
curriculum overspecialized......	24.5	29.0	14.3	40.8	34.3	25.1	21.2	25.6	18.8	16.9	14.6	7.5
many students don't "fit in"....	23.4	25.7	18.2	27.5	29.6	24.3	24.6	28.2	18.0	24.4	17.9	24.5
fac committed to welfare of coll	78.2	76.2	82.6	66.4	81.2	73.6	87.4	83.4	88.4	92.4	82.5	84.9
courses incl minority perspect..	39.6	38.5	42.0	34.0	35.4	41.1	40.4	43.8	41.8	34.6	43.0	23.1
admin consider student concerns.	61.0	59.5	64.3	47.4	49.8	61.4	71.6	68.0	74.8	74.3	63.7	77.4
fac interest in stdnts acad prob	79.0	76.6	84.6	60.3	69.7	79.7	90.4	86.9	92.2	94.0	84.0	96.2
a lot of racial conflict here...	13.8	17.1	6.5	28.0	15.4	12.8	12.7	16.8	7.2	11.1	6.6	3.8
students resent required courses	42.2	41.4	43.9	41.3	35.0	44.9	39.1	38.0	41.1	39.2	43.4	52.8
ethnic groups communicate well.	58.4	52.8	70.8	44.1	44.2	55.7	60.1	57.2	63.2	62.1	70.6	75.5
admin care little about students	21.4	22.1	19.9	32.1	19.2	23.2	12.0	15.1	9.3	9.5	20.1	17.0
low trust btwn minorities/admin.	25.7	29.2	18.0	44.2	33.5	25.1	19.0	23.1	14.5	16.4	18.2	15.1
fac positive about gen ed pgm...	74.7	70.0	85.3	60.2	74.8	67.9	80.6	75.5	83.5	85.5	85.3	84.9
courses incl feminist perspect..	26.3	25.9	27.3	23.9	30.0	21.7	32.0	35.1	42.7	19.9	28.1	11.3
oppty for fac/stdnt socializing.	36.1	36.4	35.4	21.5	35.5	30.1	59.6	54.1	58.2	68.2	34.3	58.5
admin consider faculty concerns.	49.1	49.0	49.2	39.4	50.7	46.7	60.8	56.0	60.1	68.0	49.3	47.2
stdnts well prep academically...	29.5	32.1	23.5	25.4	53.7	25.5	40.1	37.7	37.5	45.2	23.7	18.9
Stdnt Aff staff supported by fac	63.0	62.6	63.9	58.8	58.8	61.5	68.8	66.2	68.2	72.8	63.1	79.2
research interferes w/teaching..	26.2	35.0	6.0	49.4	44.5	34.8	18.4	21.3	20.3	12.8	6.1	3.8
unionization enhances teaching..	37.7	34.6	44.2	35.6	30.9	37.0	31.6	39.3	26.0	25.1	45.1	27.8
tenure is an outmoded concept...	45.4	46.0	44.1	49.6	45.0	42.7	47.2	45.7	53.9	44.2	44.0	46.3
Issues Noted as Being of High or Highest Priority												
promote intellectual development	77.6	77.6	77.5	71.3	81.7	74.6	86.4	83.8	86.7	90.1	77.3	81.5
help students understand values.	51.7	51.6	51.9	35.9	45.9	47.3	74.4	64.5	84.1	81.1	50.6	77.8
increase minorities in fac/admin	49.0	49.4	47.9	54.6	35.6	55.2	41.2	47.3	40.9	33.0	49.0	25.9
devel community among stdnts/fac	46.5	44.1	52.0	25.9	34.5	43.5	65.6	62.0	69.2	68.0	51.6	59.3
devel leadership abil in stdnts.	43.0	43.7	41.3	27.3	38.1	44.1	60.7	57.0	63.6	63.9	40.2	63.0
conduct basic & applied research	38.4	50.8	10.1	78.6	69.1	45.7	24.7	31.7	18.9	19.0	10.3	7.4
raise money for the institution.	61.2	68.1	45.3	68.1	82.7	59.2	75.2	78.0	69.9	75.1	45.0	50.9
devel leadership abil in faculty	28.9	27.0	33.1	23.0	18.7	29.1	30.9	28.8	31.8	33.0	33.6	24.1
increase women in fac/admin.....	34.8	35.6	33.0	37.3	24.3	38.1	34.2	40.7	35.4	24.2	33.9	14.8
facilitate comm svcs involvement	28.4	30.2	24.4	16.5	34.4	27.3	45.9	42.3	50.5	47.6	24.6	22.2
teach students how to change soc	25.3	25.9	24.1	18.3	18.3	26.4	35.0	34.2	39.2	33.0	24.2	22.2
help solve soc/environ problems.	27.2	28.5	24.3	24.3	26.9	27.8	33.8	32.8	38.8	31.7	24.4	22.2
allow airing of diff opinions...	48.5	48.4	48.6	45.9	43.8	47.4	53.8	54.8	56.2	50.6	48.9	42.6
increase/maintain inst prestige.	76.2	78.3	71.3	80.5	89.4	72.8	79.9	82.7	76.3	78.6	71.3	71.7
devel apprec of multi-cultul soc	51.5	51.8	50.7	50.2	40.1	51.9	57.1	58.3	59.4	53.9	50.7	50.0
hire faculty "stars"............	26.4	32.2	13.0	54.1	50.1	24.1	16.1	20.1	11.6	13.8	13.2	9.4
economize and cut costs.........	58.3	59.5	55.4	67.0	64.7	57.2	53.8	55.1	55.3	50.8	55.1	61.1
recruit more minority students..	49.7	51.3	46.2	52.1	42.2	56.7	46.2	51.0	47.6	38.5	46.8	34.0
enhance inst's national image...	59.6	67.4	41.8	75.4	88.5	57.2	66.2	74.3	52.2	65.0	41.9	38.9
create positive undergrad exp...	72.1	69.9	77.1	49.9	71.8	71.6	86.4	82.3	89.2	90.0	76.7	84.9
create multi-cultural environ...	44.3	44.5	43.9	41.4	30.5	48.1	47.5	50.4	50.1	41.5	44.0	40.7
enhance stdnt's out-of-class exp	32.6	32.5	32.8	19.6	29.4	32.1	46.3	45.9	42.8	49.5	32.0	48.1

FEMALE FACULTY

	ALL			Universities		Four-year Colleges					Two-year Colleges	
	Insts	4-yr	2-yr	Pub	Priv	Pub	All Priv	Nons	Cath	Prot	Pub	Priv
Attributes Noted as Being Very Descriptive of Institution												
easy to see fac outside ofc hour	33.7	33.0	35.0	18.9	30.8	29.2	52.7	48.7	54.5	57.0	34.3	50.0
great conformity among students	23.3	27.3	14.4	27.0	31.9	21.0	34.4	32.9	31.6	38.6	13.7	28.6
most students very bright	8.6	11.3	2.6	7.8	35.1	5.9	14.1	19.5	5.3	13.0	2.7	0.0
admin open about policies	13.0	12.1	15.2	8.5	8.4	11.6	17.5	17.8	14.4	19.3	15.7	5.4
keen competition for grades	19.0	22.8	10.4	24.7	49.8	15.8	21.5	21.8	22.0	20.7	10.6	5.4
courses more theoret than pract	6.6	8.6	2.2	8.0	22.0	4.9	9.8	12.0	6.1	9.3	2.3	0.0
fac rewarded for advising skills	2.2	2.7	1.2	1.3	2.2	2.0	5.1	5.7	4.2	5.0	1.2	1.8
little std contact out-of-class	12.0	9.2	18.3	11.4	3.4	13.2	2.8	3.6	3.0	1.5	19.1	0.0
faculty at odds with admin	17.5	17.1	18.3	20.1	14.3	18.2	13.7	19.1	10.5	8.6	18.5	14.3
intercoll sports overemphasized	13.5	16.7	6.4	32.2	9.3	13.2	8.9	10.4	5.4	9.4	5.6	21.4
classes usually informal	19.8	18.1	23.9	13.8	15.9	18.1	22.9	26.7	19.2	20.3	23.8	25.0
faculty respect each other	35.7	33.3	41.0	23.0	38.0	28.2	48.6	44.0	50.2	53.6	40.3	55.4
most stdnts treated like numbers	4.8	6.0	2.1	12.2	8.5	4.4	1.5	2.5	0.6	0.6	2.2	0.0
social activities overemphasized	5.6	7.6	1.0	7.7	8.8	5.9	9.5	11.8	5.4	9.4	0.6	7.1
little student/faculty contact	4.3	4.7	3.4	6.9	6.6	4.9	1.7	2.5	1.8	0.7	3.5	1.8
student body apathetic	13.7	10.5	20.8	9.6	8.0	15.0	6.1	6.9	4.6	6.0	21.3	10.7
stdnts don't socialize regularly	6.4	4.9	9.6	5.0	0.8	8.5	1.2	2.2	1.0	0.1	10.1	0.0
fac rewarded for good teaching	10.2	11.1	8.2	5.3	11.0	9.5	18.8	18.5	16.4	21.0	8.6	1.8
student services well supported	19.4	19.1	19.9	14.5	16.4	16.6	27.8	31.3	24.6	25.3	19.7	23.2
Personal Goals Noted as Very Important or Essential												
become authority in own field	66.1	66.9	64.3	70.2	76.7	66.9	60.3	62.6	57.1	59.5	64.7	57.1
influence political structure	23.6	24.2	22.2	24.4	24.3	25.4	22.2	23.1	24.7	19.0	22.1	25.0
influence social values	57.1	58.0	55.1	56.0	59.2	56.1	62.1	59.7	63.4	64.4	54.5	66.1
raise a family	61.0	57.7	68.4	57.5	60.2	55.8	59.6	60.2	53.7	63.1	68.2	71.4
have admin responsibility	14.2	13.4	16.2	11.8	10.1	13.3	16.1	18.3	14.7	14.0	16.4	12.5
be very well-off financially	34.4	31.5	41.2	33.0	23.6	35.2	27.7	31.9	23.2	25.1	41.6	32.1
help others in difficulty	74.3	72.9	77.5	68.1	66.4	74.2	78.2	75.0	80.1	81.3	77.4	78.6
be involved in environ clean-up	46.8	45.8	49.0	46.2	33.1	46.9	48.1	49.9	48.7	45.2	49.1	48.2
develop philosophy of life	85.1	84.4	86.5	83.5	76.8	84.1	88.2	85.8	91.1	89.5	86.8	82.1
promote racial understanding	68.3	69.2	66.1	70.6	60.9	68.2	72.2	73.4	71.8	70.9	66.2	64.3
obtain recog from colleagues	53.3	58.4	41.8	65.3	78.5	55.0	49.1	54.8	44.9	44.4	42.0	39.3
Aspects of Job Noted as Very Satisfactory or Satisfactory (4)												
salary and fringe benefits	44.9	40.6	54.8	40.8	49.5	39.6	38.6	41.7	34.7	37.0	55.6	36.5
oppty for scholarly pursuits	37.8	36.3	41.5	39.8	50.5	31.9	33.8	33.6	32.6	35.0	42.0	31.4
teaching load	47.7	46.6	50.3	52.5	55.0	40.7	45.9	46.0	45.3	46.0	50.6	45.3
quality of students	42.5	45.6	35.3	47.4	58.8	38.0	49.6	49.2	46.9	52.1	35.8	25.9
working conditions	62.0	61.3	63.4	60.5	67.6	57.6	65.0	65.8	64.0	64.6	63.4	62.3
autonomy and independence	81.9	82.5	80.6	83.0	86.6	79.8	84.3	82.3	84.8	86.8	80.2	88.7
relationships with other faculty	76.5	74.3	81.7	67.3	70.9	76.0	79.8	77.1	81.0	83.0	81.8	79.6
competency of colleagues	69.0	67.2	72.9	63.7	66.8	63.6	75.7	73.1	77.1	78.2	73.2	67.9
visibility for jobs	41.7	41.1	43.3	42.3	49.9	38.5	39.8	38.8	40.9	40.6	43.3	44.4
job security	66.9	62.1	77.6	56.6	57.2	67.4	62.3	57.4	64.8	67.2	78.2	65.4
undergraduate course assignments	76.8	75.4	80.3	73.1	79.3	73.1	79.3	79.1	77.5	80.9	80.0	86.0
graduate course assignments	66.0	68.4	37.6	70.5	73.1	65.5	65.7	66.8	64.0	65.2	37.0	100.0
relationships with admin	54.4	54.4	54.3	51.2	60.4	51.6	59.2	56.3	60.5	62.2	54.0	60.4
overall job satisfaction	69.8	66.9	76.5	62.3	72.9	65.9	70.8	67.6	73.5	73.3	76.4	77.8

FEMALE FACULTY

	ALL			Universities		Four-year Colleges					Two-year Colleges	
	Insts	4-yr	2-yr	Pub	Priv	Pub	All Priv	Nons	Cath	Prot	Pub	Priv
Sources of Stress												
household responsibilities	73.3	73.1	73.5	77.1	71.0	69.3	75.1	77.5	70.9	74.9	73.4	77.4
child care	28.6	28.0	30.0	28.3	31.1	25.0	30.7	31.6	29.0	30.6	29.6	37.0
care of elderly parent	28.4	27.3	30.9	26.1	23.3	28.9	27.6	25.9	30.2	27.9	30.6	37.0
my physical health	42.7	42.9	42.3	45.1	41.0	42.1	42.4	42.7	42.9	41.4	42.5	37.0
review/promotion process	50.5	55.8	38.5	63.1	51.3	54.9	51.5	54.7	50.3	47.6	38.1	45.3
subtle discrimination	47.9	51.8	38.8	54.9	58.5	52.2	46.0	50.3	39.0	45.0	39.4	27.8
long-distance commuting	22.8	23.3	21.7	19.6	24.7	25.5	23.7	26.5	22.4	20.6	21.7	22.2
committee work	61.9	62.7	59.9	63.5	49.5	66.9	61.0	61.2	62.0	60.0	59.3	72.2
faculty meetings	52.3	53.0	50.6	55.4	46.9	53.8	51.5	51.7	54.8	48.9	49.9	64.8
colleagues	57.3	59.1	53.2	62.7	54.1	57.9	59.0	60.1	57.7	58.3	53.4	50.0
students	55.6	54.5	58.2	55.5	49.0	53.3	56.9	56.2	54.4	59.7	57.8	66.7
research or publishing demands	47.8	64.2	10.4	77.2	78.1	63.7	47.5	54.7	47.4	37.6	10.5	9.3
fund-raising expectations	18.0	20.3	12.8	25.4	18.1	19.8	16.8	16.8	17.6	16.1	12.8	13.0
teaching load	72.1	73.2	69.8	71.2	70.8	73.5	75.5	73.9	75.8	77.5	69.6	74.1
children's problems	29.0	26.0	35.7	25.8	23.5	25.1	28.2	29.3	24.1	29.7	35.5	38.9
marital friction	21.5	21.6	21.4	22.6	28.1	19.1	21.7	23.9	17.9	21.2	21.7	14.8
time pressures	90.5	92.1	87.0	93.7	92.7	90.6	92.5	92.3	91.8	93.3	86.9	87.0
lack of personal life	88.7	89.7	86.2	89.1	93.0	88.5	90.9	90.0	92.3	91.1	86.0	90.7
Still Want to Be College Professor?												
definitely yes	41.7	40.5	44.4	33.3	48.2	40.4	45.1	42.9	46.9	46.9	44.6	41.1
probably yes	37.4	37.9	36.3	40.6	33.8	38.2	36.2	35.9	36.0	36.9	36.3	37.5
not sure	12.9	13.4	11.9	15.4	12.9	12.4	13.0	14.5	12.2	11.4	11.7	16.1
probably no	6.3	6.6	5.7	8.8	3.4	7.0	4.8	5.4	4.4	4.4	5.7	5.4
definitely no	1.6	1.6	1.6	1.9	1.7	1.9	0.9	1.3	0.6	0.4	1.7	0.0
Field of Highest Degree Held												
agriculture	0.4	0.5	0.2	1.1	0.4	0.3	0.1	0.1	0.0	0.2	0.2	0.0
architecture or urban planning	0.2	0.2	0.0	0.6	0.2	0.1	0.1	0.3	0.1	0.0	0.0	0.0
bacteriology, molecular biology	0.8	0.8	0.8	0.8	1.0	0.6	1.2	1.6	1.2	0.5	0.8	0.0
biochemistry	0.3	0.3	0.2	0.3	0.5	0.1	0.5	0.6	0.6	0.2	0.2	0.0
biophysics	0.0	0.0	0.0	0.1	0.0	0.0	0.0	0.1	0.0	0.0	0.0	0.0
botany	0.4	0.5	0.1	0.5	0.1	0.5	0.7	0.4	1.0	0.7	0.1	0.0
marine life sciences	0.1	0.2	0.0	0.0	0.0	0.7	0.5	0.2	0.0	0.0	0.0	0.0
physiology, anatomy	0.6	0.6	0.5	0.6	0.2	0.7	0.5	0.6	0.5	0.5	0.5	0.0
zoology	0.6	0.7	0.6	0.4	0.5	0.8	0.8	0.7	0.9	0.8	0.6	0.0
general, other biological science	1.2	1.1	1.4	1.4	0.8	1.0	1.2	1.2	1.4	1.1	1.2	5.7
accounting	1.3	1.4	1.1	1.2	1.1	1.6	1.4	1.3	1.5	1.6	1.1	0.0
finance	0.3	0.3	0.2	0.1	0.3	0.5	0.4	0.1	0.6	0.5	0.3	0.0
marketing	0.6	0.7	0.5	0.8	0.8	0.7	0.5	0.5	0.8	0.2	0.5	0.9
management	1.5	1.5	1.5	2.5	1.3	1.4	0.9	0.5	1.1	1.3	1.5	1.9
secretarial studies	0.4	0.5	1.1	0.1	0.0	0.0	0.1	0.1	0.0	0.0	1.2	0.0
general, other business	1.0	0.8	1.5	0.7	0.5	0.8	1.0	0.8	0.6	1.7	1.3	5.7
computer science	0.6	0.6	0.7	0.4	0.8	0.4	0.8	0.6	1.7	0.5	0.8	0.0

FEMALE FACULTY

Field of Degree (continued)	ALL			Universities		Four-year Colleges					Two-year Colleges	
	Insts	4-yr	2-yr	Pub	Priv	Pub	All Priv	Nons	Cath	Prot	Pub	Priv
business education	2.9	1.5	6.1	0.7	0.1	2.5	1.3	1.4	1.0	1.3	6.0	7.5
elementary education	2.2	2.6	1.5	1.4	0.2	3.9	2.8	2.4	2.3	3.6	1.2	5.7
educational administration	1.9	1.7	2.5	1.4	0.6	2.0	1.9	1.6	2.7	1.7	2.6	0.0
educational psych, counseling	1.9	1.6	2.6	1.3	0.9	2.1	1.3	1.2	1.1	1.5	2.7	1.9
music or art education	0.5	0.6	0.3	0.3	0.3	0.9	0.5	0.4	0.1	0.8	0.3	0.0
physical or health education	4.0	4.2	3.6	4.0	0.7	5.4	4.0	3.9	1.9	5.7	3.7	0.0
secondary education	1.8	1.5	2.3	1.0	0.6	1.7	2.0	1.9	1.9	2.3	2.0	1.9
special education	1.2	1.4	0.9	1.0	0.2	1.5	1.9	2.4	2.1	1.2	0.8	9.4
general, other education fields	7.4	6.4	9.9	7.7	1.5	6.9	6.1	6.3	6.3	5.7	9.8	11.3
aeronautical, astronautical eng.	0.0	0.0	0.0	0.0	0.0	0.0	0.0	0.0	0.0	0.0	0.0	0.0
chemical engineering	0.1	0.1	0.0	0.1	0.1	0.1	0.0	0.1	0.0	0.0	0.0	0.0
civil engineering	0.1	0.2	0.1	0.5	0.2	0.1	0.0	0.0	0.1	0.0	0.0	0.0
electrical engineering	0.1	0.1	0.0	0.1	0.1	0.1	0.1	0.1	0.2	0.0	0.1	0.0
industrial engineering	0.1	0.2	0.0	0.1	0.1	0.2	0.0	0.1	0.0	0.0	0.0	0.0
mechanical engineering	0.0	0.0	0.0	0.4	0.6	0.0	0.0	0.1	0.0	0.0	0.0	0.0
nuclear engineering	0.0	0.0	0.0	0.2	0.3	0.0	0.0	0.1	0.0	0.0	0.0	0.0
general, other engineering field	0.1	0.1	0.1	0.2	0.3	0.1	0.1	0.2	0.0	0.0	0.1	0.0
ethnic studies	0.1	0.1	0.0	0.2	0.0	0.1	0.1	0.1	0.2	0.0	0.0	0.0
art	2.7	2.9	2.5	2.5	1.8	3.6	2.7	2.9	2.3	2.6	2.2	7.5
dramatics or speech	1.8	1.9	1.7	1.8	1.3	1.9	2.2	1.5	2.4	3.0	1.8	0.0
music	1.8	2.4	0.6	2.1	1.2	2.2	3.4	2.5	3.0	5.1	0.6	0.0
other fine arts	1.0	1.2	0.7	1.6	1.0	0.9	1.2	1.9	1.2	0.2	0.8	0.0
forestry	0.0	0.0	0.0	0.0	0.0	0.0	0.0	0.0	0.0	0.0	0.0	0.0
geology	0.3	0.3	0.3	0.4	0.2	0.4	0.2	0.1	0.0	0.5	0.3	0.0
dentistry	0.1	0.0	0.4	0.0	0.1	0.0	0.0	0.1	0.0	0.0	0.4	0.0
health technology	0.2	0.1	0.6	0.1	0.1	0.1	0.0	0.1	0.0	0.0	0.6	0.0
medicine or surgery	0.2	0.2	0.2	0.3	0.0	0.4	0.0	0.0	0.0	0.1	0.2	0.0
nursing	9.5	7.3	14.6	6.2	3.3	9.0	7.4	3.9	9.7	10.5	15.0	5.7
pharmacy, pharmacology	0.7	0.3	0.1	0.5	0.1	0.1	0.2	0.2	0.3	0.1	0.1	0.0
therapy (speech, physical, occup)	0.2	0.9	0.4	0.8	0.2	1.2	0.7	0.5	1.3	0.5	0.4	1.9
veterinary medicine	0.2	0.2	0.1	0.2	0.3	0.3	0.2	0.4	0.0	0.1	0.1	0.0
general, other health fields	1.4	1.1	2.0	1.3	0.4	1.3	1.0	1.4	0.8	0.6	2.1	0.0
home economics	2.2	2.6	1.2	4.7	0.8	2.6	1.2	1.5	1.5	0.6	1.2	0.0
English language & literature	9.0	8.5	10.2	8.5	7.4	7.4	10.2	11.4	7.9	10.4	10.2	9.4
foreign languages & literature	0.8	0.9	0.4	1.1	1.6	0.5	1.0	1.5	0.5	0.8	0.5	0.0
French	1.5	1.9	0.5	1.7	3.8	1.2	2.4	2.9	1.2	2.5	0.4	1.9
German	0.5	0.7	0.1	0.9	1.8	0.3	0.8	0.9	0.5	0.8	0.1	0.0
Spanish	1.4	1.7	0.6	1.0	4.3	1.2	2.4	2.1	2.2	2.9	0.7	0.0
other foreign languages	0.8	1.1	0.1	1.3	3.6	0.7	0.8	1.2	0.1	0.6	0.1	0.0

FEMALE FACULTY

Field of Degree (continued)

	ALL			Universities		Four-year Colleges					Two-year Colleges	
	Insts	4-yr	2-yr	Pub	Priv	Pub	All Priv	Nons	Cath	Prot	Pub	Priv
history	2.2	2.4	1.8	2.6	5.5	1.5	2.3	2.4	2.6	1.9	1.8	1.9
linguistics	0.8	0.9	0.5	1.1	2.0	0.8	0.7	1.0	0.6	0.3	0.6	0.0
philosophy	0.7	0.9	0.3	0.7	1.7	0.6	1.1	1.0	2.2	0.4	0.3	0.0
religion & theology	0.6	0.8	0.1	0.3	2.0	0.2	1.7	1.1	3.8	0.9	0.1	0.0
general, other humanities fields	1.5	1.8	0.8	2.4	4.9	1.1	1.2	1.6	0.7	1.0	0.9	0.0
journalism	0.4	0.4	0.4	0.3	0.4	0.4	0.3	0.3	0.3	0.2	0.5	0.0
law	0.5	0.5	0.7	0.8	0.3	0.4	0.3	0.2	0.7	0.1	0.7	0.0
law enforcement	0.1	0.0	0.1	0.0	0.1	0.1	0.0	0.0	0.0	0.0	0.1	0.0
library science	0.5	0.6	0.3	0.4	0.2	0.8	0.7	0.5	0.6	1.0	0.3	0.0
mathematics and/or statistics	3.7	3.2	4.7	1.7	2.3	4.0	4.0	3.4	5.6	3.7	4.6	5.7
military science	0.0	0.0	0.0	0.0	0.0	0.0	0.0	0.0	0.0	0.1	0.0	0.0
astronomy	0.1	0.2	0.0	0.2	0.0	0.3	0.1	0.2	0.0	0.1	0.0	0.0
atmospheric sciences	0.0	0.0	0.0	0.0	0.0	0.1	0.0	0.0	0.0	0.0	0.0	0.0
chemistry	1.2	1.4	0.9	0.7	1.8	1.4	1.8	1.7	2.5	1.5	1.0	0.0
earth sciences	0.3	0.3	0.2	0.6	0.1	0.2	0.3	0.3	0.1	0.3	0.2	0.0
marine sciences	0.0	0.0	0.0	0.0	0.0	0.0	0.0	0.0	0.0	0.0	0.0	0.0
physics	0.3	0.3	0.1	0.3	0.2	0.3	0.4	0.4	0.2	0.6	0.1	0.0
general, other physical sciences	0.0	0.0	0.1	0.1	0.0	0.0	0.0	0.0	0.0	0.0	0.1	0.0
clinical psychology	0.6	0.7	0.2	0.9	0.5	0.6	0.9	0.8	0.8	1.1	0.2	0.0
counseling & guidance	1.0	0.6	2.1	0.3	0.2	0.8	0.7	0.5	1.0	0.6	2.0	3.8
experimental psychology	0.8	1.0	0.3	0.9	1.2	0.9	1.1	1.3	0.8	1.0	0.3	0.0
social psychology	0.8	1.1	0.3	0.7	5.8	0.2	0.8	1.1	0.8	0.5	0.3	0.0
general, other psychology	1.3	1.3	1.2	1.1	1.0	1.2	1.7	2.2	1.1	1.5	1.3	0.0
anthropology	1.0	1.3	0.3	2.1	2.0	1.1	0.6	0.9	0.5	0.4	0.3	0.0
archaeology	0.3	0.4	0.0	0.1	3.1	0.1	0.1	0.2	0.0	0.0	0.0	0.0
economics	1.4	1.8	0.6	1.6	6.2	1.0	1.5	1.8	2.1	0.6	0.5	1.9
political science, government	1.1	1.4	0.4	1.2	4.0	1.1	1.2	1.8	0.7	0.8	0.4	0.0
sociology	2.2	2.6	1.3	4.5	2.2	1.8	2.1	2.1	1.7	2.4	1.3	1.9
general, other social sciences	0.5	0.7	0.2	1.1	0.6	0.5	0.5	0.4	0.7	0.4	0.3	0.0
social work, social welfare	1.0	1.1	0.7	0.4	1.6	1.3	1.1	0.8	0.8	1.9	0.6	1.9
building trades	0.0	0.0	0.0	0.0	0.0	0.0	0.0	0.0	0.0	0.0	0.0	0.0
data processing, computer prog	0.1	0.0	0.3	0.0	0.0	0.0	0.1	0.1	0.1	0.0	0.3	0.0
drafting/design	0.1	0.0	0.3	0.0	0.0	0.0	0.0	0.1	0.0	0.0	0.3	0.0
electronics	0.0	0.0	0.0	0.0	0.0	0.0	0.0	0.0	0.0	0.0	0.0	0.0
industrial arts	0.0	0.0	0.0	0.0	0.0	0.0	0.0	0.1	0.0	0.0	0.0	0.0
mechanics	0.0	0.0	0.0	0.0	0.0	0.0	0.0	0.0	0.0	0.0	0.0	0.0
other technical	0.1	0.1	0.2	0.0	0.0	0.2	0.1	0.1	0.0	0.0	0.1	1.9
other vocational	0.5	0.1	1.3	0.1	0.0	0.2	0.0	0.1	0.0	0.0	1.4	0.0
women's studies	0.1	0.2	0.0	0.1	0.0	0.3	0.1	0.1	0.1	0.0	0.0	0.0
all other fields	2.5	2.9	1.6	3.2	1.8	3.5	2.0	2.7	1.9	1.0	1.6	1.9

FEMALE FACULTY

Department of Current Faculty Appointment	ALL			Universities		Four-year Colleges					Two-year Colleges	
	Insts	4-yr	2-yr	Pub	Priv	Pub	All Priv	Nons	Cath	Prot	Pub	Priv
agriculture	0.5	0.6	0.2	1.4	0.2	0.6	0.0	0.0	0.0	0.0	0.2	0.0
architecture or urban planning	0.2	0.3	0.0	0.6	0.4	0.4	0.0	0.1	0.0	0.0	0.0	0.0
bacteriology, molecular biology	0.4	0.4	0.3	0.6	0.9	0.2	0.4	0.2	0.6	0.5	0.3	0.0
biochemistry	0.0	0.0	0.0	0.1	0.0	0.0	0.0	0.0	0.0	0.0	0.0	0.0
biophysics	0.1	0.0	0.0	0.0	0.0	0.0	0.0	0.0	0.0	0.0	0.0	0.0
botany	0.1	0.2	0.0	0.5	0.0	0.0	0.1	0.2	0.0	0.0	0.0	0.0
marine life sciences	0.2	0.1	0.0	0.1	0.0	0.0	0.2	0.1	0.0	0.0	0.0	0.0
physiology, anatomy	0.1	0.1	0.5	0.1	0.0	0.1	0.1	0.1	0.2	0.4	0.5	0.0
zoology	0.1	0.1	0.0	0.2	0.0	0.1	0.1	0.2	0.0	0.2	0.0	0.0
general, other biological science	2.7	2.8	2.5	1.6	1.4	3.1	4.1	4.6	4.7	3.0	2.3	5.8
accounting	1.7	1.7	1.8	1.4	1.2	2.2	1.5	1.1	1.8	1.9	1.8	1.9
finance	0.2	0.3	0.0	0.2	0.4	0.3	0.4	0.2	0.8	0.4	0.0	0.0
marketing	0.8	0.9	0.7	1.0	1.0	0.9	0.7	1.4	0.3	0.1	0.7	0.0
management	1.7	2.3	0.5	3.7	1.8	1.8	1.6	1.3	2.6	1.1	0.5	1.9
secretarial studies	1.8	0.4	5.0	0.1	0.0	0.4	0.7	0.7	0.6	0.8	5.1	1.9
general, other business	1.8	1.4	2.7	1.1	0.8	1.6	1.7	1.4	2.2	1.9	2.4	7.7
computer science	1.2	1.0	1.8	0.5	1.8	1.0	1.1	0.9	2.1	0.5	1.8	1.9
business education	1.5	0.7	3.3	0.4	0.4	1.3	0.4	0.3	0.4	0.4	3.1	5.8
elementary education	2.2	3.1	0.1	1.7	0.4	4.4	3.6	2.5	3.8	5.2	0.0	1.9
educational administration	0.1	0.1	0.0	0.1	0.1	0.2	0.1	0.1	0.1	0.1	0.0	0.0
educational psych, counseling	0.4	0.5	0.4	0.6	0.4	0.6	0.2	0.4	0.2	0.5	0.4	0.0
music or art education	0.3	0.3	0.3	0.1	0.3	0.5	0.3	0.2	0.2	0.5	0.2	1.9
physical or health education	4.4	5.0	3.0	4.8	1.1	6.4	4.6	4.4	2.0	6.8	3.0	3.8
secondary education	0.6	0.8	0.2	0.5	0.3	1.2	0.7	0.5	0.6	1.0	0.2	0.0
special education	0.9	1.1	0.5	1.4	0.2	1.5	0.7	0.5	1.3	0.4	0.5	0.0
general, other education fields	3.0	2.9	3.2	2.1	0.8	3.1	4.1	4.7	3.7	3.6	2.9	9.6
aeronautical, astronautical eng.	0.0	0.0	0.0	0.0	0.0	0.0	0.0	0.0	0.0	0.0	0.0	0.0
chemical engineering	0.0	0.1	0.0	0.5	0.1	0.1	0.0	0.1	0.0	0.0	0.0	0.0
civil engineering	0.1	0.2	0.0	0.1	0.2	0.1	0.0	0.0	0.1	0.0	0.0	0.0
electrical engineering	0.1	0.2	0.0	0.1	0.1	0.3	0.1	0.1	0.2	0.0	0.0	0.0
industrial engineering	0.1	0.1	0.0	0.2	0.0	0.2	0.0	0.0	0.0	0.0	0.0	0.0
mechanical engineering	0.1	0.1	0.0	0.1	0.0	0.0	0.0	0.1	0.0	0.0	0.0	0.0
nuclear engineering	0.0	0.0	0.0	0.1	0.0	0.0	0.0	0.0	0.0	0.0	0.0	0.0
general, other engineering field	0.2	0.2	0.1	0.4	0.1	0.2	0.1	0.2	0.0	0.0	0.2	0.0
ethnic studies	0.2	0.3	0.0	0.4	0.3	0.2	0.1	0.1	0.1	0.1	0.0	0.0
art	2.8	3.3	1.7	3.3	2.4	3.8	2.9	3.3	1.9	2.9	1.5	5.8
dramatics or speech	1.9	2.1	1.3	2.3	1.3	1.9	2.5	2.0	2.4	3.2	1.4	0.0
music	1.9	2.5	0.7	2.2	1.3	2.4	3.2	2.2	2.6	5.1	0.8	0.0
other fine arts	0.8	1.0	0.6	1.3	1.2	0.6	1.1	1.7	1.1	0.1	0.6	0.0
forestry	0.0	0.0	0.0	0.1	0.0	0.0	0.0	0.0	0.0	0.0	0.0	0.0

FEMALE FACULTY

	ALL			Universities		Four-year Colleges					Two-year Colleges	
	Insts	4-yr	2-yr	Pub	Priv	Pub	All Priv	Nons	Cath	Prot	Pub	Priv
Current Department (contuned)												
geology............................	0.2	0.2	0.2	0.3	0.0	0.1	0.2	0.1	0.0	0.5	0.2	0.0
dentistry..........................	0.6	0.1	1.8	0.1	0.1	0.1	0.0	0.1	0.0	0.0	1.8	0.0
health technology..................	0.9	0.3	2.1	0.4	0.2	0.5	0.2	0.5	0.0	0.0	2.2	0.0
medicine or surgery................	0.2	0.3	0.1	0.4	0.0	0.4	0.0	0.0	0.0	0.0	0.1	0.0
nursing............................	11.8	9.4	17.1	8.6	4.2	11.7	9.0	5.0	11.8	12.6	17.8	3.8
pharmacy, pharmacology.............	0.2	0.3	0.1	0.6	0.7	0.1	0.2	0.2	0.2	0.2	0.1	0.0
therapy (speech,physical,occup)....	1.1	1.3	0.7	1.2	0.7	1.7	1.0	0.7	2.3	0.3	0.6	3.8
veterinary medicine................	0.1	0.1	0.7	0.3	0.3	0.0	0.0	0.1	0.0	0.0	0.1	0.0
general, other health fields.......	1.8	1.0	3.7	1.0	0.4	1.5	0.7	1.0	0.8	0.1	3.9	0.0
home economics.....................	2.8	3.5	1.2	6.1	0.9	3.9	1.1	0.9	1.9	1.0	1.1	1.9
English language & literature......	10.2	9.4	12.1	9.2	7.6	8.3	11.7	12.7	8.4	12.7	12.2	9.6
foreign languages & literature.....	2.3	3.0	0.7	2.2	6.5	2.0	4.0	4.7	2.9	3.7	0.7	0.0
French.............................	0.8	1.1	0.3	1.1	2.7	0.6	1.1	1.3	0.5	1.3	0.2	1.9
German.............................	0.3	0.4	0.1	0.8	0.8	0.1	0.3	0.4	0.2	0.3	0.1	0.0
Spanish............................	0.9	1.1	0.4	0.9	2.0	0.6	1.5	1.5	0.7	2.1	0.4	0.0
other foreign languages............	0.9	1.2	0.2	1.6	4.5	0.3	0.9	1.4	0.3	0.6	0.2	0.0
history............................	1.8	2.1	1.1	2.4	3.1	1.7	2.1	2.3	2.1	1.9	1.0	1.9
linguistics........................	0.2	0.3	0.0	0.4	0.6	0.3	0.1	0.2	0.0	0.0	0.0	0.0
philosophy.........................	0.6	0.8	0.2	0.5	1.6	0.6	1.0	0.9	2.1	0.4	0.2	0.0
religion & theology................	0.6	0.8	0.1	0.3	2.6	0.2	1.4	0.6	3.5	0.9	0.1	0.0
general, other humanities fields...	1.8	2.1	1.0	1.4	8.0	1.1	2.1	3.0	1.7	1.1	1.0	0.0
journalism.........................	0.5	0.5	0.4	0.7	0.4	0.5	0.4	0.5	0.4	0.2	0.4	0.0
law................................	0.1	0.0	0.1	0.1	0.0	0.0	0.0	0.0	0.2	0.0	0.1	0.0
law enforcement....................	0.1	0.0	0.3	0.0	0.1	0.1	0.0	0.0	0.0	0.0	0.3	0.0
library science....................	0.4	0.4	0.3	0.3	0.1	0.4	0.6	0.5	0.4	0.9	0.3	0.0
mathematics and/or statistics......	5.1	4.6	6.4	4.2	1.8	5.3	4.8	4.3	6.4	4.5	6.1	13.5
military science...................	0.0	0.0	0.0	0.0	0.0	0.0	0.0	0.0	0.0	0.0	0.0	0.0
astronomy..........................	0.0	0.1	0.0	0.1	0.0	0.0	0.0	0.1	0.1	0.0	0.0	0.0
atmospheric sciences...............	0.0	0.0	0.0	0.0	0.0	0.0	0.0	0.0	0.0	0.0	0.0	0.0
chemistry..........................	1.3	1.3	1.3	0.5	1.7	1.4	2.1	1.9	2.7	1.8	1.3	0.0
earth sciences.....................	0.3	0.4	0.2	0.7	0.1	0.3	0.2	0.2	0.0	0.3	0.3	0.0
marine sciences....................	0.0	0.0	0.0	0.0	0.0	0.0	0.0	0.6	0.0	0.4	0.0	0.0
physics............................	0.2	0.3	0.1	0.3	0.1	0.2	0.4	0.0	0.1	0.0	0.1	0.0
general,other physical sciences....	0.1	0.1	0.2	0.1	0.0	0.1	0.1	0.0	0.2	0.0	0.2	0.0

FEMALE FACULTY

Current Department (contuned)	ALL			Universities		Four-year Colleges					Two-year Colleges	
	Insts	4-yr	2-yr	Pub	Priv	Pub	All Priv	Nons	Cath	Prot	Pub	Priv
clinical psychology............	0.3	0.4	0.0	0.5	0.5	0.5	0.1	0.0	0.2	0.2	0.0	0.0
counseling & guidance..........	0.6	0.2	1.5	0.1	0.1	0.2	0.2	0.2	0.3	0.2	1.5	0.0
experimental psychology........	0.4	0.6	0.1	0.6	1.4	0.5	0.4	0.3	0.2	0.5	0.1	0.0
social psychology..............	0.5	0.7	0.0	0.1	6.1	0.1	0.1	0.1	0.2	0.1	0.0	0.0
general,other psychology.......	2.1	2.1	2.2	1.3	0.9	1.9	3.6	4.1	2.9	3.4	1.9	7.7
anthropology...................	0.7	1.0	0.1	1.7	1.3	0.8	0.4	0.7	0.3	0.1	0.2	0.0
archaeology....................	0.0	0.0	0.0	0.0	0.0	0.0	0.0	0.0	0.0	0.0	0.0	0.0
economics......................	1.3	1.6	0.5	1.1	6.6	1.0	1.2	1.6	1.3	0.6	0.5	0.0
political science, government..	0.9	1.2	0.3	1.0	3.5	0.8	1.1	1.6	0.6	0.8	0.3	0.0
sociology......................	2.2	2.5	1.4	4.0	2.0	1.8	2.2	2.4	1.7	2.8	1.4	1.9
general,other social sciences..	1.2	1.1	1.6	1.3	1.2	0.9	1.2	1.3	1.7	0.6	1.6	0.0
social work, social welfare....	0.8	0.9	0.5	0.5	1.6	1.2	0.9	0.4	1.0	1.4	0.5	1.9
building trades................	0.0	0.0	0.0	0.0	0.0	0.0	0.0	0.0	0.0	0.0	0.0	0.0
data processing,computer prog..	0.3	0.1	0.7	0.1	0.0	0.0	0.3	0.1	0.8	0.1	0.8	0.0
drafting/design................	0.2	0.0	0.5	0.0	0.0	0.0	0.1	0.3	0.0	0.0	0.5	0.0
electronics....................	0.1	0.0	0.2	0.0	0.0	0.0	0.0	0.2	0.0	0.0	0.2	0.0
industrial arts................	0.0	0.0	0.0	0.0	0.0	0.0	0.1	0.0	0.0	0.0	0.0	0.0
mechanics......................	0.0	0.0	0.0	0.0	0.0	0.0	0.0	0.0	0.0	0.0	0.0	0.0
other technical................	0.3	0.2	0.7	0.2	0.0	0.3	0.2	0.4	0.0	0.0	0.6	1.9
other vocational...............	0.6	0.1	1.7	0.0	0.0	0.0	0.3	0.6	0.0	0.0	1.7	0.0
women's studies................	0.2	0.3	0.0	0.2	0.3	0.5	0.2	0.4	0.0	0.0	0.0	0.0
all other fields...............	3.5	3.4	3.9	4.2	2.4	3.4	2.7	3.8	3.3	0.9	4.1	0.0

Notes

1. Percentages will sum to more than 100 if any respondents checked more than one category.

2. Recategorization of this item from a longer list is shown in the American College Teacher.

3. Nine-month salaries converted to twelve-month.

4. Respondents marking "not applicable" are not included in tabulations.

Appendix A

Representativeness of the Sample

Appendix A

Representativeness of the Results

How accurate and representative are the data obtained from this survey? We are fortunate to have available a comparison sample from a national faculty survey conducted in 1988 by the National Center for Educational Statistics (NCES, 1990). While the NCES survey sample was much smaller (N=8,798), their response rate was higher (75 percent). Also, the HERI survey used a more sophisticated stratification scheme for sampling institutions, whereas the NCES used a more sophisticated scheme for sampling faculty within institutions. The principal difference between the two survey populations was that the NCES survey included institutions not offering undergraduate degrees (e.g., free standing professional schools) and their tabulations included faculty who did not teach undergraduates.

Table A1 compares the HERI and NCES sample results in terms of four basic indicators: age, race, academic rank, and the percent holding doctorate or advanced professional degrees. In general, the results agree very closely. In the case of the two-year colleges, the percentages on all items are either identical or agree within one percent in all categories except one: the percentage of faculty in the 30-44 age range which differs from the HERI sample by two percent. Among the four-year colleges and university faculty, only three of the sixteen percentage comparisons differed by more than one percent: the NCES sample produced two percent more Asian faculty (5 versus 3 percent for the HERI sample), two percent fewer associate professors (27 versus 29) and five percent more with doctorate or advanced professional degrees. In all likelihood, at least some of these differences can be explained by population differences. The NCES sample, for example, has more faculty with advanced degrees because it includes medical and law schools, most of whose faculty would be expected to have advanced professional (e.g., J.D., M.D.) degrees. The NCES sample may also contain more Asians because it includes medical school faculty. This latter possibility is supported by the fact that one of the NCES sampling categories, "private doctoral" institutions, is said to include medical schools. As it happens, this category also has by far the largest percentage of Asians -- ten percent -- of all the NCES categories.

In short, the data in Table A1 suggest that the HERI sample is adequately representative of teaching faculty in general in terms of age, race, academic rank, and highest degree held.

Table A1
Comparison of Results from Faculty Surveys of HERI and NCES (percentages)

Comparison Item	Four-Year Institutions		Two-Year Public Colleges	
	HERI Survey	NCES Survey	HERI Survey	NCES Survey
Age				
Less than 30	2	1	2	2
30-44	40	40	36	38
45-54	33	33	40	39
55 or more	25	25	24	23
Race				
White	90	89	91	91
Black	4	3	4	3
Asians	3	5	2	2
Hispanic	1	2	2	3
American Indian	1	1	1	1
Academic Rank				
Professor	36	37	25	b
Associate Professor	29	27	16	
Assistant Professor	26	26	12	
Lecturer	2	2	1	
Instructor	5	6	41	
Other	2	2a	5	
Doctorate or Advanced Professional Degree	75	80	19	18

a Includes 1 percent "not applicable: no ranks designated at this institution."
b Not comparable because 28 percent checked "not applicable: no rank designated at this institution," a category not included in the HERI survey.

Appendix B

1989 Faculty Survey Instrument

1989 Faculty Survey
Higher Education Research Institute, UCLA

DIRECTIONS

r responses will be read by an optical mark
er. Your observance of these few direc-
s will be most appreciated.

e only a black lead pencil (No. 2 is ideal).
ke heavy black marks that fill the oval.
ase cleanly any answer you wish to change.
ke no stray markings of any kind.

**MPLE: Will marks made with a ball-point
or felt-tip pen be properly read?**
○ Yes   ● No

**hat is your principal activity in your current
osition at this institution?** (Mark one)
○ Administration
○ Teaching
○ Research
○ Services to clients and patients
○ Other

**re you considered a full-time employee of
ur institution for at least nine months of
e current academic year?** (Mark one)
○ Yes   ○ No

hat is your present academic rank?
○ Professor
○ Associate Professor
○ Assistant Professor
○ Lecturer
○ Instructor
○ Other

hat is your administrative title?
○ Not applicable
○ Director, coordinator, or administrator of
   an institute, center, lab, or specially-
   funded program
○ Department Chair
○ Dean
○ Associate or Assistant Dean
○ Vice-President, Provost, Vice-Chancellor
○ President, Chancellor
○ Other

ur sex:
○ Male   ○ Female

ur marital status:
○ Married (currently)
○ Separated
○ Single (never married)
○ Single (with partner)
○ Single (divorced)
○ Single (widowed)

**you were to begin your career again, would
u still want to be a college professor?**
○ Definitely yes
○ Probably yes
○ Not sure
○ Probably no
○ Definitely no

---

8. Racial/Ethnic group: (Mark all that apply)
○ White/Caucasian
○ Black/Negro/Afro-American
○ American Indian
○ Asian-American
○ Mexican-American/Chicano
○ Puerto Rican-American
○ Other

**9. Do your interests lie primarily in teaching
or research?**
○ Very heavily in research
○ In both, but leaning toward research
○ In both, but leaning toward teaching
○ Very heavily in teaching

**10. Which of these statements applies to your
current research or scholarly endeavors?**
(Mark one)
○ I am essentially working alone
○ I am working with one or two colleagues
○ I am a member of a larger group

**11. On the following list,
please mark:** (Mark
one in each column)

	Highest Degree Earned	Degree Currently Working On
Bachelor's (B.A., B.S., etc.)	○	○
Master's (M.A., M.S., etc.)	○	○
LL.B., J.D.	○	○
M.D., D.D.S., (or equivalent)	○	○
Other first professional degree beyond B.A. (e.g., D.D., D.V.M.)	○	○
Ed.D.	○	○
Ph.D.	○	○
Other degree	○	○
None	○	○

**12. During the past two years, have you
engaged in any of the following
activities?** (Mark one for each item)

	Yes	No
Taught an honors course	○	○
Taught an interdisciplinary course	○	○
Taught a general education course	○	○
Taught a developmental/remedial course	○	○
Taught an ethnic studies course	○	○
Taught a women's studies course	○	○
Team-taught a course	○	○
Worked with students on a research project	○	○
Attended a racial/cultural awareness workshop	○	○
Participated in a faculty seminar to integrate women's and minorities' perspectives in regular courses	○	○
Held a faculty senate or council office	○	○
Used intra- or extramural funds for research	○	○
Served as a paid consultant	○	○

**13. In the two sets of ovals shown below, please
mark the most appropriate code from the
fields listed on the back of the accompanying
letter.** (Please see example on back of
accompanying letter)

Major of highest degree held
Department of current faculty appointment

(Ovals 0–9 for each set)

**14. In the set of ovals to
the right, please mark
the dollar value of
your base institutional
salary, rounded to
the nearest $1,000
(Note: Amounts above
$99,000 should be
marked "99").**

(Ovals 0–9)

The above salary is based on:
○ 9/10 months   ○ 11/12 months

**15. In the four sets of circles below, please
mark the last two digits of the year of
each of the following:**

Year of birth   (Ovals 0–9)
Year of highest degree now held   (Ovals 0–9)

Year of appointment at present institution   (Ovals 0–9)   ○ Not Tenured
If tenured, year tenure awarded at current institution   (Ovals 0–9)

NOTE: If you are now between terms (quarters, semesters, trimesters), on leave, or in an interim term, please answer questions 16 and 17 as they apply to the full term most recently completed at this institution.

16. During the present term, how many hours per week on the average do you actually spend in connection with your present position on each of the following activities?

(Mark one for each activity)

	Hours Per Week								
	None	1-4	5-8	9-12	13-16	17-20	21-34	35-44	45+
Scheduled teaching (give actual, not credit, hours)	○	○	○	○	○	○	○	○	○
Preparing for teaching (including reading student papers and grading)	○	○	○	○	○	○	○	○	○
Advising and counseling of students	○	○	○	○	○	○	○	○	○
Committee work and meetings	○	○	○	○	○	○	○	○	○
Other administration	○	○	○	○	○	○	○	○	○
Research and scholarly writing	○	○	○	○	○	○	○	○	○
Consultation with clients/patients	○	○	○	○	○	○	○	○	○

17. How many of the following courses are you teaching this term?
(Mark one for each item)

General education courses	⓪	①	②	③	④	⑤⁺
Other BA or BS undergraduate credit courses	⓪	①	②	③	④	⑤⁺
Non-BA credit courses (developmental and/or remedial)	⓪	①	②	③	④	⑤⁺
Graduate courses	⓪	①	②	③	④	⑤⁺

18. How would you characterize your political views?

- ○ Far Left
- ○ Liberal
- ○ Moderate
- ○ Conservative
- ○ Far Right

19. Indicate the importance to you of each of the following:

(Mark one for each item)

Education Goals for Undergraduate Students:

	Essential	Very Important	Somewhat Important	Not Important
Develop ability to think clearly	Ⓔ	Ⓥ	Ⓢ	Ⓝ
Increase desire and ability to undertake self-directed learning	Ⓔ	Ⓥ	Ⓢ	Ⓝ
Prepare students for employment after college	Ⓔ	Ⓥ	Ⓢ	Ⓝ
Prepare students for graduate or advanced education	Ⓔ	Ⓥ	Ⓢ	Ⓝ
Develop moral character	Ⓔ	Ⓥ	Ⓢ	Ⓝ
Provide for students' emotional development	Ⓔ	Ⓥ	Ⓢ	Ⓝ
Prepare students for family living	Ⓔ	Ⓥ	Ⓢ	Ⓝ
Teach students the classic works of Western civilization	Ⓔ	Ⓥ	Ⓢ	Ⓝ
Help students develop personal values	Ⓔ	Ⓥ	Ⓢ	Ⓝ
Enhance the out-of-class experience of students	Ⓔ	Ⓥ	Ⓢ	Ⓝ
Enhance students' self-understanding	Ⓔ	Ⓥ	Ⓢ	Ⓝ

Personal/Professional Goals:

	Essential	Very Important	Somewhat Important	Not Important
Engage in research	Ⓔ	Ⓥ	Ⓢ	Ⓝ
Engage in outside activities	Ⓔ	Ⓥ	Ⓢ	Ⓝ
Provide services to the community	Ⓔ	Ⓥ	Ⓢ	Ⓝ
Participate in committee or other administrative work	Ⓔ	Ⓥ	Ⓢ	Ⓝ
Be a good colleague	Ⓔ	Ⓥ	Ⓢ	Ⓝ
Be a good teacher	Ⓔ	Ⓥ	Ⓢ	Ⓝ

For questions 20-24, please mark only one response for each question.

	None	1-2	3-4	5-10	11-20
20. How many articles have you published in academic or professional journals?	○	○	○	○	○
21. How many chapters have you published in edited volumes?	○	○	○	○	○
22. How many books, manuals, or monographs have you written or edited, alone or in collaboration?	○	○	○	○	○
23. How many of your professional writings have been published or accepted for publication in the last two years?	○	○	○	○	○
24. About how many days during the past (1988-89) academic year were you away from campus for professional activities (e.g., professional meetings, speeches, consulting)?	○	○	○	○	○

25. What is the highest level of education reached by your spouse/partner and your parents?
(Mark one in each column)

	Spouse/Partner	Father
8th grade or less	Ⓢ	Ⓕ
Some high school	Ⓢ	Ⓕ
Completed high school	Ⓢ	Ⓕ
Some college	Ⓢ	Ⓕ
Graduated from college	Ⓢ	Ⓕ
Attended graduate or professional school	Ⓢ	Ⓕ
Attained advanced degree	Ⓢ	Ⓕ
Does not apply (No spouse or partner)	Ⓢ	

26. For each of the following items, please mark either Yes or N

	Yes
Have you ever held an academic administrative post?	○
Have you ever received an award for outstanding teaching?	○
Is your spouse or live-in partner an academic?	○
Do you commute a long distance to work?	○
Has any of your research or writing focused on women or gender?	○
Has any of your research or writing focused on racial or ethnic minorities?	○
Do you have dependent children?	○
Are you a U.S. citizen?	○
Have you ever interrupted your professional career for more than one year for health or family reasons?	○
Have you ever considered a career in academic administration?	○
Do you plan on working beyond age 70?	○

During the Last Two Years, Have You:

Received at least one firm job offer?	○
Participated in a faculty development program?	○
Developed a new course?	○
Considered early retirement?	○
Considered leaving academe for another job?	○

27. Indicate how important you believe each priority listed below is at your college or university.

(Mark one for each item)

	Highest Priority	High Priority	Medium Priority	Low Priority
To promote the intellectual development of students	④	③	②	①
To help students examine and understand their personal values	④	③	②	①
To increase the representation of minorities in the faculty and administration	④	③	②	①
To develop a sense of community among students and faculty	④	③	②	①
To develop leadership ability among students	④	③	②	①
To conduct basic and applied research	④	③	②	①
To raise money for the institution	④	③	②	①
To develop leadership ability among faculty	④	③	②	①
To increase the representation of women in the faculty and administration	④	③	②	①
To facilitate student involvement in community service activities	④	③	②	①
To help students learn how to bring about change in American society	④	③	②	①
To help solve major social and environmental problems	④	③	②	①
To maintain a campus climate where differences of opinion can be aired openly	④	③	②	①
To increase or maintain institutional prestige	④	③	②	①
To develop among students and faculty an appreciation for a multi-cultural society	④	③	②	①
To hire faculty "stars"	④	③	②	①
To economize and cut costs	④	③	②	①
To recruit more minority students	④	③	②	①
To enhance the institution's national image	④	③	②	①
To create a positive undergraduate experience	④	③	②	①
To create a diverse multi-cultural environment on campus	④	③	②	①
To enhance the out-of-class experience of students	④	③	②	①

28. Please indicate the extent to which each of the following has been a source of stress for you during the last two years.

(Mark one for each item)

	Extensive	Somewhat	Not At All
Managing household responsibilities	Ⓔ	Ⓢ	Ⓝ
Child care	Ⓔ	Ⓢ	Ⓝ
Care of elderly parent	Ⓔ	Ⓢ	Ⓝ
My physical health	Ⓔ	Ⓢ	Ⓝ
Review/promotion process	Ⓔ	Ⓢ	Ⓝ
Subtle discrimination including prejudice, racism, sexism	Ⓔ	Ⓢ	Ⓝ
Long-distance commuting	Ⓔ	Ⓢ	Ⓝ
Committee work	Ⓔ	Ⓢ	Ⓝ
Faculty meetings	Ⓔ	Ⓢ	Ⓝ
Colleagues	Ⓔ	Ⓢ	Ⓝ
Students	Ⓔ	Ⓢ	Ⓝ
Research or publishing demands	Ⓔ	Ⓢ	Ⓝ
Fund-raising expectations	Ⓔ	Ⓢ	Ⓝ
Teaching load	Ⓔ	Ⓢ	Ⓝ
Children's problems	Ⓔ	Ⓢ	Ⓝ
Marital friction	Ⓔ	Ⓢ	Ⓝ
Time pressures	Ⓔ	Ⓢ	Ⓝ
Lack of personal time	Ⓔ	Ⓢ	Ⓝ

29. How satisfied are you with the following aspects of your job?

(Mark one for each item)

	Very Satisfied	Satisfied	Marginally Satisfied	Not Satisfied	Not Applicable
Salary and fringe benefits	Ⓥ	Ⓢ	Ⓜ	Ⓝ	◯
Opportunity for scholarly pursuits	Ⓥ	Ⓢ	Ⓜ	Ⓝ	◯
Teaching load	Ⓥ	Ⓢ	Ⓜ	Ⓝ	◯
Quality of students	Ⓥ	Ⓢ	Ⓜ	Ⓝ	◯
Working conditions (hours, location)	Ⓥ	Ⓢ	Ⓜ	Ⓝ	◯
Autonomy and independence	Ⓥ	Ⓢ	Ⓜ	Ⓝ	◯
Relationships with other faculty	Ⓥ	Ⓢ	Ⓜ	Ⓝ	◯
Competency of colleagues	Ⓥ	Ⓢ	Ⓜ	Ⓝ	◯
Visibility for jobs at other institutions/organizations	Ⓥ	Ⓢ	Ⓜ	Ⓝ	◯
Job security	Ⓥ	Ⓢ	Ⓜ	Ⓝ	◯
Undergraduate course assignments	Ⓥ	Ⓢ	Ⓜ	Ⓝ	◯
Graduate course assignments	Ⓥ	Ⓢ	Ⓜ	Ⓝ	◯
Relationships with administration	Ⓥ	Ⓢ	Ⓜ	Ⓝ	◯
Overall job satisfaction	Ⓥ	Ⓢ	Ⓜ	Ⓝ	◯

30. Below are some statements about your current college. Indicate the extent to which you agree or disagree with each of the following:

(Mark one for each item)

	Agree Strongly	Agree Somewhat	Disagree Somewhat	Disagree Strongly
Faculty here are interested in students' personal problems	④	③	②	①
Most faculty here are sensitive to the issues of minorities	④	③	②	①
The curriculum here has suffered from faculty overspecialization	④	③	②	①
Many students feel like they do not "fit in" on this campus	④	③	②	①
Faculty are committed to the welfare of this institution	④	③	②	①
Many courses include minority group perspectives	④	③	②	①
Administrators consider student concerns when making policy	④	③	②	①
Faculty here are strongly interested in the academic problems of undergraduates	④	③	②	①
There is a lot of campus racial conflict here	④	③	②	①
Students here resent taking courses outside their major	④	③	②	①
Students of different racial/ethnic origins communicate well with one another	④	③	②	①
Campus administrators care little about what happens to students	④	③	②	①
There is little trust between minority student groups and campus administrators	④	③	②	①
Faculty here are positive about the general education program	④	③	②	①
Many courses include feminist perspectives	④	③	②	①
There are many opportunities for faculty and students to socialize with one another	④	③	②	①
Administrators consider faculty concerns when making policy	④	③	②	①
Faculty feel that most students are well-prepared academically	④	③	②	①
Student Affairs staff have the support and respect of faculty	④	③	②	①
Institutional demands for doing research interfere with my effectiveness as a teacher	④	③	②	①

31. Indicate how well each of the following describes your college or university.

(Mark one for each item)

	Very Descriptive	Somewhat Descriptive	Not Descriptive
It is easy for students to see faculty outside of regular office hours	Ⓥ	Ⓢ	Ⓝ
There is a great deal of conformity among the students	Ⓥ	Ⓢ	Ⓝ
Most of the students are very bright	Ⓥ	Ⓢ	Ⓝ
The administration is open about its policies	Ⓥ	Ⓢ	Ⓝ
There is keen competition among most of the students for high grades	Ⓥ	Ⓢ	Ⓝ
Course work is definitely more theoretical than practical	Ⓥ	Ⓢ	Ⓝ
Faculty are rewarded for their advising skills	Ⓥ	Ⓢ	Ⓝ
Students have little contact with each other outside of class	Ⓥ	Ⓢ	Ⓝ
The faculty are typically at odds with the campus administration	Ⓥ	Ⓢ	Ⓝ
Intercollegiate sports are overemphasized	Ⓥ	Ⓢ	Ⓝ
The classes are usually informal	Ⓥ	Ⓢ	Ⓝ
Faculty here respect each other	Ⓥ	Ⓢ	Ⓝ
Most students are treated like "numbers in a book"	Ⓥ	Ⓢ	Ⓝ
Social activities are overemphasized	Ⓥ	Ⓢ	Ⓝ
There is little or no contact between students and faculty	Ⓥ	Ⓢ	Ⓝ
The student body is apathetic and has little "school spirit"	Ⓥ	Ⓢ	Ⓝ
Students here do not usually socialize with one another	Ⓥ	Ⓢ	Ⓝ
Faculty are rewarded for being good teachers	Ⓥ	Ⓢ	Ⓝ
Student services are well supported on this campus	Ⓥ	Ⓢ	Ⓝ

32. In how many of the undergraduate courses that you teach, do you require each of the following?

(Mark one for each item)

Evaluation Methods:

	All	Most	Some	None
Multiple-choice mid-term and/or final exams	Ⓐ	Ⓜ	Ⓢ	Ⓝ
Essay mid-term and/or final exams	Ⓐ	Ⓜ	Ⓢ	Ⓝ
Short-answer mid-term and/or final exams	Ⓐ	Ⓜ	Ⓢ	Ⓝ
Multiple-choice quizzes	Ⓐ	Ⓜ	Ⓢ	Ⓝ
Short-answer quizzes	Ⓐ	Ⓜ	Ⓢ	Ⓝ
Weekly essay assignments	Ⓐ	Ⓜ	Ⓢ	Ⓝ
Student presentations	Ⓐ	Ⓜ	Ⓢ	Ⓝ
Term/research papers	Ⓐ	Ⓜ	Ⓢ	Ⓝ
Student evaluations of each others' work	Ⓐ	Ⓜ	Ⓢ	Ⓝ
Grading on a curve	Ⓐ	Ⓜ	Ⓢ	Ⓝ
Competency-based grading	Ⓐ	Ⓜ	Ⓢ	Ⓝ
Student evaluations of teaching	Ⓐ	Ⓜ	Ⓢ	Ⓝ

Instructional Techniques/Methods:

	All	Most	Some	None
Class discussions	Ⓐ	Ⓜ	Ⓢ	Ⓝ
Computer or machine-aided instruction	Ⓐ	Ⓜ	Ⓢ	Ⓝ
Cooperative learning (small groups)	Ⓐ	Ⓜ	Ⓢ	Ⓝ
Experiential learning/Field studies	Ⓐ	Ⓜ	Ⓢ	Ⓝ
Graduate teaching assistants	Ⓐ	Ⓜ	Ⓢ	Ⓝ
Undergraduate teaching assistants	Ⓐ	Ⓜ	Ⓢ	Ⓝ
Group projects	Ⓐ	Ⓜ	Ⓢ	Ⓝ
Independent projects	Ⓐ	Ⓜ	Ⓢ	Ⓝ
Extensive lecturing	Ⓐ	Ⓜ	Ⓢ	Ⓝ
Multiple drafts of written work	Ⓐ	Ⓜ	Ⓢ	Ⓝ
Readings on racial and ethnic issues	Ⓐ	Ⓜ	Ⓢ	Ⓝ
Readings on women and gender issues	Ⓐ	Ⓜ	Ⓢ	Ⓝ
Student-developed activities (assignments, exams, etc.)	Ⓐ	Ⓜ	Ⓢ	Ⓝ
Student-selected topics for course content	Ⓐ	Ⓜ	Ⓢ	Ⓝ

33. Please indicate your agreement with each of the following statements.

(Mark one for each item)

	Agree Strongly	Agree Somewhat	Disagree Somewhat	Disagree Strongly
The death penalty should be abolished	④	③	②	①
A national health care plan is needed to cover everybody's medical costs	④	③	②	①
Abortion should be legalized	④	③	②	①
Grading in colleges has become too easy	④	③	②	①
Wealthy people should pay a larger share of taxes than they do now	④	③	②	①
College officials have the right to ban persons with extreme views from speaking on campus	④	③	②	①
The chief benefit of a college education is that it increases one's earning power	④	③	②	①
Racial discrimination is no longer a problem in America	④	③	②	①
Colleges should be actively involved in solving social problems	④	③	②	①
Faculty unionization has enhanced the teaching/learning process	④	③	②	①
Tenure is an outmoded concept	④	③	②	①

34. Indicate the importance to you personally of each of the following:

(Mark one for each item)

	Essential	Very Important	Somewhat Important	Not Important
Becoming an authority in my field	Ⓔ	Ⓥ	Ⓢ	Ⓝ
Influencing the political structure	Ⓔ	Ⓥ	Ⓢ	Ⓝ
Influencing social values	Ⓔ	Ⓥ	Ⓢ	Ⓝ
Raising a family	Ⓔ	Ⓥ	Ⓢ	Ⓝ
Having administrative responsibility for the work of others	Ⓔ	Ⓥ	Ⓢ	Ⓝ
Being very well-off financially	Ⓔ	Ⓥ	Ⓢ	Ⓝ
Helping others who are in difficulty	Ⓔ	Ⓥ	Ⓢ	Ⓝ
Becoming involved in programs to clean up the environment	Ⓔ	Ⓥ	Ⓢ	Ⓝ
Developing a meaningful philosophy of life	Ⓔ	Ⓥ	Ⓢ	Ⓝ
Helping to promote racial understanding	Ⓔ	Ⓥ	Ⓢ	Ⓝ
Obtaining recognition from my colleagues for contributions to my special field	Ⓔ	Ⓥ	Ⓢ	Ⓝ

ADDITIONAL QUESTIONS: If you received additional questions, mark answers below:

35. Ⓐ Ⓑ Ⓒ Ⓓ Ⓔ	39. Ⓐ Ⓑ Ⓒ Ⓓ Ⓔ	42. Ⓐ Ⓑ Ⓒ Ⓓ Ⓔ
36. Ⓐ Ⓑ Ⓒ Ⓓ Ⓔ	40. Ⓐ Ⓑ Ⓒ Ⓓ Ⓔ	43. Ⓐ Ⓑ Ⓒ Ⓓ Ⓔ
37. Ⓐ Ⓑ Ⓒ Ⓓ Ⓔ	41. Ⓐ Ⓑ Ⓒ Ⓓ Ⓔ	44. Ⓐ Ⓑ Ⓒ Ⓓ Ⓔ
38. Ⓐ Ⓑ Ⓒ Ⓓ Ⓔ		

Please return your completed questionnaire in the postage-paid envelope to:
Higher Education Research Institute
2905 West Service Road, Eagan, MN 55121

THANK YOU!

3153-Questar/576-5432

Higher Education Research Institute/CIRP
Current Publications List
March, 1991

The American College Student

Provides information on the college student experience two and four years after college entry. Student satisfaction, talent development, student involvement, changing values and career development, and retention issues are highlighted along with normative data from student responses to the HERI Follow-up Surveys.

    1988 report: Normative data for 1984 and 1986
        freshman. August, 1990/210 pages $15.00
    1987 report: Normative data for 1983 and 1985
        freshman. Sept., 1989/130 pages $15.00
    1985 report: Normative data for 1981 and 1983
        freshman. March, 1989/44 pages $14.00

Predicting College Student Retention ($8.00)
Comparative National Data from the 1982 freshman class.
A practical guide for colleges interested in using registrar's data to predict student retention. Focus is on the entering freshmen class of 1982 using results from the 1986 Follow-up Survey. March, 1989/110 pages.

The Black Undergraduate ($8.00)
Current Status and Trends in the Characteristics of Freshmen
This study examines changes in the characteristics of black college freshmen during the past two decades. A wide variety of characteristics of black college freshmen are considered in the study: family background, academic experience in high school, reasons for attending college, finanical aid, choices of majors and careers, expectations for college, self-concept, values, attitudes, and beliefs. August, 1990/22 pages.

The American College Teacher ($12.00)
National Norms for the 1989-90 HERI Faculty Survey
Provides an informative profile of teaching faculty at American colleges and universities. Teaching, research activities and professional development issues are highlighted along with issues related to job satisfaction and stress. December, 1990/ 104 pages.

The Courage and Vision to Experiment ($10.00)
Hampshire College 1970-1990
Summarizes the results of a study of Hampshire College, an experimenting liberal arts institution located in Amherst, Massachusetts. Through an analysis of alumni outcomes, the report emphasizes how the lessons learned from the innovative approach used at Hampshire can be translated to the higher education community at large. January, 1991/190 pages.

The American Freshman: Twenty-five year Trends
Forthcoming, Spring 1991 ($25.00)
Will provide trend data for entering freshmen classes on selected items of the CIRP survey from 1966-1990. The report highlights academic skills and preparation, demographic trends, high school activities and experiences, education and career plans, and student attitudes and values.

The American Freshman: National Norms
Provides national normative data on freshmen responses to the annual freshmen survey. Please check the year you wish to receive:

Year	Price	Year	Price
1966	7.50__	1979	7.50__
1967	7.50__	1980	7.50__
1968	7.50__	1981	7.50__
1969	7.50__	1982	7.50__
1970	7.50__	1983	8.25__
1971	7.50__	1984	8.25__
1972	7.50__	1985	8.50__
1973	7.50__	1986	12.95 (out of stock)
1974	7.50__	1987	15.00__
1975	7.50__	1988	17.00__
1976	7.50__	1989	19.00__
1977	7.50__	1990	19.00__
1978	7.50__		

===

Order Form
Please send me the publication(s) checked on the listing above.

Name _____

Title _____

Institution _____

Address _____

City _____ State _____ Zip _____

Daytime Phone _____

Enclosed is: _____Personal Check _____Institutional Check _____Institutional Purchase Order

Total amount enclosed $_____